CONTEMPORARY
CHILDHOOD

Education at SAGE

SAGE is a leading international publisher of journals, books, and electronic media for academic, educational, and professional markets.

Our education publishing includes:

- accessible and comprehensive texts for aspiring education professionals and practitioners looking to further their careers through continuing professional development

- inspirational advice and guidance for the classroom

- authoritative state of the art reference from the leading authors in the field.

Find out more at: **www.sagepub.co.uk/education**

CONTEMPORARY CHILDHOOD

SEAN MACBLAIN, JILL DUNN *and* IAN LUKE

$SAGE

Los Angeles | London | New Delhi
Singapore | Washington DC | Melbourne

Los Angeles | London | New Delhi
Singapore | Washington DC | Melbourne

SAGE Publications Ltd
1 Oliver's Yard
55 City Road
London EC1Y 1SP

SAGE Publications Inc.
2455 Teller Road
Thousand Oaks, California 91320

SAGE Publications India Pvt Ltd
B 1/I 1 Mohan Cooperative Industrial Area
Mathura Road
New Delhi 110 044

SAGE Publications Asia-Pacific Pte Ltd
3 Church Street
#10-04 Samsung Hub
Singapore 049483

Editor: Jude Bowen
Associate editor: George Knowles
Production editor: Nicola Marshall
Copyeditor: Sharon Cawood
Proofreader: Kate Campbell
Indexer: Gary Kirby
Marketing manager: Lorna Patkai
Cover design: Wendy Scott
Typeset by: C&M Digitals (P) Ltd, Chennai, India
Printed in the UK

Library of Congress Control Number: 2017931157

British Library Cataloguing in Publication data

A catalogue record for this book is available from
the British Library

ISBN 978-1-4739-5199-0
ISBN 978-1-4739-5200-3(pbk)

At SAGE we take sustainability seriously. Most of our products are printed in the UK using FSC papers and boards.
When we print overseas we ensure sustainable papers are used as measured by the PREPS grading system.
We undertake an annual audit to monitor our sustainability.

Sean MacBlain: For Martin and Fiona

*Jill Dunn: In memory of my mother, Alma Reed, who was
my first and best teacher*

*Ian Luke: For Sophie and our beautiful children, Ed, Alice,
Imogen, Eliza and Isla*

CONTENTS

Companion Website   xi
About the Authors   xiii
Foreword   xv
Acknowledgements   xix

Introduction   1
   Aims of the book   2
   Why it is important to understand and study childhood   3
   Popular and historical perceptions of childhood   4
   National and global perspectives   5
   Organisation of the book   6
   How readers can get the best from the book   7

PART 1   THE CHILD   9

1 The Changing Nature of Childhood   11
   Shifting landscapes: children's security   12
   Multiculturalism   13
   Inclusion and children with additional needs   14
   Austerity and poverty   16
   Children as carers   18
   State of play in the UK   19
   Emerging curricula and proposed initiatives   22

2 The Child's Perspective   29
   Current views on children's perspectives   30
   Childhood studies and children's perspectives   31
   United Nations Convention on the Rights of the
      Child and children's perspectives   33
   Challenges and tensions in listening to young
      children's perspectives   34
   Methods for seeking children's perspectives in research 36
   Innovative methods for eliciting the views of young children 37
   Children's involvement in the research process   39

**3 Social and Emotional Functioning in the
Learning Environment**   **47**

Learning, happiness and well-being   48
Attachment and the learning environment   52
Loss in childhood: its impact on learning   53
Fear and love in the lives of children   55
Supporting children's social and emotional functioning
    outside of the home   58

**4 Creating Optimum Learning Environments
for the Child**   **65**

Today's challenges   66
Identification and assessment: reflections on practice   67
Ethical issues in the identification and assessment of children 75
Low achievement and underachievement   75
Children whose first language is not English   76
Monitoring and evaluating practice   77

PART 2 THE CHILD AND THE FAMILY   **83**

5 The Changing Nature of Families   **85**

Divorce, separation and step-families   86
The importance of fathers in families   88
Grandparents and families   91
Working with refugee and asylum-seeking families   95
Working with lesbian, gay, bisexual and transgender families 99

6 The Parent's Voice   **109**

Listening to parents   110
Working with parents   119
Parents' working patterns   120

7 Multi-professional Perspectives   **127**

Evolving perspectives   128
Safeguarding   128
Challenges of multi-agency working   134
Professionals and parents: working together   135
Recent initiatives   138

PART 3   MODERN AND EMERGING CHILDHOODS   **145**

8 Policy, Discourse and Identity   **147**

Policy and practice   148
Contemporary political ideology and philosophy   149
Regulation, control and accountability   151
Professionalism and professional identity   156

9 The Digital Child   **167**

What is a digital child?   168
Digital media   169
The affordances of digital media   173
Starting where children are: the importance of children's
    learning experiences at home   174
Children's digital lives in the new millennium   177
E-safety for children in a digital world   178

10 International Perspectives   **187**

International variations in practice   188
Children and conflict   193
Growth of technology   194
Gender   195
Provision for children throughout the world   196
Economic costs of childhood   197
The readying culture   199

11 Contemporary Issues in a Global Society   **205**

Poverty and life chances   206
Obesity   207
Sexualisation of children   208
Social fears   209
Mental health   210
Media and materialism   212
The emergence of neuroscience   213
Reflections on professionalism   215
Child-centredness in a changing world   216

Index   223

COMPANION WEBSITE

Contemporary Childhood is supported by a wealth of online resources available at **https://study.sagepub.com/contemporarychildhood**

Visit the website to:

- access a selection of **free SAGE journal articles** and other annotated readings
- follow **web links** which direct you to useful resources
- read **additional case studies** and **activities** to help you link theory to real life practice
- use **chapter PowerPoints** to help you revise.

ABOUT THE AUTHORS

Sean MacBlain is Reader in Child Development and Disability at the University of St Mark & St John, Plymouth and was previously research lead for the Centre for Professional and Educational Research. Prior to working at the University of St Mark & St John, Sean worked as a Senior Lecturer in Education and Developmental Psychology at Stranmillis University College, a College of Queen's University Belfast. Sean has also worked as an educational psychologist and continues in this field in his own private practice – SMB Associates SW Ltd (enquiries@seanmacblain.com). Other publications by Sean include: Gray and MacBlain (Sage, 2015) *Learning Theories in Childhood* now in its 2nd edition; MacBlain, Long and Dunn (Sage, 2015) *Dyslexia, Literacy and Inclusion: Child-centred Perspectives*; MacBlain (Sage, 2014) *How Children Learn*. Sean's research interests include the professional development of teachers and early years practitioners, and the social and emotional development of children and young people with special educational needs and disabilities. Sean is married to Angela and lives in Somerset, England.

Jill Dunn is a senior lecturer at Stranmillis University College, Belfast. She was a primary school teacher working in early years classrooms before moving into teacher education. Jill teaches across the BEd, MEd and PGCE Early Years programmes and her main interests lie in the teaching of literacy in the early years and in working with parents. Jill completed her EdD in 2013 and her dissertation focused on children's views on the use of popular culture to teach writing. She has been involved in a number of funded research projects on literacy and on digital technology in the early years. She has presented her work at conferences and published articles in *Literacy* and the *International Journal of Early Years Education*, among others. She is co-author of the recent book *Dyslexia, Literacy and Inclusion: Child-centred Perspectives* (Sage, 2015, with MacBlain and Long). She lives with her husband Ian and daughters Holly and Katy in Northern Ireland.

Ian Luke is Dean of Faculty: Education & Social Sciences at the University of St Mark & St John, Plymouth. Ian has worked in schools and universities across the UK and has also taught internationally. Prior to working at the University of St Mark & St John, he was based at the University of Bath. His research interests include metacognition, disability, professional development, higher education and teacher education. Ian has a strong sporting background in sports acrobatics, winning both world and European medals. He lives with his partner Sophie and their five children in Tavistock, Devon.

FOREWORD

For so many years of my childhood, I lived in a world of make believe and imagination – I was the wife of a millionaire, who was in fact my orange teddy bear and we lived in an amazing castle, i.e. an outhouse attached to the garage. I spent the most part of my childhood playing outdoors, dressed up in my mum's clothes, making mud pies and enjoying a pressure-free life. My childhood was filled with happiness, playfulness and adventure, cocooned in the safety of a loving family.

This book is about childhood, and my childhood experiences in many ways reminisce with the words of the World Summit for Children (UNICEF, 1990):

> The children of the world are innocent, vulnerable and dependent. They are also curious, active and full of hope. Their time should be one of joy and peace, of playing, learning and growing. Their future should be shaped in harmony and co-operation. Their lives should mature as they broaden their perspectives and gain new experiences.

But as this book so aptly reminds us, to believe that the above is true of all children in the twenty-first century is a complete fallacy. What makes this book distinctive is that the authors do not shy away from the controversial issues that bombard everyday childhood across the globe. They bring to the reader's attention the real challenges and tensions that many young children presently encounter in an effort to expose for critique the rosy images and naïve assumptions that are often associated with childhood. They tackle the complex issues, amongst many others, of over-commercialisation and over-sexualisation that young children in the twenty-first century are confronted with. They deal with the technological explosion that has hit society worldwide and the related controversies of obesity and social and emotional anxieties. In addition, they address the politicisation of childhood and the resulting neo-liberal discourse of efficiency, productivity and competitiveness that has invaded early childhood education, where playful opportunities and child-initiated experiences are relentlessly being overtaken by academic pressures to teach to the test. In this way the book as it stands uncovers a broad perspective on childhood which is signalled clearly in the introductory chapter with its triple focus: *The Child, The Child and the Family* and *Modern and Emerging Childhoods*. Each of these parts serves to open the reader's mind to new understandings of childhood and its associated complexities.

Towards the beginning of the book, the authors raise ideas that resonate very strongly with the underpinning topic under scrutiny: 'the potential conflict between children's right to participation and their right to protection' and the notion of children as 'being versus becoming'. For me these phrases lie at the heart of the challenges of modern childhood: in one way children are being hurried to display their independence and to showcase their competence to be readied for adulthood. But against this backdrop of forcing children to grow up too quickly and behaving in certain ways are an ever-growing concern and anxiety about shielding and sheltering children, where decisions are being made for them, instead of with them, and where their concerns and those of their families appear to be ignored and unheard. The authors embrace these polarised views of childhood as opportunities to create spaces for discussion, reflection and critical engagement. The book therefore provides a sound interplay between the theoretical and the illustrative. It offers a plethora of international evidence and theoretical justifications counterbalanced with a number of vignettes and references to policy and practice, not in an endeavour to present solutions or indeed to try and evade the ever-changing landscape, but instead to provoke engagement with and understanding of the challenges and dilemmas which invade that life stage known as childhood.

Whether we like it or not, childhood, as we once knew it, is presently under attack and is undergoing significant change, but what this book does not set out to do is to simply present a depressing picture of childhood and its changing nature. Through its eclectic approach, it attempts to go one step forward and use the controversies of contemporary childhood as mechanisms to arm and up-skill childhood practitioners and professionals to meet the needs of children more fully in their everyday environments. International evidence has shown us time and time again the importance of getting it right for all children, not only from the perspective of the child themselves but also for the wider economy and society at large. Getting it right for children does pay off (see Heckman and Raut, 2016) and this book goes some way in helping us to delve deeper into the how and why.

In summation, this is a detailed, rich and thought-provoking text. Within 11 chapters, it provides a comprehensive overview and a bringing together of those underlying issues and challenges that underpin childhood in the twenty-first century. But it does so much more and for that reason it is an essential read for all those working and hoping to work in the field of early childhood education and beyond. Children are our future and the importance of knowing and understanding their real world goes without saying. Reading this book will provide that understanding of what it really means to be a child growing up in today's society and, through its effective blend of theory and practice, it also helps to uncover how children can best be supported to meet this challenge. Childhood matters and if you want to learn more, don't delay in reading this book!

Dr Glenda Walsh
Head of Early Years Education, Stranmillis University College

REFERENCES

Heckman, James J. and Raut, Lakshmi K. (2016) 'Intergenerational long-term effects of preschool-structural estimates from a discrete dynamic programming model', *Journal of Econometrics*, 191(1): 164–75.

UNICEF (1990) World Declaration on the Survival, Protection and Development of Children. World Summit for Children. Available at: www.unicef.org/wsc/declare.htm

ACKNOWLEDGEMENTS

The authors would like to offer their thanks to Jude Bowen who from the outset was encouraging and supportive and whose help and direction were invaluable. Our thanks also go to George Knowles for his continued support throughout the process of bringing this text to completion.

Sean MacBlain would like to acknowledge Lorna Jackson and Rebecca Hall, two of his undergraduate students at the University of St Mark & St John, who so confidently brought to his attention the potential for early years practitioners and students in using the Leuven Scale for Well-being in their practice with young children. He would also like to acknowledge Caroline Snelling, a postgraduate student at the University of St Mark & St John, for drawing attention to the concepts of 'maskrosbarn' and 'orkidebarn'. Further thanks go to Fiona Welch for her shared insights into the language used by young children and for the support she offered in researching different aspects of thinking in children. Sean's thanks go to his wife Angela for her continued love and support throughout.

INTRODUCTION

AIMS OF THE BOOK

The primary aim of this book is to raise awareness amongst all those working with children of the increasingly complex nature of childhood in the twenty-first century and the need to understand childhood in all of its reality. In 1989, Loris Malaguzzi, the renowned founder of the Reggio Emilia educational philosophy, highlighted that times were so difficult, so mutable and so constantly changing for children (Cagliari et al., 2016). Fast forward to 2016 and the same sentiments about change are being echoed where those working with children today are being urged to enable them to function successfully in our culturally and linguistically diverse and increasingly connected global and digital society (Kim, 2016). Indeed, James and Prout (2015) caution that the uncertainties around childhood and society in the 1990s were accompanied by an optimistic mood; however, the current mood tends to have more pessimistic views of childhood. It is indisputable that children live differently now. Making reference to the original ideas of the philosopher Froebel's notion of a kindergarten, where early stages of childhood are akin to growing up in a garden, Sorin (2005, p. 12) cited Steinberg and Kincheloe (2004) who warned that 'Children no longer live in the secret garden of childhood, [they] possess an open door to the adult world'.

A key feature of this text will be that of supporting and directing students and practitioners towards developing a much greater understanding of the wider holistic needs of children in primary schools and early years settings. Understanding the concept of child-centredness in terms of children's rights, the child's voice, partnerships between home, school and community, and meaningful collaboration between professionals and key stakeholders will be central to this text. This is in addition to focusing on the importance of the family, children as carers, the emergence of digital technology and its impact on learning, mental health issues and the changing nature of play. A strong international perspective is taken throughout the text with particular emphasis being given to global issues in the final two chapters.

Too many practitioners continue to make assumptions about childhood rather than explicitly exploring their own professional practice in relation to children's individual and holistic needs and how social, cultural and economic environments impact on learning and social and emotional development. It is the contention of the authors that too few professionals critically engage with the theoretical and philosophical principles, which have shaped, and continue to shape, our understanding of childhood; too often, practice leads to views of childhood that fail to go far enough in their interpretations of observed behaviours in children. Too few adults fully understand why so many young children continue to fail as a direct consequence of their experiences in childhood.

WHY IT IS IMPORTANT TO UNDERSTAND AND STUDY CHILDHOOD

Children are our future. At a political level, they will be our future citizens; at an economic level, they will be future consumers and producers of wealth. Socially, they will form the very fabric of our societies. It has become increasingly acknowledged that our understanding of childhood is limited and it is only really in the past few decades that the complexity of early emotional and social development in childhood is being properly researched and understood. For too long, difficult issues relating to childhood have been largely avoided, misunderstood and all-too-often ignored. Indeed, the popularised perception that many adults hold of childhood is that it is a time of freedom and innocence, playfulness and fun and a lack of responsibility (Woodhead, 2005). Such perceptions have been fuelled largely by the media and in many regards serve to disguise and even mask what, for many children, is an all-too-different reality. Only two decades ago, Schostak (1991, p. 10) commented as follows:

> Society has a picture of the Ideal Family ... Within the Ideal Family, however, there is a contradiction since it holds at the same time the proposition that childhood is inno-cent and the vulnerability of the child should be protected ... The Ideal Family is the theme of countless films, television series and novels.

Our knowledge of how personalities are formed in the first years of childhood and how experiences and significant events in the early years come to influence and define the course of children's lives remains poorly understood and, arguably, under-researched. Popularised perceptions of childhood have been radically challenged in recent years through disturbing reports appearing almost weekly in the media about child abuse, conflict involving children across the globe, poverty, starvation and migration, and the early sexualisation and commercialisation of children. High-profile cases in the UK, such as those of *Victoria Climbié* (Laming, 2003) and *Baby P* (discussed in Chapter 7), and, more recently, investigations into child abuse in the English town of Rotherham; and the unfolding and harrowing findings following enquiries into Jimmy Savile and the extent of allegations into abuse in the Catholic Church across the globe, have shocked the public into looking more intently and more openly at the nature of childhood today. Victoria Climbié and Baby P were two very young children who were killed by adults who had responsibility for their security and care. Both children were judged to have been failed by those institutions that were in place to offer them protection. Both cases shocked the public and resulted in a whole raft of legislation, policies and changed practice. The view that all children are reared in stable and loving families fell under the micro-scope, with a growing realisation that large numbers of children in the UK are growing up in dysfunctional families and suffering from poverty and neglect and, in a number of cases, abuse. Within the last decade, Cowie (2012, pp. 1–2) has indicated that:

> In comparison with other countries, children in the UK are more likely to have been drunk. Rates of underage sex are high, as is the incidence of teenage pregnancy … Today's young people seem to face severe stresses that were unknown a generation ago. Suicidal thoughts are common among young people, as are feelings of hopelessness and futility … There are disturbing statistics on the number of children and young people who run away from home or care … These amount to around 100,000 episodes each year in the UK, with around a quarter running away before the age of 13, and one in 10 running away before the age of 10.

Cowie went on to indicate how in 2012 the National Society for the Prevention of Cruelty to Children (NSPCC) dealt with some 30,000 cases, or around 0.25 per cent of the population.

If we are to have a better understanding of childhood, then we need to ensure that the views of children themselves have a more central place in our consideration of what it means to be a child in the twenty-first century. Young children remain hidden in the majority of literature relating to early childhood (Eckhoff, 2015), yet the inclusion of young children's voices can illuminate and bring fresh and unique perspectives to our understanding of being a child in today's world. Considering children's perspectives is not without its own challenges, and Clark (2016) urges that we need to be reminded about whose voices count and which young children's voices are underrepresented or missing from global narratives about early childhood.

POPULAR AND HISTORICAL PERCEPTIONS OF CHILDHOOD

Research into childhood has really been confined to recent times. Ariès (1962/1986) and Zelizer (1985/1994), amongst others, have suggested that in earlier times, such as those of John Locke and Jean-Jacques Rousseau, childhood was viewed very differently, not as a distinct stage of development but more as a time of children being 'adults-in-waiting'. With the growth of industrialisation in the UK and the opening of large numbers of factories, new legislation needed to be introduced in order to slow down and prevent the exploitation of children and to give them much greater means of protection, which previously was all but non-existent. With the changes in legislation came an increasing awareness that childhood was, in fact, a different and discrete stage from adulthood.

In a highly influential and seminal contribution to the wider literature, *Pricing the Priceless Child: The Changing Social Value of Children*, Zelizer (1985/1994, cited in Gray and MacBlain, 2015, p. 150) drew attention to how in those years between the nineteenth and twentieth centuries, the perception of childhood changed significantly from 'economically "useful" to economically "useless" but emotionally "priceless"', with Zelizer making the case that 'the real "value" of children lies in their ability to give meaning and fulfilment to their parents' lives'. Some years earlier, McDowall Clark (2010, p. 1) drew attention to how children have become the focus of 'unprecedented attention from all quarters of society', notably, parents and educators, politicians and manufacturers, with the media increasingly turning a spotlight on children over the past few decades. McDowall Clark has also drawn attention to the increased focus in universities on childhood with a substantial growth in academic subjects with childhood as their focus.

NATIONAL AND GLOBAL PERSPECTIVES

McDowall Clark (2010), amongst others, has proposed that there is no universally agreed definition of childhood, suggesting that perceptions of childhood vary greatly across the world and even within cultures. Some years earlier, Prout (2005, p. 3) had proposed how the already diverse nature of childhood was increasing and becoming more visible through the media, and suggested that we need to revise our perceptions of childhood and view this period in the lives of individuals as a 'unitary phenomenon'. Gray and MacBlain (2015) have commented on how social inequity presents itself in many forms and perhaps most notably in the nature of employment across the globe. In the UK, for example, children who are aged 14 years may be employed on a part-time basis, whilst full-time employment is only legal for children aged 16 years and above. In contrast, children across the globe are employed at far younger ages, as was the case historically in the UK and across all western industrialised societies. A report by the International Labour Organisation in 2015 noted how some 168 million children across the globe were trapped in child labour, accounting for almost 11 per cent of the overall child population. Children are being exposed to types of work that cause irreversible damage both physically and/or mentally and even pose a risk to life. McKinney (2014) discusses how child labour is often associated with sweatshops, mining, soldiering or exploitation in the sex industry and these forms of child labour are connected to coercion, abuse and hazardous conditions. However, most child labour is located in rural and agricultural contexts. Yet any form of child labour that affects attendance at school will have an impact on the child's future welfare.

All too frequently, we are confronted with images of childhood that arguably desensitise us to the realities that many children experience whilst growing up. In large part, this is to do with historical perceptions of childhood that have come to internalise and, in many respects, dominate our thinking about this period in the lives of others as well as ourselves. Ask anyone to explain what they understand by childhood and you are likely to encounter a range of descriptions, leading, in most cases, to memories and recollections from their own years of growing up; always anecdotal and almost always happy. For many children, however, the reality of growing up is less than happy. Indeed, for a significant number, it can be a time of pain and suffering.

ORGANISATION OF THE BOOK

This text is divided into three parts: *The Child*, *The Child and the Family* and *Modern and Emerging Childhoods*, with each section offering chapters on key aspects of childhood. The text is organised in such a way that it begins by looking at the changing nature of childhood before examining childhood from the perspective of a child and then exploring key features of childhood at an international level.

Chapter 1 examines the changing nature of childhood and children's security. Multiculturalism and children with additional needs are explored as are children as carers. Recent, current and proposed initiatives are examined with particular attention being given to curricula and play. The importance of listening to children and hearing their voice is addressed in Chapter 2, which explores children's rights, focusing on the role of the child in research, methods and methodologies and innovative ways of eliciting the views of young learners, including the 'Mosaic Approach'. Diversity, and its impact on young children and their families, is also explored in this chapter with case studies offering the views of children, one of whom has additional needs. Chapter 3 then explores social and emotional functioning in the learning environment, with sections on children in care, happiness and well-being, attachment, love and fear in young children, developing emotional intelligence and self-efficacy. This chapter also looks at how children are being supported outside of the home, focusing on nurture groups, breakfast clubs, buddy systems and children in hospital. Chapter 4 addresses the importance of creating and maintaining optimum learning environments for children, focusing on identification and assessment in the early years and the primary school, multi-agency frameworks, working in partnership with parents, ethical issues in the identification and assessment of children, low achievement and under-achievement, co-morbidity, the needs of children whose first language is not English and the monitoring, evaluation and inspection of practice across the UK.

Chapter 5 examines key issues regarding the changing and complex nature of many families and the impact on children, before examining in detail the importance of understanding childhood from the perspective of parents, in Chapter 6 where case studies illuminate the difficulties that parents and professionals might experience in working with one another. Chapter 7 then explores childhood through multi-professional perspectives, with a particular focus on safeguarding and the challenges of multi-agency working, the Integrated Review at 2–2½ Years, children's safeguarding boards and the Statutory Framework for the Early Years Foundation Stage. Illustrative case studies are offered to assist readers in exploring further the nature of the issues raised and to support them in reflecting on their own thinking and professional practice.

Chapter 8 addresses issues of policy, discourse and identity, focusing particularly on discourses associated with childhood educators' identities, how government policy can influence and place strain on identity, the impact for childhood education when identity is challenged, and contestation and hope in childhood education. Chapter 9 addresses the concept of the digital child and focuses on how the rapid growth and availability of digital technology is impacting on the lives of children, whilst Chapters 10 and 11 go on to examine international perspectives and contemporary issues in childhood across the globe.

Links to websites and YouTube videos are offered to readers alongside *Points for Discussion*, with references being given in each chapter to relevant texts and journal articles. In addition, chapters contain case studies through which readers will be able to see the relevance of the points being made by the authors. Reflecting the authors' theoretical approach, the text will not argue the superiority of any one theoretical perspective. Instead, throughout the book readers will be encouraged to arrive at their own conclusions, supported by appropriate and focused references and discussion points.

HOW READERS CAN GET THE BEST FROM THE BOOK

Though this text can be read from beginning to end, it can also be used as a valuable resource for referencing. Students, for example, who are exploring the impact of digital technology on children, may wish to explore issues in Chapter 9 where these are discussed in detail, in addition to looking at issues in Chapter 3 which focuses on the emotional aspects of childhood, and Chapter 10 which looks at key factors such as diet and nutrition. An initial reading of the whole text will allow the reader to locate particular areas of interest relevant to their own practice. Throughout the text, readers are provided with a range of examples, which are intended to act as reference points for their own experience. Points for Discussion are offered throughout the text, which are aimed at further extending readers' own reflections on issues explored in the chapters. These points can be used not only to facilitate reflection on the content of the book but also to provide opportunities to consider one's own observations and make critical interpretations of professional practice.

Don't forget to visit **https://study.sagepub.com/contemporarychildhood** for a selection of free SAGE journal articles, web links, additional case studies, activities, and PowerPoints to help you revise.

REFERENCES

Ariès, P. (1986 [1962]) *Centuries of Childhood: A Social History of Family Life*. London: Penguin.

Cagliari, P., Castagnetti, M., Giudici, C., Rinaldi, C., Vecchi, V. and Moss, P. (2016) *Loris Malaguzzi and the Schools of Reggio Emilia: A Selection of his Writings and Speeches 1945–1993*. London: Routledge.

Clark, A. (2016) 'Editorial: Take a walk following the complexities of young children's lives', *European Early Childhood Education Research Journal*, 24(3): 330–41.

Cowie, H. (2012) *From Birth to Sixteen: Children's Health, Social, Emotional and Linguistic Development*. London: Routledge.

Eckhoff, A. (2015) 'Ethical considerations of children's digital image-making and image-audiancing in early childhood environments', *Early Child Development and Care*, 185(10): 1617–28.

Gray, C. and MacBlain, S.F. (2015) *Learning Theories in Childhood* (2nd edn). London: Sage.

International Labour Organisation (ILO) (2015) *World Report on Child Labour: Paving the Way to Decent Work for Young People*. Geneva: ILO.

James, A. and Prout, A. (2015) *Constructing and Reconstructing Childhood: Contemporary Issues in the Sociological Study of Childhood*. London: Routledge.

Kim, M. (2016) 'Uncovering one trilingual child's multi-literacies development across informal and formal learning contexts', *European Early Childhood Education Research Journal*, 24(3): 414–38.

Laming, Lord (2003) *The Victoria Climbié Inquiry: Report of an Inquiry by Lord Laming*. London: The Stationery Office.

McDowall Clark, R. (2010) *Childhood in Society: For Early Childhood Studies*. Exeter: Learning Matters.

McKinney, S. (2014) 'The relationship of child poverty to school education', *Improving Schools*, 17(3): 201–16.

Prout, A. (2005) *The Future of Childhood: Towards the Interdisciplinary Study of Children*. London: RoutledgeFalmer.

Schostak, J. (1991) *Youth in Trouble*. London: Kogan Page.

Sorin, R. (2005) 'Changing images of childhood: reconceptualising early childhood practice', *International Journal of Transitions in Childhood*, 1: 12–21.

Steinberg, S.R. and Kincheloe, J.L. (eds) (2004) *Kinderculture: The Corporate Construction of Childhood* (2nd edn). Oxford: Westview Press.

Woodhead, M. (2005) 'Children and development', in J. Oates, C. Wood and A. Grayson (eds), *Psychological Development and Early Childhood*. Oxford: Open University Press.

Zelizer, V. (1994 [1985]) *Pricing the Priceless Child: The Changing Social Value of Children*. Princeton, NJ: Princeton University Press.

PART 1
THE CHILD

1

THE CHANGING
NATURE OF
CHILDHOOD

Why you should read this chapter

To properly understand childhood in the twenty-first century, we need to examine changing perspectives of childhood and explore the changing nature of families. We must also examine the shifting nature of cultures and the impact of inclusion. In addition, we must examine the nature of emerging curricula and current and proposed initiatives such as the new Statutory Framework for Early Years, all of which impact hugely on the work of practitioners and the lives of children today.

By the end of this chapter you should:

- have a clear understanding of key issues underpinning the changing nature of childhood
- have knowledge of the relevance of multiculturalism on the changing landscape of childhood
- be aware of some examples of best practice when working with families
- have explored issues relating to children with additional needs
- have examined the impact of poverty on the lives of children and the working patterns of parents and primary care givers
- explored the state of 'play' today, in the UK.

SHIFTING LANDSCAPES: CHILDREN'S SECURITY

For many children living today, the realities of modern life can at best be challenging and at worst deeply distressing (Cawson, 2002; Colverd and Hodgkin, 2011; MacBlain, 2014). Childhood has become increasingly complex and continues to grow in its complexity. While most children grow up in stable environments that offer love and security and prepare them for adulthood, many do not. Cowie (2012, p. 2) commented as follows in relation to the UK:

> Today's young people seem to face severe stresses that were unknown a generation ago. Suicidal thoughts are common among young people, as are feelings of hopelessness and futility ... There are disturbing statistics on the number of children and young people who run away from home or care ... These amount to around 100,000 episodes each year in the UK, with around a quarter running away before the age of 13, and one in ten running away before the age of ten.

Cowie has gone on to indicate how in 2012 the National Society for the Prevention of Cruelty to Children (NSPCC) found itself dealing with some 30,000 cases, amounting to 0.25 per cent of the population. In a review undertaken by the NSPCC (Cuthbert et al., 2011), it was estimated that in 2010 some 19,500 infants under the age of 1 year in the UK were living in a home with a parent who was a user of Class A drugs, and that around 93,500 infants under the age of 1 year were living in a home with a parent who was a problem drinker. Such statistics are worrying and challenge the often popularly expressed view in the media that childhood is a time characterised by freedom and fun, security and stability and a carefree existence with little, if any, responsibility.

 —— POINTS FOR DISCUSSION ————————

Take time to view this excellent YouTube video clip of Sir Al Aynsley Green, entitled 'Should the Nurture of Children be Everybody's Business?', at www.youtube.com/watch?v=HqYSS1nxOeA, in which Sir Al makes the case for a new and more collective approach to securing the best prospects for all children in the UK today. Then consider the following:

> How might practitioners in early years settings and primary schools work to develop environments where all children feel nurtured? What personal, as well as professional, qualities might practitioners need to do this effectively?

There are significant numbers of children growing up today who are forced to witness physical abuse in their homes, often as early as in their first months. It has been recognised (Walker et al., 2009), for example, that domestic violence accounts for around 14 per cent of all violent incidents in England and Wales. Elsewhere, it has been reported (Cawson, 2002) that 6 per cent of children receive maltreatment at the hands of their parents or carers, with 7 per cent of children experiencing serious physical abuse. An estimated 6 per cent of children have been the subject of serious absence of care throughout their childhood, with the same percentage of children experiencing frequent and severe emotional maltreatment (Colverd and Hodgkin, 2011). Many children, then, entering early years settings and primary schools will have already internalised models of behaviour from those whom they should be able to trust, that fall well short of what can be considered to be stable and nurturing. It is with these internalised models in place that children then commence their education and begin relating to those adults outside of the home who will then be largely responsible for their education and learning and their social and emotional development.

MULTICULTURALISM

The nature and cultural make-up of many schools and early years settings and, therefore, the experiences of children have been changing dramatically over the past few years as many 'new arrivals' enter the education system across the UK. This has been exacerbated in more recent years and months by the repositioning across Europe of large numbers of migrants escaping conflict in the Middle East.

Prior to the Coalition Government in the UK coming to power in 2010, there were some 856,670 pupils learning English as an Additional Language (EAL) in England, representing 15.2 per cent of the primary school population and 11.1 per cent of the secondary school population in England, with an estimation of over 200 languages being spoken (DCSF, 2009). In inner London, it was further estimated at this time that 54.1 per cent of pupils were learning English as an additional language (DCSF, 2009). In 2012, the National Association for Language Development in the Curriculum (NALDIC, 2012) reported on its website how the results of the annual school census in January of that year had shown that:

> one in six primary school pupils in England – 577,555 – do not have English as their first language. In secondary schools the figure stands at 417,765, just over one in eight. Once special schools and pupil referral units are taken into account, the total rises to just over a million at 1,007,090. These figures have doubled since 1997.

In other parts of the UK, the picture has been similar. Northern Ireland, for example, has, over the last few decades, seen much inward migration, which has had a marked impact on schools across the region. Statistics from the Department of

Education Northern Ireland (DENI, 2010) indicated a six-fold increase in what was termed 'newcomer children' between 2001/2 (1366 children) and 2009/10 (7899 children) across schools in Northern Ireland, with over 50 per cent of these children being in primary schools in 2009–10 (DENI, 2010). Such a development has had significant implications for teachers preparing to enter the profession (Skinner, 2010) and for the continuing professional development of experienced teachers across the region (DENI, 2005, 2006, 2007, 2009b; ETI, 2005; NISRA, 2009). One particular challenge facing many teachers has been the increased numbers of children entering schools with little, if any, English. In 2012, for example, the National Association for Language Development in the Curriculum (NALDIC) again reported on its website as follows:

> There are more than a million children between 5-16 years old in UK schools who speak in excess of 360 languages between them in addition to English. Currently there are 1,061,010 bilingual 5-16 year olds in English schools, 26,131 in Scotland, 8674 'newcomer' pupils in Northern Ireland and 30,756 EAL learners in Wales.

Clearly, such an increase brings with it both benefits and challenges.

INCLUSION AND CHILDREN WITH ADDITIONAL NEEDS

In September 2014, the Children and Families Act came into effect in England and was followed in January 2015 by a new Code of Practice. This Act, and the subsequent Code of Practice, will, some would argue, change the face of special educational needs and/or disability education. Of note is the fact that the Act encompasses health with education and social services and places particular emphasis on the legal obligations on local authorities and professionals to view their interventions with children and young people aged 0 to 25 years. Most importantly, the Act places children at the centre of decision making and involves families much more than before in any processes affecting their children (see www. gov.uk/government/news/landmark-children-and-families-act-2014-gains-royal-assent for a detailed account of what the Act aims to offer children and families).

The increase in diversity that has occurred across the UK in recent decades can be closely associated not only with increasing numbers of pupils with special educational needs (SEN) being educated in mainstream schools, following an international shift towards greater inclusion (UNESCO, 1994; UNICEF, 1989), but also with a number of legislative landmarks such as the 1981 Education Act (which was subsequently repealed), the Special Education Needs Disability Act (SENDA 2001) and, of course, the new Children and Families Act (DfE, 2014), all of which have endeavoured to strengthen the rights of children with SEN and/or disabilities.

There has been a significant change in attitude to children with additional needs over the past few decades, with increasing numbers of children with additional needs being educated in mainstream schools. In England, for example, it was estimated that in 2008 there were 1,614,300 children with SEN in mainstream schools or around 20 per cent of the school population (DCSF, 2008). The statistics for other parts of the UK yielded a similar picture, with figures in Northern Ireland during 2009 indicating that there were some 60,000 children with SEN, amounting to around 17 to 18 per cent of the entire school population in mainstream schools. In Northern Ireland, the number of children with formalised Statements of Special Educational Needs rose from 2.5 per cent of the total school population in 1996/7 to around 3.9 per cent in 2007, with over two thirds of pupils with Statements being educated within mainstream schools or units attached to mainstream schools (DENI, 2009a). The number of children with additional needs in mainstream schools across the UK is now considerable (MacBlain, 2014; MacBlain et al., 2015) and, unlike in previous generations, is seen as being the norm. Indeed, the recent Children and Families Act (DfE, 2014a) and the subsequent Code of Practice (DfE, 2015) have gone further in determining the rights of children with additional needs, putting them at the centre of decision making and placing much greater emphasis on multi-agency working.

Whilst moves towards greater inclusion of children with SEN into mainstream settings have been generally welcomed (Booth and Ainscow, 2002), such increases in inclusion have presented significant challenges for teachers and early years practitioners in mainstream settings, as they have sought to meet their pupils' increasingly diverse needs. One example of the type of challenges facing early years practitioners can be found in the case of those children who struggle with the acquisition of literacy and who might have underlying cognitive deficits typical of children with dyslexia. These children may pose significant problems for adults working with them; they may, for example, require more individual and one-to-one support at the expense of time being spent on other children. A decade ago, Hartas (2006, p. 15), for example, commented in regard to this group of children as follows:

> Able young children with dyslexia are likely to experience difficulties with short-term memory and hand-eye co-ordination, as well as frustration emanating from not being able to show their good intellect in their academic work. Motor skills, especially fine motor skills, often lag behind cognitive abilities, particularly in gifted children ... Regarding their self-esteem, gifted young children with dyslexia tend to be highly self-critical in that they evaluate themselves on what they are unable to do, rather than on their substantial abilities, impacting on their sense of self-worth and emotional maturity and adjustment.

Hartas has further emphasised the need for practitioners to pay particular attention to key characteristics that can alert them to learning difficulties in those children that are very able but might be perceived as less able because of their underlying specific learning difficulties.

AUSTERITY AND POVERTY

Less than a decade ago, Cullis and Hansen (2009, p. 13) quite worryingly reported in relation to lower-income families in the UK that every £100 of extra income in the first nine months of children's lives made the difference of around a month's development by the age of 5. They also drew attention to the fact that the poorest families in society are often unable to afford books and computers, in addition to extra-curricular activities; their children's education is also more likely to be adversely affected by poor nutrition, overcrowding in the home and stress. A year later, Field (2010, p. 28) drew public attention to how:

> Children from low income families in the UK often grow up to be poor adults ... [they] are more likely to have preschool conduct and behavioural problems; more likely to experience bullying and take part in risky behaviours as teenagers; less likely to do well at school; less likely to stay on at school after 16; and more likely to grow up to be poor themselves.

Many children growing up in the 'poorest' families, as Cullis and Hansen have indicated, will too often fail to have access to computers in their homes, have a lack of good reading material and may have limited learning activities, which in the case of more well-off children would in turn benefit their learning whilst in school. The implications of this can be many for significant numbers of children who may fail to have their potential realised. In a report entitled *Deprivation and Risk: The Case for Early Intervention* (Action for Children, 2010, p. 12), Dr Ruth Lupton wrote:

> The relationship between deprivation and educational attainment is striking. Across the UK, children from the poorest homes start school with more limited vocabularies and greater likelihood of conduct problems and hyperactivity ... During primary school UK children fall further behind, and even the brightest children from the most disadvantaged backgrounds are overtaken by the age of 10 by their better-off peers who start off behind them.

One further and very worrying feature of poverty, more recently accentuated by the growth in austerity across most economies, has been the extent to which children from the poorest families who are intellectually very able, fail to find their way into high-achieving and academically inspiring schools. In his annual report, *Unsure Start: HMCI's Early Years Annual Report 2012/13 Speech 2014*, Sir Michael Wilshaw, Her Majesty's Chief Inspector (Ofsted), emphasised in the starkest of ways how poverty and low income, especially in the early years, can impact significantly on children's future realisations of potential and ultimately their life choices:

> The poorest children are less likely to follow instructions, make themselves understood, manage their own basic hygiene or play well together. By age five, many children have started reading simple words, talking in sentences and can add single numbers. But far fewer of the poorest can do these things well. Children from low-income families are far more likely than their better-off peers to lag behind at age three ... Too many do badly by the end of primary, and carry on doing badly at the end of secondary. (Wilshaw, 2014, p. 3)

Sir Michael then went on to emphasise the financial cost to the nation, which at a time of growing austerity and increased economic competition amongst countries across the globe is, again, very concerning:

> If the gap isn't closed, the costs to our nation will run into billions. The Sutton Trust estimates that the UK's economy would see cumulative losses of up to £1.3 trillion in GDP [Gross domestic product] over the next 40 years if the country fails to bring the educational outcomes of children from poorer homes up to the UK average. (p. 3)

It has been recognised (Sharma, 2007) that by 6 years of age children who are intellectually less able and who grow up in rich families are likely to have overtaken intellectually able children growing up in poor families. In one part of the UK, Northern Ireland, a report entitled *The Way Forward for Special Educational Needs and Inclusion* (DENI, 2009a, p. 12), which provided an analysis of underachievement in schools, offered the following quite worrying statistics:

> Statistics show a pattern of underachievement among children living in or at risk of poverty. Using entitlement to free school meals (FSM) as an indicator of social and economic deprivation, it was reported that in 2006/07, only 27 percent of pupils who were entitled to FSM gained at least 5 or more GCSEs at grades A–C ... including English and mathematics by the time they left school, compared with 60 percent of those who were not entitled to FSM ... 'poor educational attainment can reinforce the cycle of deprivation that many ... marginalised groups experience throughout their lives'.

Three years after this report in 2012, Sir Michael Wilshaw, in addressing concerns regarding the underachievement of children in England, called for changes in the way that many children from low-income families are taught. In particular, he was openly critical of the quality of teaching that many children who experience economic deprivation and who live in more affluent rural coastal areas were receiving. His criticisms were reported at the time in the popular media and reflected concerns at a national level regarding education. Sir Michael was especially critical of those schools with the worst record of attainment in teaching disadvantaged children who were now no longer those in inner cities but, rather, in 'mediocre' schools in deprived coastal towns and rural areas across England, where children were being incorrectly labelled and consigned to 'indifferent' teaching. Worryingly, an increasing polarisation in the UK and across the globe is being witnessed between the economic status of families, which in part is seen by some to be increasing the division between the 'well off' and those from lower socio-economic backgrounds and, even more worryingly perhaps, between two-parent families where both parents are earning and lone-parent families with only one income (Baker, 2006; Bianchi and Milke, 2010). A further group of children whose needs have only recently come to be recognised are those children, of all ages, who have to care for a parent and/or an older sibling (Barnardo's, 2015).

CHILDREN AS CARERS

The number of children caring for adults in the UK and across the globe is increasing. This is a feature of modern societies and particularly childhood that has only recently come to be properly acknowledged and addressed in recent years (MacBlain, 2014). In 2015, the Barnardo's organisation reported that the average age of a young carer in the UK was 12, and defined young carers as those children and young people below the age of 18 who 'provide regular and on-going care and emotional support to a family member who is physically or mentally ill, disabled or misuses substances'. Barnardo's cited the 2001 census, which identified 175,000 young carers in the UK, of which, astonishingly, some 13,000 were caring for someone for over 50 hours per week. Somewhat alarmingly, Barnardo's also indicated that ten years later, the 2011 census had identified 178,000 young carers in England and Wales alone, representing a staggering increase of 83 per cent in the number of young carers aged between 5 and 7 years of age and a 55 per cent increase in the number of children as carers aged between 8 and 9 years. These figures represent substantial increases and reveal how within most schools there will be children who are caring for someone else. The effects on their lives will, in most cases, be huge. It is certain that their education will be affected and it will be important, therefore, that adults tasked with managing and supporting the learning of this group of children fully recognise and understand the impact that caring will have on their learning and on their social and emotional development.

— —— POINTS FOR DISCUSSION —————————————

View the following YouTube video entitled 'Young Carers How Young is Young?' at www.youtube.com/watch?v=UMa7odqOEQw (The Lowry, 2015). Then consider the following:

1 How might teachers in primary schools and early years practitioners work with parents and outside agencies to determine how best to support children in their learning?

2 What steps might teachers and early years practitioners take to gain a better understanding of the impact of caring on a young person in their class and how might they create situations where they can talk about the practicalities of what they deal with each day, whilst maintaining dignity and confidentiality for the 'cared for' person?

STATE OF PLAY IN THE UK

Everywhere one looks one sees examples of children who don't seem to know how to play. Children's play is now radically different to that of even a few years ago. Indeed, much of children's play today would be unrecognisable to parents living only a few decades ago. It is different; some would argue, too different and often lacking in quality, most particularly creativity and social and physical activity and experiences. Nearly two decades ago, McDowall Clark (2010, p. 1) highlighted what is potentially a worrying trend:

> Children do not play out in the street anymore, they are rarely allowed to travel to school on their own ... Children spend an increasing proportion of their time in specially designated places such as day nurseries, out-of-school clubs and their own bedrooms, frequently fitted out with the latest technology. Childhood is progressively more regulated so that instead of being a natural part of public life, it takes place in private.

Central to the nature of children's play is an increased reliance on technology (Beauchamp, 2006, 2012), which though not a bad thing can bring problems if it dominates children's play and reduces other means of playful activities. Recently, Cook (2016, p. 3) urged caution when viewing the nature of play today:

> There exists a rather strong vector of sentiment, discourse and ideology at the current moment which takes 'play' – particularly, but not exclusively, children's play – as something of an all-inclusive cure for a wide swath of social ills. Lack of creativity, learning difficulties, the polluting effects of media and commerce, the debilitations of racism and sexism, together with a variety of therapeutics, are regularly presented at the altar of play in the hope of realising some sort of transformation, some kind of conversion.

Cook goes further in proposing how:

> the pilgrimage to the play deity extends seemingly in all directions without end in sight. Adults are urged to engage in playful parenting ... teachers in playful teaching ...When conceptions of play (re)essentialize the child, the definitive problematic of childhood studies becomes compromised, weakened. The 'problem of the child' – that is, what (or who) a child is, how to apprehend different childhoods – dissipates and diffuses in the presence of tacit agreements about the nature and, often, the benefits of play. (2016, p. 3)

The extent of tensions surrounding the place that play has had in the education of young children was brought to the attention of the public in February 2012 when Graeme Paton, education editor for the national online UK newspaper *The Telegraph*, reported as follows:

> In a letter to The Daily Telegraph, academics and authors said that controversial education reforms are robbing under-fives of the ability to play and leading to the 'schoolification' of the early years ... today's letter ... warned of 'widespread concern about the direction of the current revision' ... The experts ... suggested the system was 'too inflexible to cater for the highly diverse developmental needs of young children'. They are now creating a new group – Early Childhood Action – with the support of around 50 leading academics, authors and childcare organizations to push for an alternative curriculum.

Such tensions and the fact that they were reported in a national daily newspaper suggest major concerns regarding how children should be taught and the type of curricula they should have access to in their first years of formal education. It is recognised and accepted by most practitioners that, through play, children learn to communicate and cooperate with others and to form and manage relationships; through play they come to understand the world in which they live. The nature of play is, however, changing. Through play, children develop abilities and skills with language and, in doing so, their capacity to think (Gray and MacBlain, 2015). Play lies at the very heart of children's cognitive and emotional and social development; it is for this reason that many practitioners, academics and parents are becoming increasingly concerned that too many children today are not having enough opportunities to engage in active, meaningful and creative play activities. We now have a much better understanding of the nature of play and its importance in child development, but it remains a controversial area as witnessed by recent and current attempts by some in government within the UK to introduce more formal assessment at the age of 7!

FOCUS ON THEORY

Smith et al. (2003, p. 218) proposed what they considered to be a key distinction between play and exploration in young children, which has arisen from the ideas of the behaviourists and the Piagetians:

> Both exploration and play were awkward for traditional learning theorists, as neither was obviously goalseeking or under the control of reinforcers. It is also true that with very young children, during sensorimotor development ... the distinction between exploration and play is difficult to make, as for young infants, all objects are novel. By the preschool years, however, the distinction is clearer.

In emphasising this distinction, Smith et al. offered a conceptual framework through which it is possible to explore what is commonly understood as play. They have suggested three kinds of play: *locomotor*, *sociodramatic* and *language* play. The first of these involves physical exercise play and what is often referred to as rough-and-tumble play. The second refers to play with objects, which might include fantasy play and/or play of a sociodramatic nature. The final type has language at its core. With locomotor play, young children can be observed to engage in physical activities such as rough and tumble, running and jumping. Readers might like to reflect on how a lack of physical play might impact on a child's coordination and sensory integration and, more particularly, on their cognitive development such as problem solving and the development of logic. Readers might also reflect on the growth of Forest Schools and 'outdoor' play over the last few decades and how it can work to facilitate locomotor or physical development in children.

With regard to physical play, Pellegrini and Smith (1998, cited in Smith et al., 2003, pp. 220–1) have proposed that in physical activity play three developmental stages can be identified: (1) 'rhythmical stereotypes' such as the kicking of legs and waving of arms, as is typical of young babies; (2) 'exercise play' such as running and jumping, where the child is using their whole body, typical of children in pre-school settings, which frequently overlaps with (3) rough-and-tumble play, so often observed by adults in playground settings and by parents at home. Here, it is worth reflecting on the limited nature and experience of many young children today who spend much of their time before coming to pre-school and primary school watching television and computer screens for long periods of time (these concerns are addressed in more depth in Chapter 9 on the digital child).

Smith et al. (2003) suggest that sociodramatic play can be observed in children as young as 12 months, with the earliest type of pretend play including such behaviours as directing actions towards themselves and being dependent on the use of objects found around the home. The final type of play is language play. It is worth reflecting on how few opportunities many children have to engage in verbal communication with other children. Drawing directly on the work of Bruner, Brown (1977) suggests:

> Before the child can write or read he must be able to identify the symbols and the sounds they represent ... For written language the child must also have a high degree of motor coordination ... He [Bruner] suggested that the mind of a person who spent much of his time in these activities [reading and writing] might be 'profoundly different' from that of one who was involved in nonlinguistic activities such as drawing or building, and perhaps even different from that of one who mostly talked and listened. (p. 119)

It must be emphasised that children learn a great deal from listening to rhyming poems, riddles, nursery rhymes, and so on. As they grow, they move towards playing games that have rules with clearly defined structures. Through this type of play, they learn to manage relationships with others and understand the importance of boundaries. This latter type of play provides opportunities to be active outside of their homes and to join local clubs. Children also learn a great deal through playing outdoors (MacBlain and Bowman, 2016).

EMERGING CURRICULA AND PROPOSED INITIATIVES

In September 2012, a major initiative was introduced in England, though not in the rest of the UK, entitled *The Statutory Framework for the Early Years Foundation Stage* (DfE, 2012). This became mandatory for all early years providers in England working in maintained and non-maintained schools, independent schools, and all providers on the Early Years Register, though it was acknowledged that there might be exemptions to this final group. Though generally welcomed across the sector, this initiative has divided practitioners and academics, due in the main to a perceived emphasis on the introduction of more formalised teaching and learning approaches. Though the Framework has now been superseded by the more recent EYFS *Statutory Framework for the Early Years Foundation Stage: Setting the Standards for Learning, Development and Care for Children from Birth to Five* (2014), it is, nonetheless, worth visiting the key elements of the original 2012 Framework as it is in this document that we can identify the key ideas that worked towards promoting change.

Statutory framework for the early years foundation stage: Setting the standards for learning, development and care for children from birth to five (EYFS, 2014):

www.gov.uk/government/uploads/system/uploads/attachment_data/file/335504/EYFS_framework_from_1_September_2014__with_clarification_note.pdf

The 2012 Framework built on existing good practice and at its core was the belief that all children should have available to them the best possible start in life and the necessary level and type of support which would enable them to fulfil their potential. In addition, the Framework embraced the notion that children today are developing at a rate more quickly than ever before and that life experiences in their first years prior to commencing formal schooling at around the age of 5 are crucial to their future lives. Positive and effective parenting was also highlighted within the 2012 Framework as being central to the holistic development of children during the early years, as was the need for children to have access to learning experiences and environments of a high quality. It was especially notable that under the Framework, Ofsted were to have particular regard to the Early Years Foundation Stage (EYFS) in as much as it would inspect both the implementation and application of the new Framework and then report on the quality and standards of provision that are being offered. Following the inspections, Ofsted would be tasked with publishing its findings and, in some instances, issuing *notices to improve* or *welfare requirements notices*. Any provider subsequently not complying with a welfare requirements notice would be committing an offence. The Framework proposed four over-arching principles, which were to be central to practice in early years settings:

- every child is a unique child, who is constantly learning and can be resilient, capable, confident and self-assured
- children learn to be strong and independent through positive relationships
- children learn and develop well in enabling environments, in which their experiences respond to their individual needs and there is a strong partnership between practitioners and parents and/or carers
- children develop and learn in different ways and at different rates. (DfE, 2012, p. 3)

The Framework also proposed seven areas which would be at the core of learning and development in all young children: communication and language; physical development; personal, social and emotional development; literacy; mathematics; understanding the world; and expressive arts and design. The first three of these were to be viewed as 'Prime' areas, which would be particularly crucial, with the next four being seen as 'Specific' areas, which providers should take close account of in supporting children with the development of the Prime areas. The Framework stressed the importance of providers paying particular attention to the individual needs of children, in addition to the stage of development at which children are perceived to be functioning. With the introduction of the Framework, particular attention was to be given to the Prime areas, and especially when managing the learning experiences of very young children, which, the Framework proposed, 'reflect the key skills and capacities all children need to develop and learn effectively, and become ready for school' (DfE, 2012, p. 6).

The Framework also pays particular attention to children with special educational needs and/or disabilities where specialist intervention may be called for. Purposeful and effective links with families are highlighted as important, especially when supporting parents and children in accessing appropriate support from external agencies. Particularly encouraging is the fact that the Framework places particular emphasis on the importance of assessment:

> Ongoing assessment (also known as formative assessment) is an integral part of the learning and development process. It involves practitioners observing children to understand their level of achievement, interests and learning styles, and to then shape learning experiences for each child reflecting those observations. (DfE, 2012, p. 10)

Also included within the Framework is a significant and wholly welcome departure from one factor that has been a major challenge for many practitioners – the amount of paperwork they have felt it necessary to complete: 'Assessment should not entail prolonged breaks from interaction with children, nor require excessive paperwork. Paperwork should be limited to that which is absolutely necessary to promote children's successful learning and development' (p. 10).

A further welcome emphasis within the Framework has been that placed on child protection and safeguarding: 'Providers must have and implement a policy, and procedures, to safeguard children' (p. 13). The Framework has also placed significance on the training and qualifications and skill levels of providers, in addition to their active and meaningful role in the induction of new staff and subsequent effective, purposeful and appropriate continuing professional development. At the time of the introduction of the Framework, the British Association for Early Childhood Education (2012) produced an excellent publication, *Development Matters in the Early Years Foundation Stage* (EYFS), which offered clear guidance for providers in a most accessible format. It offered clear information relating to the learning of children in the Prime and Specific areas from birth through 40–60 months, offering providers and parents, in addition to other relevant professionals, a focus on what they ought to expect from children at differing ages and stages of development.

In Northern Ireland, *Learning to Learn: A Framework for Early Years Education and Learning* was published in 2013 (DENI, 2013) and set out the way forward for the early years education of children from birth through to the end of the Foundation Stage; in particular, it recognises and stresses how children's later success in school and in their future lives is determined at a very young age. It is similar to the *Statutory Framework for the Early Years Foundation Stage* in England (DfE, 2014b) in that it emphasises the importance of children growing up in positive and supportive home learning environments. It also emphasises how education and learning begin at birth and that working in partnership with parents is essential if society's goals for children are to be achieved, the two over-arching goals being 'raising standards for all' and 'closing the performance gap, increasing access and equality'. In order to achieve these, the Northern Ireland Framework pointed towards three enabling goals, namely: *developing the education workforce, improving the learning environment* and *transforming the governance and management of education.*

It is encouraging to note that today the importance of play in its own right and as a pedagogical tool is recognised as being fundamental to high quality early years education. Maintaining play at the centre of learning in the early years is essential. Practitioners feel strongly about this and are robust in their opposition to any proposed initiatives by government seeking to lessen the emphasis play has on the learning of children in the early years. Collaborative working amongst statutory, voluntary and professional bodies, therefore, and agreed aims and goals are critical to securing improved outcomes for young children.

SUMMARY

It is important for practitioners to examine and reflect on the changing nature of childhood and the perspectives that are popularly held of this time in the lives of individuals. Importantly, it is essential that practitioners working with young children examine their own perceptions and how these might account for meeting the individual needs of all children in their care. Exploring the changing nature of families and the shifting cultures within which children are now growing up and being educated is also a fundamental part of understanding the holistic needs of children.

 EXTENDED AND RECOMMENDED READING

Bianchi, S.M. and Milke, M.A. (2010) 'Work and family research in the first decade of the 21st century', *Journal of Marriage and Family*, 72: 705-25.

Marzano, R. and Kendall, J.S. (2006) *The New Taxonomy of Educational Objectives* (2nd edn). Thousand Oaks, CA/London: Sage.

Don't forget to visit **https://study.sagepub.com/contemporarychildhood** for a selection of free SAGE journal articles, web links, additional case studies, activities, and PowerPoints to help you revise.

REFERENCES

Action for Children (2010) *Deprivation and Risk: The Case for Early Intervention*. London: Action for Children.

Baker, M. (2006) *Restructuring Family Policies: Convergences and Divergences*. Toronto, Ontario, Canada: University of Toronto Press.

Barnardo's (2015) Child Poverty Statistics and Facts (www.barnardos.org.uk/what_we_do/ our_work/child_poverty/child_poverty_what_is_poverty/child_poverty_statistics_facts. htm).

Beauchamp, G. (2006) 'New technologies and "new teaching": a process of evolution?' In R. Webb (ed.), *Changing Teaching and Learning in the Primary School*. Maidenhead: Open University Press.

Beauchamp, G. (2012) *ICT in the Primary School: From Pedagogy to Practice*. London: Pearson.

Bianchi, S.M. and Milke, M.A. (2010) 'Work and family research in the first decade of the 21st century', *Journal of Marriage and Family*, 72: 705–25.

Booth, T. and Ainscow, M. (2002) *Index for Inclusion: Developing Learning and Participation in Schools*. Bristol: CSIE.

British Association for Early Childhood Education (BAECE) (2012) *Development Matters in the Early Years*. London: BAECE.

Brown, G. (1977) *Child Development*. Shepton Mallet: Open Books.

Cawson, P. (2002) *Child Maltreatment in the Family*. London: NSPCC.

Colverd, S. and Hodgkin, B. (2011) *Developing Emotional Intelligence in the Primary School*. London: Routledge.

Cook, D. (2016) 'Disrupting play: a cautionary note', *Childhood*, 23(1): 3–6.

Cowie, H. (2012) *From Birth to Sixteen: Children's Health, Social, Emotional and Linguistic Development*. London: Routledge.

Cullis, A. and Hansen, K. (2009) *Child Development in the First Three Sweeps of the Millennium Cohort Study*, DCSF Research Report RW-007. London: DCSF.

Cuthbert, C., Rayns, G. and Stanley, K. (2011) *All Babies Count: Prevention and Protection for Vulnerable Babies – A Review of the Evidence*. London: NSPCC.

Department for Children, Schools and Families (DCSF) (2008) *Special Educational Needs in England*. London: DCSF.

Department for Children, Schools and Families (DCSF) (2009) *Statistical First Release, August 2009*. London: DCSF. (www.dcsf.gov.uk, accessed 18 December 2009).

Department for Education (DfE) (2012) *Statutory Framework for the Early Years Foundation Stage: Setting the Standards for Learning, Development and Care for Children from Birth to Five*. Runcorn: DfE.

Department for Education (DfE) (2014a) *Children and Families Act 2014*. London: The Stationery Office.

Department for Education (DfE) (2014b) *Statutory Framework for the Early Years Foundation Stage: Setting the Standards for Learning, Development and Care for Children from Birth to Five*. London: DfE.

Department for Education (DfE) (2015) *Special Educational Needs and Disability Code of Practice: 0 to 25 Years*. London: The Stationery Office.

Department of Education Northern Ireland (DENI) (2005) *Review of English as an Additional Language (EAL)*. Bangor: DENI.

Department of Education Northern Ireland (DENI) (2006) *English as an Additional Language: Summary of Principal and Teacher Interviews*. Bangor: DENI.

Department of Education Northern Ireland (DENI) (2007) *Supporting Ethnic Minority Children who have English as an Additional Language*. Bangor: DENI.

Department of Education Northern Ireland (DENI) (2009a) *The Way Forward for Special Educational Needs and Inclusion*. Bangor: DENI.

Department of Education Northern Ireland (DENI) (2009b) *Every School a Good School: Supporting Newcomer Pupils*. Bangor: DENI.

Department of Education Northern Ireland (DENI) (2010) *Statistics on Education*. Bangor: DENI.

Department of Education Northern Ireland (DENI) (2013) *Learning to Learn: A Framework for Early Years Education and Learning*. Bangor: DENI.

Education and Training Inspectorate (ETI) (2005) *The Quality of Learning and Teaching and the Standards and Outcomes Achieved by Learners in Relation to the Provision for English as an Additional Language*. Belfast: Department of Education.

EYFS (2014) *Statutory Framework for the Early Years Foundation Stage: Setting the Standards for Learning, Development and Care for Children from Birth to Five.* London: DfE.

Field, F. (2010) *The Foundation Years: Preventing Poor Children Becoming Poor Adults – Report of the Independent Review on Poverty and Life Chances.* London: Cabinet Office.

Gray, C. and MacBlain, S.F. (2015) *Learning Theories in Childhood* (2nd edn). London: Sage.

Hartas, D. (2006) *Dyslexia in the Early Years: A Guide to Teaching and Learning.* London: Routledge.

MacBlain, S.F. (2014) *How Children Learn.* London: Sage.

MacBlain, S.F. and Bowman, H. (2016) 'Teaching and learning', in D. Wyse and S. Rodgers (eds), *A Guide to Early Years and Primary Teaching.* London: Sage.

MacBlain, S.F., Long, L. and Dunn, J. (2015) *Dyslexia, Literacy and Inclusion: Child-centred Perspectives.* London: Sage.

McDowall Clark, R. (2010) *Childhood in Society: For Early Childhood Studies.* Exeter: Learning Matters.

National Association for Language Development in the Curriculum (NALDIC) (2012) Research and Information (www.naldic.org.uk/research-and-information/eal-statistics/eal-pupils).

Northern Ireland Statistics and Research Agency (NISRA) (2009) *Long-term International Migration Estimates for Northern Ireland* (2007–8). Belfast: NISRA.

Paton, G. (2012) 'New-style "nappy curriculum" will damage childhood', *The Telegraph*, 6 February (www.telegraph.co.uk/education/educationnews/9064870/New-style-nappy-curriculum-will-damage-childhood.html).

Pellegrini, A. and Smith, P. K. (1998) 'Physical activity play: the nature and function of a neglected aspect of play', *Child Development, 69,* 557–598.

Sharma, N. (2007) *'It doesn't Happen Here': The Reality of Child Poverty in the UK.* Ilford: Barnado Press.

Skinner, B. (2010) 'English as an Additional Language and initial teacher education: views and experiences from Northern Ireland', *Journal of Education for Teaching*, 36(1): 75–90.

Smith, K.S., Cowie, H. and Blades, M. (2003) *Understanding Children's Development* (4th edn). Oxford: Blackwell.

United Nations Educational, Scientific and Cultural Organization (UNESCO) (1994) The Salamanca Statement and Framework for Action on Special Needs Education (http://unesdoc.unesco.org/images/0009/000984/098427eo.pdf).

United Nations Children's Fund (UNICEF) (1989) Convention on the Rights of the Child (www2.ohchr.org/english/law/crc.htm#art12).

Walker, A., Flatley, J. and Kershaw, C. (eds) (2009) *Crime in England and Wales 2008/09, Vol. 1: Findings from the British Crime Survey and Police Recorded Crime.* London: HMSO.

Wilshaw, M. (2014) *Unsure Start: HMCI's Early Years Annual Report 2012/13 Speech 2014.*

2

THE CHILD'S PERSPECTIVE

Why you should read this chapter

If you work with children, or are studying to work with children, then you probably already view childhood as a special phase in life and children as unique, exceptional and different from the rest of humankind. There has been considerable change over the last couple of decades in how children are viewed and this has had an undeniable impact in the field of early childhood. The ratification of, awareness and support for the United Nations Convention on the Rights of the Child (UN, 1989) has also had a major influence on these shifting perceptions of the child. This has all culminated in much greater concerns for and promotion of the child's perspective. However, this current trend can be problematic and has the potential to provide oversimplified views of listening to children (Palaiologou, 2014).

By the end of this chapter you should:

- have an awareness of the significance and impact of the United Nations Convention on the Rights of the Child in early childhood
- have developed your understanding of the rhetoric and the reality of seeking to listen to children's perspectives
- have a growing understanding of the role of the child in research and innovative methods of participatory research.

CURRENT VIEWS ON CHILDREN'S PERSPECTIVES

In recent years, young children's perspectives and their active participation has been high on the UK's political, research and policy agendas (Konstantoni, 2013). Indeed, James and Prout (2015) suggest that at no other time have children been so highly profiled nor had such a prominent place in policy and practice. It is argued that if we want to improve children's lives, then we must focus on childhood as a life stage in its own right and value children's subjective experience of childhood. In the recent 'Good Childhood Report' (2015), the Children's Society suggests that children's priorities are refreshing because they challenge polarised narratives and their views are often more balanced and nuanced than many adults give them credit for. In the UK, children are encouraged to participate in and shape policies which affect their lives and many such policies are published in a variety of formats including age-appropriate versions for children to access. For example, in Northern Ireland, the *Early Years (0–6) Strategy* (DENI, 2010) went through a period of consultation before being published, which included consultation with children aged from 0 to 6 years old. The creative approaches used to uncover these young children's views can be seen at www.deni.gov.uk/publications/report-early-years-consultation-young-children-0-6-strategy. Similarly, Young Minds, which is the UK's leading charity for improving the well-being and mental health of children and young people, was recently commissioned by NHS England and the Department of Health to consult with children and young people on a range of mental health issues. Over 1100 children and young people took part in the survey and their findings contributed to the government's report 'Future in Mind' (Department of Health, 2015), which also included an open letter to children and young people. You can find this report at www.gov.uk/government/uploads/system/uploads/attachment_data/file/414024/Childrens_Mental_Health.pdf. This commitment to sharing policy findings with children who have contributed their perspectives is also essential in ensuring that consultation with children is not tokenistic but helps them to see that they are part of the team of experts and they are 'another chair ... around the decision making tables' (Lancaster and Kirby, 2010, p. 12).

There has also been a growing literature on children's participation in research. This not only involves them as research participants but it also involves them as co-researchers where they can be involved in any number of research phases (Dunn, 2015). Indeed, this shift in seeking children's perspectives and giving them a voice has been referred to as 'irresistible' and a 'social epidemic' by Palaiologou (2014: 690), since this idea of children as participants in matters which affect them is so widespread in the field of early childhood. There is a growing literature on making children's voices much more visible in both pedagogy and in research as it is suggested that, until recently, children have often been invisible and voiceless. So what has brought about this shift in seeking children's perspectives? In answering this question, it is important to consider changing theoretical perspectives within the field of Childhood Studies and also the impact of the ratification of the United Nations Convention on the Rights of the Child.

CHILDHOOD STUDIES AND CHILDREN'S PERSPECTIVES

The field of Childhood Studies recognises that childhoods are not unitary; rather, they are plural and that even within a single nation there is great diversity in the social construction of childhood. The idea of a standard childhood is no longer acceptable and it is widely agreed that the conditions of contemporary childhood have undoubtably changed in the twenty-first century (Prout, 2011). Childhood Studies draws on a range of disciplines, including anthropology, psychology and sociology, and what is referred to as the 'new sociology of childhood' (James and Prout, 1997; James, Jenks and Prout, 1998) appeared during the 1980s and 1990s. This had a huge impact on how children were viewed. James and Prout (2015) discuss how the history of the study of childhood was marked by the silence of children and how children were a 'muted group'. However, the new sociology of childhood led to a move from adults' constructions of childhood to a focus on children's own perspectives and an increasing participation of children in all aspects of life (Smith, 2011). Children are now recognised as social actors and informants in their own right (Hendrick, 2008) and as 'being' rather than 'becoming'. Therefore, children are no longer seen as passive subjects in the world but rather as active in the construction of their social lives. Childhood is recognised as a special phase of life rather than simply a preparation for adulthood and children themselves are recognised as being competent and capable (Christensen and Prout, 2005). Agency is one of the key features of the new sociology of childhood where children are perceived to have the capacity to understand and act on their world. Therefore, children are viewed as active agents who construct their own cultures (Corsaro, 2005).

— —— POINTS FOR DISCUSSION ——————————————

In their book *Global Childhoods*, Cregan and Cuthbert (2014) discuss current views of children including 'children in crisis' and 'endangered childhoods'. They highlight the anxiety about children's lives including issues such as child obesity, the sexualisation of children, the impact of technology, children's mental health and many others. The notion of children in crisis does not sit comfortably alongside the notion of children as autonomous and strong. Discuss your view of this dichotomy and how you view children in the UK today.

However, it is suggested that the new sociology of childhood led to the creation of 'mantras' within the UK, such as recognition of and a focus on children's agency, voice, experience and participation (Tisdall and Punch, 2012). It is also argued that some of these perspectives put forward by the new sociology of childhood are unsustainable in postmodernism, and Prout (2011) returned to discuss some of the dualisms that the sociology of childhood presented and to argue for more flexible concepts. One of these dualisms was children as 'being' versus 'becoming' and he posited that both views had commendable features. However, he argued that emphasising children as 'beings' risked endorsing the myth that children are autonomous and independent. Rather, both children and adults should be seen as 'becomings' in which all are incomplete and dependent. Similarly, the concept of the child as expert is one that has been critiqued within the literature. Gallacher and Gallagher (2008) argued that notions of expertise are unhelpful and claimed that all humans are unfinished subjects in the making. However, Levy and Thompson (2015) counter-argue that it is inappropriate to insist that children are not experts in their own lives, on the grounds that no human being achieves complete expertise. Rather, they believe that child expertise should be welcomed.

Theoretical perspectives which are associated with socioculturalism have also made a major contribution to the changing perspective of children (Merewether and Fleet, 2014). Both Vygotsky (1978) and Rogoff (2003) stressed the importance of the context and social environment on learning and they advocated that children learn alongside others, both adults and children. The sociocultural approach emphasises the shared construction of knowledge leading to shared understanding.

FOCUS ON THEORY

Barbara Rogoff (2003) argues that individuals develop as participants in their cultural communities and, therefore, development happens not just within individuals but within group and community processes. Therefore, if we want to understand learning and development, we have to study it within family life and community practices. She highlights the importance of taking different perspectives of people from different cultures and communities and she highlights the value of learning from both 'insiders' and 'outsiders' from these communities. All of these perspectives provide an angle on the phenomena being studied which helps to build understanding. Therefore, we can see that Rogoff's view of human development requires us to consider the perspectives of a wide range of individuals who are part of families and communities and this includes children. Children are positioned as social actors who are capable of holding opinions and ideas. Their perspectives as insiders in families, in schools and in the wider community are essential in building understanding about a wide range of issues.

UNITED NATIONS CONVENTION ON THE RIGHTS OF THE CHILD AND CHILDREN'S PERSPECTIVES

This changing view of children as competent, strong and knowledgeable, which we have been reading about in the previous section on Childhood Studies, also owes much to the mandates of the United Nations Convention on the Rights of the Child (UNCRC) (UN, 1989). The UNCRC is the most ratified international convention and its 54 articles cover civil, economic, social and cultural rights for children and young people. Ratifying countries are obligated to turn the rights into reality (Tisdall and Punch, 2012). The ratification of the UNCRC in the UK in 1991 represented a potentially dramatic shift in approaches to children's rights, including the right to be heard. Article 12 (para. 1) states:

> States' parties shall assure to the child who is capable of forming his or her own views the right to express those views freely in all matters affecting the child, the views of the child being given due weight in accordance with the age and maturity of the child.
> (UN, 1989)

However, the Committee on the Rights of the Child recognised that there was a lack of focus on early childhood by the states' parties and a concomitant lack of understanding on the broader implications of the UNCRC for young children. Therefore, they produced General Comment No. 7, Implementing Child Rights in Early Childhood (UN, 2005), which gave prominence to the view that young children are holders of all rights enshrined in the Convention and that early childhood is a critical period for the realisation of these rights. It specifically draws attention to the rights of children to participate in decision making that affects their lives and to be empowered to communicate their own views (Harcourt and Einarsdottir, 2011). Further to this, in 2006 the Committee on the Rights of the Child held its annual Day of General Discussion on the Right of the Child to be Heard and highlighted the importance of Article 12 and recognised the right of the child to express views and to participate in various activities, stating that this was 'beneficial for the child, for the family, for the community, the school, the State, for democracy' (UN, 2006, p. 2). Similarly, General Comment No. 12, The Right of the Child to be Heard (UN, 2009), clearly elucidated that the right of all children to be heard and taken seriously constituted one of the fundamental values of the Convention. In the more recent General Comment No. 14, The Committee on the Rights of the Child emphasises that the fact that the child is very young does not deprive him or her of the right to express his or her views, nor reduce the weight given to the child's views in determining his or her best interests (UN, 2013).

Therefore, from this brief look at the UNCRC and the associated General Comments from the Committee on the Rights of the Child, we can be in no doubt that consulting with children is not just an aspiration but is an obligation for professionals working with young children. Indeed, Lundy (2007, p. 931) asserts that inviting children's perspectives is 'not an option which is the gift of adults, but a legal imperative which is the right of the child'. Freeman (1983, p. 32) highlights how rights are particularly valuable 'moral coinage' for those without other means of power, and the UNCRC has been advantageous for children in that it has brought together international law pertaining to children and young people into one binding instrument. It has led to advocacy for children and young people at local, national and international levels and, at its core, it promotes the rights of children and young people (Tisdall and Punch, 2012). However, despite the legal pressure and the strong vision outlined in government policy, there is still a divide between the rhetoric and the reality of listening to the views and interests of very young children (Dunn, 2015). Despite the UNCRC being popular in its ratification, Tisdall and Punch (2012) point out that it 'lacks teeth' in terms of enforceability and that the phrasing in the UNCRC allows for considerable interpretation and even manipulation, and Livingstone (2014) agrees that the UNCRC is often more notable for its lack of implementation than its achievements. There are also a number of challenges, paradoxes and dilemmas in relation to children in research which impact on the reality of children's perspectives.

CHALLENGES AND TENSIONS IN LISTENING TO YOUNG CHILDREN'S PERSPECTIVES

Although children's rights are presented as the new norm in policy and practice, there are some 'troublesome consequences' (Quennerstedt and Quennerstedt, 2014, p. 117). It is suggested that questions, tensions and challenges continually emerge as part of the dynamic relationship between children's rights, children and society (Jones, 2011). One of these challenges is the potential conflict between children's right to participate and their right to protection. Einarsdottir (2011) addresses this potential conflict and highlights how listening to children can be seen to be potentially obtrusive and could be seen as a way for adults to control children and have them under constant surveillance. Kanyal and Gibbs (2014) also believe it is critical to understand the delicate balance between participation and protection. However, they caution that this conflicting view of children as competent and autonomous and children as vulnerable can encroach and impact negatively on children's participatory rights. Alderson and Morrow (2011, p. 36) assert that whilst protection is important, 'over-protection can lead to children being treated as passive objects of concern rather than as active moral agents in their own right' and they further highlight the dangers of silencing children and ending their hope of influencing policy and practice. If research is conducted within an ethical framework, then concerns about harming participants should be minimised (Meehan, 2016). Indeed, many researchers argue that if research is going to influence practice within the classroom, then it must be situated within classrooms, the presence of children as research participants must be taken seriously and there must be a balance between protection and voice (Rogers et al., 2016).

 POINTS FOR DISCUSSION

Children's safety in the online world is a current challenge and digital exposure for most children is increasingly inevitable (Binford, 2015). You can read more about this in Chapter 9: The Digital Child.

Sexting, child pornography, cyberbullying, grooming and trolling are all potentially devastating issues that may involve young children. Consider the following points:

- If we take the view that children are experts with autonomy and agency, then should we be consulting them about these issues and how they think they might be made more aware of how to protect themselves online?
- Is encouraging their perspectives on this issue in their best interests (UN, 2013) or do we need to protect children from even discussing such issues?
- Is it possible to encourage children's perspectives in these areas in age-appropriate and child-friendly ways?

Consider the following videos and how they might be used in such discussions:

- This video is a sensitive animation presenting the findings of a report on child sexual exploitation in Northern Ireland (Marshall, 2014) to children and young people (www.youtube.com/watch?v=kGcn8wWVOuM&feature=youtu.be).
- This video was produced by the NSPCC to help children understand the dangers of sexting (www.nspcc.org.uk/preventing-abuse/keeping-children-safe/share-aware/).

Another potential dilemma that arises in seeking children's perspectives is the generational divide and power differentials that exist when adults carry out research with children (Smith, 2011). Dockett, Einarsdottir and Perry (2011) maintain that children's social status is subordinate to adults and therefore power relationships are inherent and may impact on the nature of research. It is undeniable that the presence of an adult as a researcher seeking children's perspectives changes the environment 'however lightly the researcher steps' (Eckhoff, 2015, p. 1617) and children's views are open to being misrepresented and distorted by adults who have a more powerful position than children. This brings us to the debates on seeking children's perspectives in research studies.

METHODS FOR SEEKING CHILDREN'S PERSPECTIVES IN RESEARCH

There is a lot of discussion in the literature about whether participatory research with children needs to use different methods to those used in research with adults. Should they be the same or different and does participatory research with children really require 'child-friendly' methods? Punch (2002) suggests that child-friendly methods are necessary due to children's lack of power in interactions with adults. However, Christensen and Prout (2002) argue for the concept of 'ethical symmetry' which is grounded in the belief that children are both similar to adults and unique. Therefore, commonality and difference are recognised. Dockett, Einarsdottir and Perry (2011) further explain that assuming ethical symmetry does not mean that researchers regard adults and children as the same, but that it focuses on using appropriate methods that emphasise the particular competency of the research participants.

Participatory research is about respecting and understanding those being researched and it aims to break down the distinction between the researcher and research participants. It has democratic underpinnings which emphasise the complementary expertise of researcher and participants. However, the inability of adults to choose appropriate research methods to use with young children, which will help us to listen effectively to what they want to say, is often seen as a barrier to true participation (Kanyal and Gibbs, 2014). Listening to children can imply a passive process but 'listening is an active verb, which involves giving an interpretation, giving meaning to the message and value to those who are being listened to' (Rinaldi, 2001, p. 4). Listening may also suggest verbal interactions; however, with very young children this may not always be an appropriate way to access their views. Malaguzzi created the phrase 'the hundred languages of children' (Edwards et al., 1998), which indicates the potential of children to express themselves in a wide range of ways.

If we return to the Committee on the Rights of the Child, we can see that it recognises that, if children are going to achieve their right of participation, there is a variety of ways that children can express themselves. The Committee recognises the evolving capacities of young children and states that adults (researchers) should adopt a child-centred attitude and 'show patience and creativity by adapting their expectations to a young child's interests, level of understanding and preferred ways of communicating' (UN, 2005, para. 14). The importance of the environment in which the child is expressing their views is highlighted as being one in which the child should feel respected and secure, and a recognition of and respect for non-verbal forms of communication, including play, body language, facial expressions and drawing and painting, are urged (UN, 2009, para. 21). It is also asserted that children are not a homogenous group and therefore diversity must be taken into account when assessing their best interests (UN, 2013). Therefore, responsibility lies with the researcher to know the children in the research study, their level of understanding, their interests and how they may prefer to share their perspectives.

 **POINTS FOR DISCUSSION** ──────────

Merewether and Fleet (2014) highlight that their experiences in research led them to believe that some researchers' lack of expertise in working with young children can limit the potential of children's perspectives:

- From your standpoint of having experience in working with young children, why do you think this may be?
- How might greater expertise in working with children enhance the research of children's experiences and perspectives?
- How does your experience in working with children help you to understand how particular methods might or might not work well with young children?

INNOVATIVE METHODS FOR ELICITING THE VIEWS OF YOUNG CHILDREN

Due to the changing perspectives on childhood and the increasing recognition of children's rights, as already discussed at the beginning of this chapter, there has been a plethora of research which seeks to uncover children's views and perspectives on a wide range of topics. In some literature, it has been likened to a social epidemic (Palaiologou, 2014). It has also given rise to concerns about an oversimplified view of the child and listening (Kjørholt et al., 2005), mono-layered approaches to research with children (Palaiologou, 2014) and an uncensored celebration of voice (Silin, 2005). Further to this, Palaiologou (2014) cautions that seeking children's perspectives through participatory research is in danger of becoming an 'illusion of participation' with narrow views on listening to children's voices. This 'mantra' of valuing children's voices (Tisdall and Punch 2012), whilst commendable, is not simple in practice. Rather, it is a complex process which requires continuous critical reflection.

The Mosaic approach (Clark and Moss, 2001) is very well known in the field of early childhood as a framework for listening to young children. The principles of this framework are that it is: *multi-method*, in that it recognises the different voices of children; *participatory*, in treating children as experts; *reflexive*, including children's, practitioners' and parents' views in the overall interpretation; *adaptable*, within a wide range of settings; *focused on children's lived experiences* and *embedded into practice*, rather than seen as a bolt-on activity. The different pieces of the Mosaic involve observation, child conferencing, using cameras to take photographs, tours led by children, map making by children and role play. Clark and Moss recognised the need to imaginatively re-think appropriate methods of consultation with very young children and you can read more of their research in other texts. Many current research studies have used and adapted this approach in their work.

Many of these studies adopt the combined use of photographs and accompanying narrative about the pictures to elicit children' views. In their research, Alaca et al. (2016) wanted to gain insights into young children's (aged 3 to 5 years) perspectives on their communities. They used photovoice methodology where the children took photographs with disposable cameras and then selected a number of the photos to discuss with their teacher while researchers recorded the narrative. Christensen and James (2008) believe that the use of cameras not only evokes children's enthusiasm and interest in the research topic but that, when used alongside other methods, it can form part of a methodological triangulation. Indeed, Alaca et al. (2016) highlighted that it was the combination of visual and verbal which allowed the children's views to be heard, as they suggest that children's inner worlds are unique to them and it would be nearly impossible for researchers to interpret their perspective from the photographs alone. They also suggested that the active engagement of the children in photovoice was a particularly appropriate methodology in the school environment as it did not disrupt the children's learning space.

In another recent study, Mykkänen et al. (2016) discuss how they use photo-elicitation to investigate how children explain factors that lead to success in classroom learning activities. In this study, the children used camera-equipped devices (iPod Touch) to take pictures of their classroom activities and then used the photos as part of discussions with a researcher. But these authors recognised the importance of engaging the children's interest in the task and made the activity playful by presenting the data collection as a detective course where the participants acted as 'detectives of success' in their classroom (2016, p. 100). This approach demonstrates a child-centred attitude, creativity and an awareness of how young children may be engaged in tasks without disrupting learning within the classroom setting. However, some authors criticise the over-use of participatory methods which privilege verbal communication, which therefore means that only children who can verbally formulate their views can have their voices heard (Quennerstedt, 2016). In her study, Quennerstedt works with children aged 1–3 years and accesses their perspectives on human rights in the pre-school setting through detailed observations of the children's interactions with each other and the environment. As well as children being involved as research participants, they are also increasingly being involved in different stages of the process. So let us turn our attention to why this is also becoming an increasing trend in research with children.

CHILDREN'S INVOLVEMENT IN THE RESEARCH PROCESS

A number of arguments have been presented on the benefits of involving children in research. These include pedagogical benefits (what children themselves learn from the experience), political potential (the potential for children to change policy) and epistemological benefits (the potential for children to produce improved understandings and therefore better research) (Davis, 2009). These perceived benefits have led to researchers working with children as co-researchers where children may be involved in any number of research phases from design to dissemination (Kellett, 2010). We have already mentioned, earlier in this chapter, the challenge of the power differential that exists between the adult researcher and the child participants. This power differential can have implications for the research and may impact on the perspectives shared by the children on the issues under investigation. One way of reducing the power divide can be in children themselves carrying out the research with other children. In a recent study, Levy and Thompson (2015) took a 'buddy partnership' approach and involved 11- and 12-year-old boys (the buddies) in working with 5- and 6-year-old boys to understand the factors that influenced the younger boys' engagement and confidence in reading. They allocated significant time for the buddy partnership to be developed in a playful and relaxed manner before any data was gathered and they highlighted the crucial role that relationships play in participatory research.

Children's involvement as co-researcher has growing recognition in participatory research, but do very young children understand what is being researched and how can we assist them in doing so?

--- ○ --- **CASE STUDY 2.1** ----------------------------------

In her work on children's views on popular culture to teach writing in the primary classroom (Dunn et al., 2014), Dunn adapted the use of a Children's Research Advisory Group (CRAG). The CRAG was to be involved in advising on appropriate research methods to use with the children in the study and also in interpreting the research findings. However, before this they were involved in capacity building where they were familiarised with the issues surrounding the research and assisted in developing their views on these issues, one of which was popular culture. Bobby the puppet 'talked' to the children in the CRAG about his favourite television programmes, children's films and computer games. He showed some of his favourite toys and games from

(Continued)

(Continued)

his toy bag which were associated with some of the films; for example, he showed his Woody and Buzz Lightyear toys and dressing-up clothes from the film *Toy Story*. He encouraged the children in the CRAG to tell their talking partner about their favourite television programmes and why they enjoyed them. The children later had opportunities to draw something from their favourite film and showcase their drawings on a board and also to talk about them in front of their peers. The children in the CRAG were also encouraged to bring in toys and other artefacts from their favourite TV programmes and films, and show-and-tell sessions were held as well as discussions using a circle-time approach about their favourite toys and games. The purpose of all of these sessions was to assist the children to further develop their understanding of the issue of popular culture before they would then become involved in advising on the research process which focused on garnering children's views on the use of popular culture to teach writing.

FOCUS ON THEORY

This involvement of children as co-researchers fits very well with children's rights' perspectives and Article 12 of the UNCRC where children have a voice in the full spectrum of research from design through to dissemination (Lundy and McEvoy, 2009). However, Lundy and McEvoy (2012) urge caution that whilst the UNCRC gives children the right to express their views, it also requires that children are assisted in forming their views. It cannot be assumed that children will understand the issue being researched and Article 12 of the UNCRC should be interpreted in line with other rights including Article 5, which highlights the right to be supported and guided by adults, and Article 13, which states the right to seek, receive and impart information. That is not to suggest that children are incompetent; rather we can take the perspective that young children are neither incompetent nor fully competent and they will benefit from adult guidance (Lundy and McEvoy, 2012; Lundy, McEvoy and Byrne, 2011). Smith (2011) concurs with this and argues that it is possible to be respectful of children's agency while also being aware of their evolving capacity and their need for direction and guidance at times.

The following case offers an example of a highly intelligent child who, though having his extremely high levels of intellectual functioning identified before he attended school, ended up being perceived by his teachers as a child who was presenting with behavioural issues.

─ 🔍 ── CASE STUDY 2.2 ────────────────────────

Simon was referred to an educational psychologist following a request from his parents who felt that he was highly intelligent and hoped that his high levels of ability would be recognised by his teachers when he commenced school a month later. The educational psychologist's report offered the following: *Assessment involved observation of Simon working through a range of activities in his home, discussion with his father and mother and information gained from psychometric assessment using the Wechsler Preschool and Primary Scale of Intelligence - Third Edition (WPPSI - III). When I met with Simon, he presented as a lovely little boy who was very engaging and outgoing. Simon was keen to talk with me and I was very impressed by his willingness to attempt all of the tasks I set. I was very impressed with Simon's levels of language and he engaged in a range of problem-solving situations, which indicated that he was applying logic at quite a sophisticated level and beyond that expected of someone of his age. I observed Simon to be very well coordinated and he demonstrated high levels of concentration and attention. In order to gain further information regarding Simon's intellectual functioning, I administered selected sub-tests from the Wechsler Preschool and Primary Scale of Intelligence - Third Edition (WPPSI - III). He achieved the following scores: Verbal: Percentile score 99; and Performance (sometimes referred to as non-verbal): Percentile score 99.*

It is generally agreed that two-thirds of children are considered to function within the average range of ability and this range is represented between the 16th and 84th centiles, where the 16th centile lies at the lowest end of the average range and the 84th centile the highest. The 85th centile upwards represents increasingly higher ability with the 95th centile representing the top 1 per cent of ability. At the other end of the range, the 1st centile represents the lowest 1 per cent of ability. The above results, therefore, clearly indicate that Simon is a child of exceptional ability. The educational psychologist offered a number of recommendations and strongly recommended that when Simon began school, his abilities, as indicated in this report, should be made known to the teacher with responsibility for children who are gifted and talented. The educational psychologist also drew attention to the *Good Schools Guide*, which has advised that one possible feature of children who are gifted and talented is their frustration with handwriting due to poor handwriting, which can arise from frustration caused by not being able to get their ideas down quickly enough on paper. She also emphasised that

Simon was very young and that it would be important that each aspect of his development be carefully monitored. A year and a half later, Simon's parents contacted the educational psychologist concerned, that his teachers were raising concerns about his behaviour, the very poor presentation of written work and his inattentiveness due, they felt, to boredom. Increasingly, Simon was becoming viewed as a child not of extremely high levels of intellectual functioning but rather as a child of average ability with poor motivation. To this extent, his voice was not being heard and those natural rights that would have been accorded to him because of his talents were being lost.

SUMMARY

Seeking children's perspectives is an increasing trend in policy and research but Mayes (2016) cautions that we must not romanticise participatory processes. This chapter has indicated the potential for using a wide variety of approaches for uncovering children's perspectives but there are still challenges and dilemmas in relation to ethics, power differences and the choice of methodologies. Innovative methods need to be continually scrutinised to ensure methodological rigour is not lost in the quest for participation. However, the current drive to champion children's perspectives can only be welcomed and it is hoped that it will continue to be developed for the betterment of the lives of all children.

 EXTENDED AND RECOMMENDED READING

Dunn, J. (2015) 'Insiders' perspectives: a children's rights approach to involving children in advising on adult-initiated research', *International Journal of Early Years Education*, 23(4): 394–408.

Provides an insight into involving children as co-researchers in advising on research.

Tisdall, E.K.M. and Punch, S. (2012) 'Not so new? Looking critically at childhood studies', *Children's Geographies*, 10(3): 249–64.

Provides an interesting critique of the new sociology of childhood and children's rights.

 Don't forget to visit **https://study.sagepub.com/contemporarychildhood** for a selection of free SAGE journal articles, web links, additional case studies, activities, and PowerPoints to help you revise.

REFERENCES

Alaca, B., Rocca, C. and Maggi, S. (2016) 'Understanding communities through the eyes and voices of children', *Early Child Development and Care*, doi.org/10.1080/03004430.2016.1155567.

Alderson, P. and Morrow, V. (2011) *The Ethics of Research with Children and Young People: A Practical Handbook* (2nd edn). London: Sage.

Binford, W. (2015) *The Digital Child*, Social Science Research Network (http://ssrn.com/abstract=2563874).

Children's Society, The (2015) *The Good Childhood Report 2015*. London: The Children's Society.

Christensen, P. and James, A. (2008) 'Childhood diversity and commonality', in P. Christensen and A. James (eds), *Research with Children: Perspectives and Practices* (2nd edn). London: Routledge. pp. 156–72.

Christensen, P. and Prout, A. (2002) 'Working with ethical symmetry in social research with children', *Childhood*, 9(4): 477–97.

Christensen, P. and Prout, A. (2005) 'Anthropological and sociological perspectives on the study of children', in S. Greene and D. Hogan (eds), *Researching Children's Experience*. London: Sage. pp. 42–60.

Clark, A. and Moss, P. (2001) *Listening to Young Children: The Mosaic Approach*. London: The National Children's Bureau.

Corsaro, W.A. (2005) *The Sociology of Childhood* (2nd edn). Thousand Oaks, CA: Pine-Forge Press.

Cregan, K. and Cuthbert, D. (2014) *Global Childhoods*. London: Sage.

Davis, J. (2009) 'Involving children', in E.K.M. Tisdall, J.M. Davis and M. Gallagher (eds), *Researching with Children and Young People*. London: Sage. pp. 154–67.

Department of Education Northern Ireland (DENI) (2010) *Early Years (0–6) Strategy*. Bangor: DENI.

Department of Health (DoH) (2015) *Future in Mind*. London: DoH.

Dockett, S., Einarsdottir, J. and Perry, B. (2011) 'Balancing methodologies and methods in researching with young children', in D. Harcourt, B. Perry and T. Waller (eds), *Researching Young Children's Perspectives*. London: Routledge. pp. 68–81.

Dunn, J. (2015) 'Insiders' perspectives: a children's rights approach to involving children in advising on adult-initiated research', *International Journal of Early Years Education*, 23(4): 394–408.

Dunn, J., Niens, U. and McMillan, D. (2014) '"Cos he's my favourite character": a children's rights approach to the use of popular culture in teaching literacy', *Literacy*, 48(1): 23–31.

Eckhoff, A. (2015) 'Ethical considerations of children's digital image-making and image-audiancing in early childhood environments', *Early Child Development and Care*, 185(10): 1617–28.

Edwards, C., Gandini, L. and Forman, G. (eds) (1998) *The Hundred Languages of Children: The Reggio Emilia Approach – Advanced Reflections* (2nd edn). Norwood, NJ: Ablex.

Einarsdottir, J. (2011) 'Icelandic children's early education transition experiences', *Early Education and Development*, 22(5): 737–56.

Freeman, M.A. (1983) *The Rights and Wrongs of Children*. London: The Falmer Press.

Gallacher, L. and Gallagher, M. (2008) 'Methodological immaturity in childhood research? Thinking through participatory methods', *Childhood*, 15(4): 499–516.

Harcourt, D. and Einarsdottir, J. (2011) 'Editorial: Introducing children's perspectives and participation in research', *European Early Childhood Education Research Journal*, 19(3): 301–7.

Hendrick, H. (2008) 'The child as a social actor in historical sources', in P. Christensen and A. James (eds), *Research with Children: Perspectives and Practices* (2nd edn). London: Routledge. pp. 40–65.

James, A. and Prout, A. (1997) *Constructing and Reconstructing Childhood* (2nd edn). London: Falmer.

James, A. and Prout, A. (2015) *Constructing and Reconstructing Childhood: Contemporary Issues in the Sociological Study of Childhood*. London: Routledge.

James, A., Jenks, C. and Prout, A. (1998) *Theorising Childhood*. Cambridge: Polity Press.

Jones, P. (2011) 'Child rights and their practical application', in P. Jones and G. Walker (eds), *Children's Rights in Practice*. London: Sage. pp. 17–31.

Kanyal, M. and Gibbs, J. (2014) 'Participation? Why and how', in M. Kanyal (ed.), *Children's Rights 0–8*. London: Routledge. pp. 45–62.

Kellett, M. (2010) *Rethinking Children and Research: Attitudes in Contemporary Society*. London: Continuum.

Kjørholt, A.T., Moss, P. and Clark, A. (2005) 'Beyond listening: future prospects', in A. Clark, A.T. Kjørholt and P. Moss (eds), *Beyond Listening: Children's Perspectives on Early Childhood Services*. Bristol: The Policy Press. pp. 175–87.

Konstantoni, K. (2013) 'Children's rights-based approaches: the challenges of listening to taboo/discriminatory issues and moving beyond children's participation', *International Journal of Early Years Education*, 21(4): 362–74.

Lancaster, Y.P. and Kirby, P. (2010) *Listening to Young Children* (2nd edn). Buckingham: Open University Press.

Levy, R. and Thompson, P. (2015) 'Creating buddy partnerships with 5- and 11-year-old boys: a methodological approach to conducting participatory research with young children', *Journal of Early Childhood Research*, 13(2): 137–49.

Livingstone, S. (2014) 'Children's digital rights: a priority', *Intermedia*, 42(4/5): 20–4.

Lundy, L. (2007) 'Voice is not enough: conceptualizing Article 12 of the United Nations Convention on the Rights of the Child', *British Educational Research Journal*, 33(6): 927–42.

Lundy, L. and McEvoy, L. (2009) 'Developing outcomes for educational services: a children's rights-based approach', *Effective Education*, 1(1): 43–60.

Lundy, L. and McEvoy, L. (2012) 'Children's rights and research processes: assisting children to (in)formed views', *Childhood*, 19(1): 129–44.

Lundy, L., McEvoy, L. and Byrne, B. (2011) 'Working with young children as co-researchers: an approach informed by the United Nations Convention on the Rights of the Child', *Early Education and Development*, 22(5): 714–36.

Marshall, K. (2014) Child Sexual Exploitation in Northern Ireland: Report of the Independent Inquiry (www.cjini.org/CJNI/files/f0/f094f421-6ae0-4ebd-9cd7-aec04a2cbafa.pdf).

Mayes, E. (2016) 'Shifting research methods with a becoming-child ontology: co-theorising puppet production with high school students', *Childhood*, 23(1): 105–22.

Meehan, C. (2016) 'Every child mattered in England: but what matters to children?', *Early Child Development and Care*, 186(3): 382–402.

Merewether, J. and Fleet, A. (2014) 'Seeking children's perspectives: a respectful layered approach', *Early Child Development and Care*, 184(6): 897–914.

Mykkänen, A., Määttä, E. and Järvelä, S. (2016) 'What makes her succeed? Children's interpretations of their peers' successes in learning situations', *International Journal of Early Years Education*, 24(1): 97–112.

Palaiologou, I. (2014) 'Do we hear what children want to say? Ethical praxis when choosing research tools with children under five', *Early Child Development and Care*, 184(5): 689–705.

Prout, A. (2011) 'Taking a step away from modernity: reconsidering the new sociology of childhood', *Global Studies of Childhood*, 1(1): 4–14.

Punch, S. (2002) 'Research with children: the same or different from research with adults?', *Childhood*, 9(3): 321–41.

Quennerstedt, A. (2016) 'Young children's enactments of human rights in early childhood education', *International Journal of Early Years Education*, 24(1): 5–18.

Quennerstedt, A. and Quennerstedt, M. (2014) 'Researching children's rights in education: sociology of childhood encountering educational theory', *British Journal of Sociology of Education*, 35(1): 115–32.

Rinaldi, C. (2001) 'A pedagogy of listening: a perspective of listening from Reggio Emilia', *Children in Europe*, 1: 2–5.

Rogers, R., Labadie, M. and Pole, K. (2016) 'Balancing voice and protection in literacy studies with young children', *Journal of Early Childhood Literacy*, 16(1): 34–59.

Rogoff, B. (2003) *The Cultural Nature of Human Development*. New York: Oxford University Press.

Silin, J.G. (2005) 'Who can speak? Silence, voice and pedagogy', in N. Yelland (ed.), *Critical Issues in Early Childhood Education*. Maidenhead: Open University Press. pp. 81–95.

Smith, A.B. (2011) 'Respecting children's rights and agency', in D. Harcourt, B. Perry and T. Waller (eds), *Researching Young Children's Perspectives*. London: Routledge. pp. 11–25.

Tisdall, E.K.M. and Punch, S. (2012) 'Not so new? Looking critically at childhood studies', *Children's Geographies*, 10(3): 249–64.

United Nations (UN) (1989) *United Nations Convention on the Rights of the Child*. Geneva: United Nations.

UN (2005) *Committee on the Rights of the Child: General Comment No. 7 – Implementing Child Rights in Early Childhood (CRC/C/GC/7)*. Geneva: United Nations.

UN (2006) *Committee on the Rights of the Child: Day of General Discussion on the Right of the Child to be Heard (CRC/DGD/2006)*. Geneva: United Nations.

UN (2009) *Committee on the Rights of the Child: General Comment No. 12 – The Right of the Child to be Heard (CRC/C/GC/12)*. Geneva: United Nations.

UN (2013) *Committee on the Rights of the Child: General Comment No. 14 – On the Right of the Child to Have His or Her Best Interests Taken as a Primary Consideration (CRC/C/GC/14)*. Geneva: United Nations.

Vygotsky, L. (1978) *Mind in Society*. Cambridge, MA: MIT Press.

3

SOCIAL AND EMOTIONAL FUNCTIONING IN THE LEARNING ENVIRONMENT

Why you should read this chapter

It is only in recent decades that we have come to more fully understand how emotions impact on the learning of children. Professionals need to understand the complex nature of learning in children and how positive emotions promote better learning in children. Equally, they need to understand how emotions can act as significant barriers to learning and the realisation of potential.

By the end of this chapter you should:

- have an understanding of happiness and well-being in children
- have explored the nature of emotional intelligence and self-efficacy
- have examined how love impacts on children's learning
- have examined the nature of attachment, loss and bereavement
- have considered how children are supported outside of their homes.

LEARNING, HAPPINESS AND WELL-BEING

From birth, children display a vast range of behaviours and it is through our observations of these that we make interpretations about their emotions and about their learning. Learning, however, is a construct that is not well understood (Gray and MacBlain, 2015; MacBlain, 2014) and has in the past been all-too-often viewed by many as being simply what happens in the classroom. The result of this has been a legacy that quite often fails to address the holistic needs of children and how these impact on learning. Some years ago, Whitebread (2012, p. 15) commented on how:

> Within schools and other educational contexts, emotions are sometimes seen as a distraction, as an aspect of human behaviour which has to be coped with, but which is essentially irrelevant to the business of learning. In fact, everything we now know ... suggests that this is a misguided and potentially highly damaging view.

From 6 months of age, children can be observed to display an increasing array of behaviours and with these a much greater range of emotions, which impact on their early learning experiences. Some researchers (Gershoff, 2003; Izard, 1994; Workman and Reader, 2007) have even suggested that it is possible to observe emotions such as happiness and sadness, and anger and fear, in children at this age, which suggests that, from birth, children are engaging in quite sophisticated learning from those around them, which is affected to varying degrees by a multitude of factors. Young children, for example, who present in their first years as being happy and content will have significantly different learning experiences to those children who exhibit behaviours associated with unhappiness and poor well-being (Kokkinaki and Vasdekis, 2015; Moss, 2015; Nutbrown, 2012; UNICEF, 2014; Whitebread and Sinclair-Harding, 2014).

EMOTIONAL INTELLIGENCE

It is essential that children from as early an age as possible begin to understand and manage their own emotions and those of others; in doing so they will improve their opportunities to engage with and enhance their own future learning. This has been referred to as *emotional intelligence* or, as it is sometimes called, *emotional literacy* (Goleman, 1996; Salovey and Mayer, 1990). Salovey and Mayer (1990, p. 189) originally defined emotional intelligence as that: 'subset of social intelligence that involves the ability to monitor one's own and others' feelings and emotions, to discriminate among them and to use this information to guide one's thinking and actions.'

They proposed four key factors central to the development of emotional intelligence: perceiving emotions, reasoning with emotions, understanding emotions, and managing emotions. With the first of these, children observe, with increasing accuracy and understanding, the emotions of those around them. They then gradually become more sensitive to the behaviours of others and begin, for example, to place interpretations on the facial expressions and body language of those around them. In doing so, they come to develop a deeper and more sophisticated understanding of patterns of behaviour and, more importantly, an understanding of the power and impact of their own language and that of others. As they do so, they then come to engage increasingly with their emotions and in turn extend their own underlying cognitive abilities. With the third factor, *understanding emotions*, children begin to attach meaning to emotions by increasingly forming accurate interpretations of them. The final factor, *managing emotions*, relates to the ability in children to regulate emotions; in doing so they then learn to manage their feelings. This is clearly of great importance for young children as they enter educational environments outside of the home and expectations are placed on them by others to work in ways where they must collaborate with other children, take turns, selectively listen to adults, follow instructions and directions, and do things that they might not want to do.

Drawing on the original work of Mayer (co-author with Salovey referred to earlier), Goleman (1996, p. 48) commented on how Mayer had proposed that individuals fall into distinctive styles of attending to and dealing with emotions, namely being: *self-aware, engulfed* and *accepting*. With the first of these, children, for example, become aware of their own feelings and moods as they occur and don't ruminate or obsess over them. With the second, children may be observed typically to feel 'swamped' by their emotions and even 'helpless' in attempting to overcome them, with the result that they do little to actively escape their feelings when they are in a 'bad mood'. With the third, children typically present as being clear about and accepting of their feelings and, therefore, don't try to alter them. Such styles of attending to emotions clearly impact on how children learn to view themselves and, importantly, how in control they feel about their own learning or what many now refer to as their 'self-efficacy'.

SELF-EFFICACY

Some decades ago, Bandura (1977, 1997) introduced us to the concept of 'self-efficacy' (MacBlain and Gray, 2016), which he viewed as central to the way children behave and how they think, and, importantly, to their emotional state. Children with poor self-efficacy, he proposed, overly struggle with tasks that present them with significant challenges and all-too-often present with poor self-confidence and low self-esteem. Bandura identified four key psychological processes, which he proposed were directly influenced by those self-efficacy beliefs that are held by individuals: *cognitive, motivational, affective* and *selection* (Hayes, 1994, p. 477).

When applied to our understanding of children's learning, we can hypothesise that the first of these, the thinking or *cognitive* processing that children engage in, plays a central role in, how they behave in different educational settings. In other words, the emotional nature of their thinking affects and, more importantly, structures and drives their behaviour. When faced with a challenge, children will typically reflect initially on the challenge and how they feel they might be able to meet it and then apply their thinking to considering how they might manage it. It is by acting like this that children's thinking then comes to structure and define their behaviours. Children with low self-efficacy, however, often believe they are incapable of attempting challenges and so withdraw from engaging with these, even though they could have been very successful. Alternatively, children with high levels of self-efficacy typically believe they can at least attempt a challenge and by thinking like this come to internalise forms of success, which in turn reinforce how they come to view and think about future challenges.

With Bandura's second process, *motivational*, children may be highly motivated and may apply themselves wholeheartedly to managing challenges and persist in their attempts to overcome them. Alternatively, they may have little motivation and give up all-too-readily without applying themselves to a challenge and making little if any real effort. The implications of this type of thinking for children's learning in the early years and how they later come to engage in learning activities at primary school are highly significant. The third process, *affective*, is to do largely with feelings. Children with low self-efficacy may, for example, find themselves, when attempting or having to complete challenges, experiencing much higher levels of stress and anxiety than many of their peers. Again, the impact of children's feelings and emotions on their learning are significant and appear obvious. The final process, *selection*, refers to how children might or might not choose to attempt tasks that present them with significant challenges. Typically, children will choose to attempt tasks, which, though presenting them with a challenge, will be perceived by them to be within their capability. When children's self-efficacy is strong, they will be more likely to attempt learning tasks that may, at first hand, appear to them to be very difficult. The implications of strong self-efficacy then for children who are being introduced by their teachers to new learning and unfamiliar aspects of the curriculum are enormous.

When tasked with identifying personal learning goals, children with low self-efficacy will typically perform less well and may, for example, show limited interest in attempting tasks they feel are challenging; they may make little effort to complete them. They may, for example, demonstrate little commitment when asked to work collaboratively with other children in their classroom and may even present with high levels of anxiety when directed by adults to participate in problem-based learning tasks with their peers. They may even place limits on themselves in regard to what they believe is possible. In such instances, teachers may, as Colverd and Hodgkin (2011, p. 36) have suggested, observe children engaging in such internal dialogue as 'I can't do this, it's boring', which really signals underlying thinking processes such as 'I don't believe I can be successful with this and therefore I don't want to take the risk'.

Bandura identified a number of primary factors that can work to improve self-efficacy. In children, these can be conceived of in terms of the development of a sense of mastery through experiences such as: observing their peers attempting and then completing particular challenges and tasks, receiving affirming comments from significant adults and older children, and, importantly, being encouraged and shown how to gain a much better understanding of their own emotions and feelings. It is clear then that developing self-efficacy is an important feature of the learning experiences of all children. This, of course, is of major importance in the early years when children are in the first stages of forming their 'learning personalities' and internalising ways of behaving and thinking that will set the standards for their future learning. Whitebread (2012, p. 9) has summarised the importance of self-efficacy and its importance in children's learning as follows: 'Not surprisingly, a considerable body of research has demonstrated the clear relationship between feelings of self-efficacy and educational achievement.' For many children, however, the extent to which they can develop their self-efficacy will be limited by their initial experiences and more especially by those important relationships they form in their early years (Colverd and Hodgkin, 2011; McKee, 2004; Main and Solomon, 1986). At the very heart of these relationships and, therefore, of their early learning experiences lie two most crucial and all-defining constructs – happiness and well-being.

A decade ago, a significant contribution to our understanding of happiness and well-being in young children and how these constructs impact on children's early learning was offered by the 'Leuven Well-being and Involvement Scales' (Laevers, 2005). Developed by a team led by Ferre Laevers, these scales focus on two key indicators of quality provision in early years practice, namely *well-being* and *involvement*. The first of these refers to children feeling at ease and being spontaneous in their behaviour and being free of emotional tensions, both of which are key to effective and purposeful learning in children as well as to their longer term mental health. The second refers to the level at which children can be observed to be absorbed in activities and can be viewed as a primary condition for effective and purposeful learning. In an attempt to measure well-being and involvement, Laevers' team created a 5-point scale (for a detailed explanation of this, see www.tes.com/teaching-resource/well-being-and-involvement-leuven-scale-6340990). Practitioners begin in their assessment of well-being and involvement by observing the children individually or in a group for a few minutes and then scoring them on a 5-point scale, 1 through to 5. If children are not found to be at Level 4 or 5, then their learning can be considered to be limited. When the scales register consistently low levels of well-being and/or involvement in children's behaviours, then it is probable that their development may be threatened. The higher the well-being and involvement of children on the scales, the better will be their social and emotional development and the deeper their learning. These scales are particularly useful in that they bring to the observation process a more objective means on the part of the observer/practitioner. The scales also offer a type of currency, which allows practitioners to share their observations using an objective measure as opposed to communicating with one another using emotionally loaded and vague descriptors.

Whilst the scales offer important indicators and 'measurements' of children's learning, it also needs to be recognised that practitioners tasked with making important decisions about children's learning, most particularly their intellectual functioning and cognitive development, should have the necessary depth of knowledge and skills to make these decisions. Understanding the psychology behind children's behaviours and emotions is quite different to having and expressing subjective notions based only on experience (MacBlain, 2014). It is essential, therefore, that adults making important decisions about young children's learning are properly informed, trained and equipped to do so. Whilst the Leuven Well-being and Involvement Scales are a useful device, they also need to be viewed as a supplement to critical, objective and purposeful observation and assessment on the part of those using them. Like that of learning, happiness and well-being are complex constructs and every child will be unique in how they approach and respond to different learning situations. In addition, each and every context and physical environment where children learn will be different.

ATTACHMENT AND THE LEARNING ENVIRONMENT

Difficulties with early attachment can impact significantly on children's later learning. In the 1970s and 1980s, Mary Ainsworth, a co-researcher with the psychologist John Bowlby, a key figure in the field of attachment, proposed what is now accepted as an insightful way of understanding and classifying aspects of attachment and attachment disorder in very young children and, therefore, later social and emotional functioning. The classifications developed by Ainsworth were: *securely attached, insecurely attached: avoidant* and *insecurely attached: ambivalent*. Some years later, Main and Solomon (1986) added a further classification – *disorganised*. With the first of these, the infant displays a preference for their primary caregiver and after being separated from the primary caregiver may then be observed to interact with strangers without any degree of sustained anxiety. 'Insecurely attached: avoidant' infants may, following separation and reuniting, be observed to be excessively clingy and to demonstrate prolonged anxiety and distress. 'Insecurely attached: ambivalent' infants may be observed to demonstrate limited consistency in their responses to the primary caregiver after being separated and then reunited, or as Pearce (2009, p. 23) has commented:

Rather, they display bizarre and contradictory behaviours (such as seeking to be close to their caregiver but with their gaze averted, approaching the caregiver only to stop and stare before full physical reunion occurs, and alternately, engaging with and disengaging from their caregiver almost simultaneously).

The benefits of secure attachment, and the damaging impact of attachment disorder on the social and emotional development of young children and their learning, are well known. In the days and weeks that follow birth, children become increasingly separated from their mothers; following short periods of separation, children are comforted by their mothers and, as periods of separation become more frequent, children increasingly internalise representations of their mother and come to know that their mother will return and they will not be harmed in any way by their mother or primary caregiver's temporary absence. In this way, they become prepared for entering environments outside of the home such as playgroup, nursery and primary school. When secure attachment fails to occur and children become attachment disordered, their daily experiences of learning are inevitably impacted on, for they may come to allocate much of their attention and emotional energy to dealing with inner anxieties and feelings of loss and abandonment.

 —— POINTS FOR DISCUSSION ————————————

View the YouTube video clip entitled 'Attachment vs. Attachment Parenting' (www.youtube.com/watch?v=QHto6X7neXk).

Then consider: Are too many parents overly concerning themselves with creating what they perceive to be 'strong' attachments with their children and, if so, why?

LOSS IN CHILDHOOD: ITS IMPACT ON LEARNING

Recently, the National Children's Bureau's website (NCB, 2016) cited how the Childhood Bereavement Network (CBN) had reported that in 2014 nearly 40,000 children and young people across the UK had experienced the death of a parent. The *Children and Young People's Mental Health Coalition* (CYPMHC, 2012, p. 4) had previously suggested that in an average classroom 10 children will have witnessed the separation of their parent and one child will have experienced the death of a parent. Few teachers and practitioners in early years, however, have a clear understanding of how to manage loss and bereavement in young children and even less understanding of the longer term impact on children's learning (MacBlain, 2014).

Two decades ago, Goleman (1996, p. 22), in drawing on the work of the neuroscientist Joseph LeDoux, speculated on the existence of 'emotional memories', which, he proposed, can remain with children throughout their lives and which may result in unresolved feelings of anger and confusion and impact adversely on the formation and management of relationships and, indirectly, their learning. Indeed, he goes much further in challenging us to view loss and bereavement not just as an event that affects children in a social way but rather through a biological lens:

> LeDoux turns to the role of the amygdala [the main area in the brain where signals triggered by epinephrine and norepinephrine arrive] in childhood to support what has long been a basic tenet of psychoanalytic thought: that the interactions of life's earliest years lay down a set of emotional lessons based on the attunement and upsets in the contacts between infant and caretakers. These emotional lessons are so potent and yet so difficult to understand from the vantage point of adult life because, believes LeDoux, they are stored in the amygdala as rough, wordless blueprints for emotional life. Since these earliest emotional memories are established at a time before infants have words for their experience, when these emotional memories are triggered in later life there is no matching set of articulate thoughts about the response that takes us over. One reason we can be so baffled by our emotional outbursts, then, is that they often date from a time early in our lives when things were bewildering and we did not yet have words for comprehending events. We may have the chaotic feelings, but not the words for the memories that formed them. What is of particular interest is why some children appear to cope better with difficult emotional memories arising from loss and bereavement and demonstrate much higher levels of resilience when others do not. (Goleman, 1996, p. 22)

FOCUS ON THEORY

Some years ago, Garmezy (1985) and Grotberg (1995) proposed a number of 'protective elements', which, they considered, were central to our understanding of resilience. Those elements, identified by Garmezy, were personality features, namely *self-esteem*, *family cohesion* and the *absence of discord* and the *availability of external support*. Grotberg, on the other hand, identified different elements, namely *personality factors, family and external support structures* and *the child's own social and interpersonal skills*, with the following three key illustrations 'I am', 'I have' and 'I can' (Barnard et al., 1999, p. 57).

The first of these illustrations, 'I am', relates to the child's personality features, for example self-esteem, whereby children feel they are persons who are loved and they are happy to please others and be respectful of themselves and those they meet, and are able to take responsibility for their own actions. The second, 'I have', relates to family and external support structures, which could include children feeling there are adults around who they can trust, who love them and who actively support them in their learning and set boundaries but with lots of encouragement to be independent and autonomous. The third, 'I can', relates to children's own social and interpersonal skills, where they feel able to communicate such feelings as fear and anxiety to others and, importantly, are able to explore with others ways of determining solutions to their problems, exercising control over their behaviours and emotions and feeling able to approach others when they feel they need support. Grotberg proposed that with the first of these illustrations it is possible to strengthen these but not create them. With the 'I have' illustrations, she argued that it was possible to provide and strengthen these, though with the 'I can' factors, she proposed that these have to be learned and cannot be taught.

Like such theorists as Bruner and Vygotsky, Grotberg emphasised the importance of children being active participants and suggested that children who have experienced bereavement would need more than one of the above factors to be present in order to exercise resilience in the face of their trauma. Worryingly, she also proposed that when none of these protective elements are present in children's lives and if they are not functioning as active participants, then mental health issues may ensue. To go even further in understanding resilience in children, it is important to acknowledge the part that two very strong factors play in the lives of children, namely *love* and *fear*.

FEAR AND LOVE IN THE LIVES OF CHILDREN

Crowley (2014, p. 147) has indicated that all children articulate fear, with very young children demonstrating fear of strangers, loud noises and separation from parents and/or primary caregivers. Pre-schoolers and children from around 3 to 6 years of age typically express fear about imaginary figures and ghosts as well as about being left by themselves for lengthy periods of time. Those children who experience a great deal of fear in their daily lives will typically demonstrate significant difficulties with more formal learning and may even find themselves drawn towards types of learning that will get them into trouble (Cowie, 2012). It must be emphasised, however, that fear in childhood is not always a bad thing as it can make children cautious and in that respect insulate them from harmful situations. Whilst all children experience fear, not all experience love. The importance of this emotion in the lives of children and its impact on how children engage and purposefully interact with their learning environments has been clearly emphasised by Curran (2012, p. 5):

> IT IS EXTRAORDINARY TO ME that in the last 15 years of brain research, all those billions of dollars spent in laboratories have shown to me one single important message. It can best be set out as follows ... If a child is in an environment where they are understood as an individual human being then ... Their self-esteem will be improved,

and... If their self-esteem is good they will gain *self-confidence* ... If they are in an environment where their self-esteem is good and they have self-confidence, they will feel engaged with that environment. And what does all that add up to? Well, love as it happens.

A useful starting point in understanding the importance of love and how it impacts on the learning of children can be located in the field of psychology, which, as any student of psychology will know, offers a whole range of different theoretical perspectives (Gray and MacBlain, 2015; MacBlain, 2014). One theoretical perspective that offers an appealing interpretation of love and how it might impact on children can be found within the psychodynamic perspective. Often associated with the original ideas of Sigmund Freud and Carl Jung, this field of psychology remains, even today, very popular in many quarters, especially amongst those who work in therapeutic contexts with troubled adults, trying to understand their early life experiences and patterns of learning. Though controversial in its assumptions about the nature of emotional development and learning (MacBlain, 2014), the psychodynamic tradition does offer fruitful material for much deeper reflection and analysis, in particular the seminal work of the celebrated psychoanalyst and philosopher Erich Fromm (1975). Before examining Fromm's ideas, let us consider the case of Lucy, a young girl who has experienced significant degrees of neglect since birth.

— 🔍 —— CASE STUDY 3.1

Lucy is 8 years of age and lives with her mother, a registered Class A drug user. Lucy has never met her father. Lucy's mother is frequently intoxicated by drugs or alcohol and goes out with friends most weekends, often not returning until the early hours. Lucy spends long periods of time by herself, is undernourished and often unkempt. The family has been known to social services since a referral was made by the health visitor and the paediatrician following Lucy's birth. Shortly after starting school, Lucy's class teacher raised concerns with the head teacher about Lucy's poor state of dress and about her strong preference to play by herself and not mix with the other children.

Though writing some decades ago, Fromm's theoretical analysis of love has much to offer current practitioners. Fromm suggested that love needs to contain four key elements: *care*, *responsibility*, *respect* and *knowledge*. Consider how each of these four elements might have been lacking in Lucy's life. How well was she cared for? What level of responsibility did her mother demonstrate towards her?

How much 'real' respect was shown for her as a vulnerable child by her mother and father? And how much effort did her parents actually put into getting to 'know' her?

Pearce (2009, p. 59) has extended the ideas underpinning Fromm's work, articulating the process of care, which must have been missing in Lucy's life, in those first vital months following birth, as follows:

> When children are born they are ... innately endowed with the capacity to call attention to their fundamental needs ... The maintenance of routines is a sense of comfort and reassurance to the child as it facilitates an understanding of the predictability of events and the behaviour and responsiveness of others.

Consider the daily and nightly experiences that Lucy would have been subjected to at home and how her learning will have been affected by a lack of routine, the unpredictable nature of events in her life and her mother's behaviours, determined largely by the mother's reliance on drugs and alcohol.

Further insights into the importance of love in the lives of children can be found in the work of James (2012) who has introduced us to the very compelling notion of 'love bombing' – or, as he sees it, a means by which parents can provide their children with intense and condensed experiences, whereby they feel loved and nurtured and, importantly, in control:

> When it comes to dealing with disobedient or shy or clingy or aggressive or impatient children, love and control ... really are the answer ... because so many parents are, or have had periods of, living very busy or miserable or complicated lives, most of us need to reconnect with our children from time to time. Love Bombing does the job. (p. 2)

More recently, Morton (2015: n.p.) has drawn attention to a study led by the academic Jools Page (2014), which sought to investigate the views of early years professionals regarding the place of love in the curriculum and to establish how appropriate loving relationships with young children in early years settings manifest themselves:

> Findings from a study into 'professional love' in early years settings reveal that most practitioners ... are comfortable hugging and kissing children in their care to build security and attachment. However, some are concerned about whether parents will understand their actions and how they will respond ... When asked to describe ... professional love, practitioners chose quite broad definitions, often using words such as 'care' and 'kindness', or being 'available' and 'paying attention to the children'. Some focused on how the child should feel in a professionally loving environment, for example 'safe', 'settled', 'secure' or 'valued' ... Despite the largely positive attitude of respondents, some expressed worries ... reporting concerns about false accusations ...

> Some described practitioners as being 'vulnerable' ... Reasons for concerns included fears that parents would feel threatened, jealous or uncomfortable about early years staff developing a relationship with their children ... Dr Page said, 'As this project has demonstrated, it is the debate and theorisation of love and care that is important. Providing opportunities for practitioners to discuss and reflect on each other's viewpoints is likely to bring about a more thoughtful understanding and crucially a shift in their thinking.'

In the case of Lucy, the four key elements identified by Fromm were most likely to be experienced by her when she attended pre-school and primary learning contexts with adults who nurtured her.

SUPPORTING CHILDREN'S SOCIAL AND EMOTIONAL FUNCTIONING OUTSIDE OF THE HOME

Whilst earlier decades saw a growth in initiatives such as HighScope and Sure Start and, more recently, Children's Centres, all designed to support young children outside of the home, the situation now appears to have deteriorated across the UK. Worryingly, Stewart and Obolenska (2015, cited in Fitzgerald and Kay, 2016, p. 29) have proposed that recent financial cuts to the benefits received by families where there is a young child have been the most significant of any group in England. They go on to indicate how:

> the abolition of the Health in Pregnancy Grant and Baby Tax Credit and the restriction of Sure Start Maternity Grant to first-borns only ... together take £1,230 out of a family's budget between the sixth month of pregnancy and the baby's first birthday. (2016, p. 51)

One particular group whose social and emotional needs in the learning environment have been largely under-researched and largely unrecognised comprises those children who have been placed in care, many even from their earliest years.

CHILDREN IN CARE

Often referred to as 'Looked-after children', the NSPCC (2015) recently reported that, currently, there are 93,000 children in care in the UK, with more than half being taken into care because of neglect or abuse. The NSPCC define 'children in care' as children who are being looked after by their local authority who may be living with foster parents or at home with their parents whilst under supervision by social services, or living in residential children's homes or other residential settings such as schools or secure units. Children may be taken into care when children's services intervene because the children are viewed as being at significant risk of harm. Some children may be placed in care by their parents on a voluntary basis when their parents feel they are struggling to cope. The NSPCC have indicated that in order for children in care to be properly protected they should be provided with a secure and caring environment where they can be supported in overcoming early life experiences that have been problematic and where they can be given the best possible chances in life. The NSPCC recognises that it is critical that children in care are supported in developing 'strong, trusting and stable relationships' with those who are caring for them, including their social workers and other professionals. The NSPCC also recognises and emphasises the importance of foster and residential carers receiving training which is of a high quality, in addition to supervision and relevant support, and that birth parents should, where possible, be helped to address those problems that have resulted in their children going into care.

NURTURE GROUPS

The Nurture Group Network (NGN) (2015) organisation defines a nurture group as an 'in-school, teacher-led psychosocial intervention of groups of less than 12 students that effectively replace missing or distorted early nurturing experiences for both children and young adults' (see www.nurturegroups.org/introducing-nurture/what-nurture-group-0). The NGN reports that these groups have been founded on practice that is evidence-based and that offers to children in the early years and primary and secondary schools, short-term and inclusive interventions that benefit them as they grow older. Interestingly, the NGN emphasises how each group should be managed by two staff members and that children attending should return to their own class after 2–4 terms. Importantly, the NGN also proposes how these groups should actively assess children's learning in addition to their social and emotional needs, and where possible provide whatever support is needed to remove current and potential barriers to learning. Further, the Network emphasises the importance of language development and the opportunities these groups can present for improving communication. Food is shared at 'breakfast' or 'snack time' with much opportunity for social learning, helping children to attend to the needs of others, with time to listen and be listened to. As the children learn academically and socially, they develop confidence, become responsive to others, learn self-respect and take pride in behaving well and in achieving.

Nurture groups are not restricted to the UK and have been part of the educational landscape of other countries, for example New Zealand and Canada. The groups have received positive affirmation from inspection services in the UK such as Ofsted in England and those inspection services in Wales and Scotland.

In 2015, the Education Scotland (ES) website (www.educationscotland.gov.uk/ inclusionandequalities/relationshipsandbehaviour/approaches/nurture/index. asp) identified a number of key principles of nurture groups, including effective assessment of children and real attempts at understanding their needs. The ES also strongly advocates that children remain part of their class, that snack time and sharing are an essential part of their experience, that emotional literacy is an essential focus within the group and that skills are built formally and informally through the provision of stimulating opportunities for play. The above principles, like those of the NGN, have at their core the importance of children being seen as individuals and with discrete and individual needs. ES also emphasises the importance of establishing and managing positive and effective links between teachers, early years practitioners and parents.

BREAKFAST CLUBS

In 2015, the popular online British newspaper the *Express* (Express, 2015) drew public attention to a survey undertaken by the Association of Teachers and Lecturers (ATL), which suggested that the only way in which many children in the UK were receiving a meal before attending school was through attending a breakfast club, with more than half of teachers questioned in over 500 schools reporting that their schools were providing a breakfast club. Key reasons given for children attending these clubs included the fact that their parent(s) needed to go to work. Worryingly, it was reported by many of those interviewed that the main reason for many children attending breakfast club was because it was the only way they would get a meal in the morning. Nearly one fifth of those interviewed reported that children attended breakfast club because of a lack of money in the family, often due to unemployment. Interestingly, one in six of those interviewed felt that their pupils attended breakfast club in order to socialise with their peers.

This survey also found that many teachers considered how providing a breakfast for their pupils helped to improve their concentration and capacity to learn. The *Express* article went on to report to the general public the views of Dr Mary Bousted, general secretary of the Association of Teachers and Lecturers (ATL), who proposed that having a nutritious meal before commencing learning in the classroom had a 'huge impact' on the ability of pupils to engage effectively in the learning process. In addition, the article also cited a spokesman for the Department for Education (DfE) who commented on how the DfE was supporting schools and local authorities in using their budgets to meet the needs of their children and offer free or subsidised meals to those from 'poorer' families. The spokesman drew attention to the Pupil Premium, which he reported would double to £2.5 billion in 2014–15 as a means of targeting extra money to assist schools in providing such support as breakfast clubs to meet the needs of the most disadvantaged children in their care.

BUDDY SYSTEMS

A decade ago, in its report *Learning Behaviour Principles and Practice: What Works in Schools*, the Department for Education and Skills (DfES) (2006, p. 16) emphasised that schools need to adopt procedures and practices that will support their pupils in learning how to behave appropriately. Interestingly, the report also emphasised the modelling of good behaviour by adults as a key factor. In doing so, it recommended that all schools confront the issue of transition, most notably from primary to secondary school and 'develop buddy systems, using pupils to support each other, and allocate named staff to act as mentors for a time-limited period for new arrivals'. This, the report advocated, was especially important where children were identified in primary school as presenting with potential risks relating to their level of resilience and their coping strategies for managing their integration into their new school. Within schools and early years settings, the buddy system has been used to very good effect (Levy and Thompson, 2015), and teachers and early years practitioners have come to see its enormous value in, for example, supporting children to work more independently.

CHILDREN IN HOSPITALS

At some time in their lives, most children will find themselves experiencing some form of illness or health concern. For some, however, the illness can be major and may mean that they are faced with admission to hospital and possibly lengthy recuperation periods. Attendance at school, therefore, may be out of the question. Some unfortunate children may even find they have a terminal illness. For those children who experience a major or lengthy illness, the emotional impact can be severe and they may, for example, find themselves unable to play outdoors with their friends and confined to long periods in and out of hospital or confined to bed, with the result that they may lose out on important social experiences and bonding with peers, in addition to having few opportunities for physical play. Guidance from the Department for Education (DfE, 2013) emphasised that children with health needs should have the same opportunities as their peers, which includes access to a broad and balanced curriculum. As far as possible, children with health needs and who are unable to attend school should receive the same range and quality of education as they would have experienced at their home school. The guidance also showed how electronic media such as virtual classrooms and learning platforms can offer access to a much broader and varied curriculum. The guidance stressed how, with planned hospital admissions, local authorities (LAs) should provide the hospital teacher with as much forewarning as possible and set up a personal education plan, which should ensure that the child's school, the LA and the hospital school or other provider can work effectively together. LAs should also meet the learning needs of children when they are eventually discharged from hospital and should pay special regard to medical advice provided by relevant professionals in regard to how much education children under the care of hospitals should receive and whether or not they should return to school on a full-time basis. Importantly, LAs should also work with schools to complement the education the child receives when they are unable to attend school.

SUMMARY

Whilst the majority of children have happy and fulfilled childhoods character-ised by stability and high levels of nurture, many do not. It is essential, therefore, that all practitioners adopt a holistic approach to their work with children and take time to fully understand the social and emotional lives of the children in their care and how these factors impact on learning. Happiness and well-being are central to children's development and learning, as is the type and quality of the support they receive. All of these factors impact significantly on children's learning, not only in their early and primary years but throughout their lives and indirectly in the future lives of their own children.

 EXTENDED AND RECOMMENDED READING

Buckler, S. and Castle, P. (2014) *Psychology for Teachers*. London: Sage.

An accessible text for teachers wishing to gain a better insight into how psychology can inform their understanding of children and families and their everyday practice.

Page, J. (2014) 'Developing "professional love" in early childhood settings', in L. Harrison and J. Sumsion (eds), *Lived Spaces of Infant-Toddler Education and Care: Exploring Diverse Perspectives on Theory, Research, Practice and Policy*. New York: Springer.

An insight into the importance and relevance of professional love in early years settings.

 Don't forget to visit **https://study.sagepub.com/contemporarychildhood** for a selection of free SAGE journal articles, web links, additional case studies, activities, and PowerPoints to help you revise.

REFERENCES

Bandura, A. (1977) *Social Learning Theory*. Englewood Cliffs, NJ: Prentice Hall.
Bandura, A. (1997) *Self-efficacy: The Exercise of Control*. New York: Freeman.

Barnard, P., Morland, I. and Nagy, J. (1999) *Children, Bereavement and Trauma: Nurturing Resilience*. London: Jessica Kingsley.

Children and Young People's Mental Health Coalition (CYPMHC) (2012) *Resilience and Results: How to Improve the Emotional and Mental Well-being of Children and Young People in Your School*. London: CYPMHC.

Colverd, S. and Hodgkin, B. (2011) *Developing Emotional Intelligence in the Primary School*. London: Routledge.

Cowie, H. (2012) *From Birth to Sixteen: Children's Health, Social, Emotional and Linguistic Development*. London: Routledge.

Crowley, K. (2014) *Child Development: A Practical Introduction*. London: Sage.

Curran, A. (2012) 'Autism and the brain's working: how far have we got?', *Debate*, 144: 5–6. Leicester: The British Psychological Society.

Department for Education (DfE) (2013) *Ensuring a Good Education for Children Who cannot Attend School because of Health Needs: Statutory Guidance for Local Authorities*. London: DfE (www.gov.uk/government/publications/education-for-children-with-health-needs-who-cannot-attend-school).

Department for Education and Skills (DfES) (2006) *Learning Behaviour Principles and Practice: What Works in Schools – Section 2 of the Report of the Practitioners on School Behaviour and Discipline chaired by Alan Steer*. Nottingham: DfES.

Education Scotland (Foghlam Alba) (2015) Nurture Groups (www.educationscotland.gov.uk/inclusionandequalities/relationshipsandbehaviour/approaches/nurture/index.asp).

Express (2015) 'Breakfast club benefits highlighted', *Express Online*, 22 March 2013; updated 11 January 2015 (www.express.co.uk/news/uk/386036/Breakfast-club-benefits-highlighted).

Fitzgerald, D. and Kay, J. (2016) *Understanding Early Years Policy* (4th edn). London: Sage.

Fromm, E. (1975) *The Art of Loving*. London: Unwin Books.

Garmezy, N. (1985) 'Stress resilient children: the search for protective factors', in J. Stevenson (ed.), *Recent Research in Developmental Psychopathology*. Oxford: Pergamon Press.

Gershoff, E. (2003) *Living at the Edge: Low Income and the Development of America's Kindergarteners*. New York: National Centre for Children in Poverty.

Goleman, D. (1996) *Emotional Intelligence: Why It Can Matter More than IQ*. London: Bloomsbury.

Gray, C. and MacBlain, S.F. (2015) *Learning Theories in Childhood* (2nd edn). London: Sage.

Grotberg, E. (1995) *A Guide to Promoting Resilience in Children*. The Hague: Bernard van Leer Foundation, the Netherlands.

Hayes, N. (1994) *Foundations of Psychology: An Introductory Text*. London: Routledge.

Izard, C.E. (1994) 'Innate and universal facial expressions: evidence from developmental and cross-cultural research', *Psychological Bulletin*, 115(2): 288–99.

James, O. (2012) *Love Bombing*. London: Karnac Books.

Kokkinaki, T. and Vasdekis, V.G.S. (2015) 'Comparing emotional coordination in early spontaneous mother–infant and father–infant interactions', *European Journal of Developmental Psychology*, 12(1): 69–84.

Laevers, F. (ed.) (2005) *Well-being and Involvement in Care Settings: A Process-oriented Self-evaluation Instrument*. Leuven, Belgium: Research Centre for Experiential Learning, Leuven University.

Levy, R. and Thompson, P. (2015) 'Creating "buddy partnerships" with 5- and 11-year old-boys: a methodological approach to conducting participatory research with young children', *Journal of Early Childhood Research*, 13(2): 137–49.

MacBlain, S.F. (2014) *How Children Learn*. London: Sage.

MacBlain, S.F. and Gray, C. (2016) 'Understanding Bandura', *Early Years Educator*, May 2016. London: Early Years Educator. pp. 38–44.

McKee, B. (2004) Child protection in education: training the trainers. Paper presented at European CAPE conference, 10–12 July, Lancaster, UK.

Main, M. and Solomon, J. (1986) 'Discovery of insecure-disorganized/disorientated attachment patterns: procedures, findings and implications for the classification of behaviour', in T.B. Brazelton and M. Yogman (eds), *Affective Development in Infancy*. Norwood, NJ: Ablex.

Morton, K. (2015) Sector mostly positive on 'professional love', *Nursery World* (www.nurseryworld.co.uk/nursery-world/news/1154966/sector-mostly-positive-on-professional-love).

Moss, P. (2015) 'There are alternatives! Contestation and hope in early childhood education', *Global Studies of Childhood*, 5(3): 226–38.

National Children's Bureau (NCB) (2016) Children's Grief Awareness Week: 40,000 children bereaved of a parent each year (www.ncb.org.uk/news/childrens-grief-awareness-week-40000-children-bereaved-of-a-parent-each-year).

NSPCC (2015) Children in Care statistics (www.nspcc.org.uk/preventing-abuse/child-protection-system/children-in-care/statistics/).

Nurture Group Network (NGN) (2015) What is a Nurture Group? (www.nurturegroups.org/introducing-nurture/what-nurture-group-0).

Nutbrown, C. (2012) *Foundations for Quality: The Independent Review of Early Education and Childcare Qualifications – Final Report*. Runcorn: Department for Education (DfE).

Page, J. (2014) 'Developing "professional love" in early childhood settings', in L. Harrison and J. Sumsion (eds), *Lived Spaces of Infant-Toddler Education and Care: Exploring Diverse Perspectives on Theory, Research, Practice and Policy*. Berlin: Springer.

Pearce, C. (2009) *A Short Introduction to Attachment and Attachment Disorder*. London: Jessica Kingsley.

Salovey, P. and Mayer, J.D. (1990) Emotional Intelligence. Available at: www.unh.edu/emotional_intelligence/EIAssets/EmotionalIntelligenceProper/EI1990%20Emotional%20Intelligence.pdf (accessed 20 March 2013).

Stewart, K. and Obolenska, P. (2015) *The Coalition Record on the Under Fives: Policy, Spending and Outcomes 2010–2015*. Social Policy in a Cold Climate Working Paper 12. London: Centre for Analysis of Social Exclusion/London School of Economics.

UNICEF (2014) *Child Poverty in the Post-2015 Agenda*, UNICEF Briefs. Available at: www.unicef.org/socialpolicy/files/Issue_Brief_Child_Poverty_in_the_post-2015_Agenda_June_2014_Final.pdf (accessed 12 April 2016).

Whitebread, D. (2012) *Developmental Psychology and Early Childhood Education*. London: Sage.

Whitebread, D. and Sinclair-Harding, L. (2014) 'Neuroscience and the infant brain', *Nursery World*, 20 Oct.–2 Nov., 21–4.

Workman, L. and Reader, W. (2007) *Evolutionary Psychology: An Introduction*. Cambridge: Cambridge University Press.

4

CREATING OPTIMUM LEARNING ENVIRONMENTS FOR THE CHILD

Why you should read this chapter

The majority of children benefit from access to learning environments that meet their needs and that work to develop their cognitive abilities and skills and their social and emotional development. For others, however, their experiences of learning fall short of what should be expected for them. When entering more informal settings such as playgroups, and settings such as primary schools, it is essential that young children have available to them environments that not only optimise their academic learning but also their social, cognitive and emotional development. Practitioners working with children need to continually reflect on what makes for such positive environments and the processes by which these can be created, managed and sustained.

By the end of this chapter you should:

- have an understanding of identification and assessment
- be aware of what makes for effective teaching and learning
- appreciate the importance of multi-agency working and the importance of monitoring and evaluation of practice
- have an understanding of key factors that create optimum learning environments.

TODAY'S CHALLENGES

Only a decade ago, Palmer (2006, p. 105) offered what was a disturbing account of children entering full-time education across western industrialised societies:

> Everywhere I went it was the same story: four- and five-year-olds were coming to school with poorer language skills than ever before; they weren't arriving with the repertoire of nursery rhymes and songs little ones always used to know, and children of all ages found it increasingly difficult to sit down and listen to their teacher or to express complex ideas in speech or writing … I also discovered that this issue was bothering teachers across the developed world.

Palmer's accounts are indeed worrying and highlighted an urgency in the need to create purposeful and meaningful learning environments that offer appropriate interventions and sustain effective learning for all children. Her observations emphasised the importance of looking closely at children's early experiences in the home and how these impact on the nature and quality of their learning. Sadly, it remains the case that large numbers of children in the UK continue to leave full-time education with poor literacy and numeracy skills (Cowie, 2012; Hattie, 2008; MacBlain, 2014; Ofsted, 2013; Palmer, 2006), having endured many years of failure. In a hard-hitting and candid report, *Removing Barriers to Literacy*, Ofsted (2011, p. 14) commented some years ago on the frequency of young children who demonstrate delayed speech and language development and emotional disturbance:

> Of the barriers facing the youngest children … a common problem was some form of delay of their development in speech and language. In one nursery visited, for example, where almost all children were of White British origin, approximately 30 per cent of the three-year-olds started nursery with a marked speech delay. Another common problem that placed children at early disadvantage was a disturbed start to their lives. In one nursery visited, most of the two-year-olds had already had some form of social care intervention by the time they joined the nursery.

Such pronouncements suggest that, for many children, their home backgrounds are failing to prepare and properly equip them for more formalised learning. More specifically, the report also emphasised that visits by inspectors to schools:

> confirmed the impact of the pupils' poor socio-economic circumstances. Although the children could often learn to decode print successfully in school, they were not always able to ascribe meaning to the words they could say because they did not have the experiences that the words described. This affected their progress in literacy in the longer term because it affected their comprehension of what they were reading.

More recently, Kuczera et al. (2016, p. 9) authored an OECD report entitled *Building Skills for All: A Review of England – Policy insights from the survey of adult skills*, in which they reported that in England there were around 9 million adults of working age who had low skills in literacy or numeracy or even both. Interestingly, the report indicated that young adults in England today perform no better than adults currently in their late 50s and early 60s. Worryingly, the report also pointed to a rather concerning proposition that, over time, the level of basic skills found in the English labour force may fall below the skill levels found in other countries. This begs the question as to why so many children living in the UK today are not having difficulties with learning identified and assessed in the early stages of education prior to patterns of failure developing and becoming deeply embedded.

IDENTIFICATION AND ASSESSMENT: REFLECTIONS ON PRACTICE

In essence, approaches to identification, and more particularly assessment, take two broad forms – formal and informal. With the former, assessment most commonly employs standardised tests and takes place at a particular time and place. With informal approaches, assessment is typically continuous; each day, teachers and early years practitioners engage, wittingly or unwittingly, in assessment of their pupils' learning in all manner of ways through, for example, the observation of children acting in a range of learning situations and exploring and collaborating with their peers and other adults (MacBlain and Bowman, 2016). A teacher might, for example, observe a child's social skills during play or scrutinise the sort of errors the child is making when completing written tasks or numerical operations. This continuous type of assessment offers practitioners rich sources of data relating to how children learn that are typically not available through using standardised tests.

EARLY YEARS

It is crucial for accurate and meaningful identification and assessment to take place at an early age, for it is during this period that the foundations of future learning are laid down. This is especially the case where children may come to have additional social and emotional needs (DfE, 2015a; Snelling, 2016). Too many children, however, fail to have their learning needs properly identified and assessed in the early years and go on to experience years of failure (MacBlain, 2014; MacBlain et al., 2015). Children learn from the cultures, communities and families they are born into (Welsh, 2014). The level of active, meaningful and intelligent support they receive from adults and older siblings in their first years is highly important (Lancaster and Kirby, 2014; Lansdown, 2005; MacBlain, 2014; Noddings, 2002; Nutbrown, 2012; Woodhead, 2005). Claxton, author of the report *An Intelligent Look at Emotional Intelligence* (ATL, 2005, p. 20), commissioned by the Association of Teachers and Lecturers, has spoken of children in their first years as having an 'emotional apprenticeship', through which they observe how older individuals in their home behave and, importantly, how they manage their emotions, which, in turn, impacts on their immediate learning and, more crucially, their future learning:

> When uncertain how to respond emotionally to a new person or event, babies and toddlers take their cue from the facial expression and tone of voice of the people they trust … Whether deliberately or inadvertently, family members act as powerful role models that steer the child's emotional development … Being around an adult who continually 'loses it' is bad for a child's own emotional development.

It is now accepted by most policy makers that the quality of experiences children have in their first years is crucial to later development and learning (Beckley, 2012; Cowie, 2012; MacBlain, 2014; Miller and Pound, 2011). Thankfully, much greater recognition has increasingly been given to learning in the early years, as witnessed by recent government policies and legislation and the implementation and evaluation of successive initiatives across the UK (DfE, 2015b; Mathers et al., 2011). Recently, the *Annual Report of Her Majesty's Chief Inspector of Education, Children's Services and Skills 2015: Early Years* (Ofsted, 2015b, p. 6) indicated that parents currently researching what is available for their children in the field of early years education will now find that provision is stronger than it has ever been. Parents now have much greater choice, which ranges from private, voluntary and independent provision through to public nursery and pre-school provision, including home-based provision with a childminder, with the knowledge that standards have risen over the past few decades and most practitioners working in early years settings now have some level of formal training, which underpins their abilities and skills in identifying and assessing children's needs and then making appropriate and effective interventions. For example, over 80 per cent of the centres of provision inspected by Ofsted (2015b) were found to be currently good or outstanding.

Interestingly, Ofsted also showed how many early years practitioners now feel more appreciative that they are being tasked with 'teaching' children as opposed to 'providing' for them, which was previously the case. This underscores more recent improvements in the field of early years, in particular improvements in practitioners' abilities and skills in identifying, assessing and intervening effectively in children's learning. Counter to this, however, is the need to reflect on the changing nature of practice in early years settings and whether or not it is becoming too dominated by pedagogical styles that are overly teacher-centred, with far greater emphasis now being placed on formal learning, often at the expense of the informal and effective identification of learning needs through play and creative learning activities. Miller and Pound (2011, p. 165) have commented thus:

External pressures from government guidance or a management hierarchy can lead practitioners to focus on curriculum 'delivery' or 'coverage' as the main focus of their practice. Such a view would have been anathema to the foundational theorists … but in England it has become a feature of the Early Years Foundation Stage (EYFS) (DfES, 2008) and the National Curriculum in primary schools, causing uncertainty for many practitioners.

Similarly, Wood (2014) highlights the increasing tensions between play-based approaches and the structured curriculum goals in national policy frameworks. She argues that child-centred discourses maintain significant power, but there are many challenges that practitioners encounter when trying to implement curricula that combine freedom and structure. It is encouraging to note that the report celebrated how the field of early years education is now benefiting from having a very high political profile, as evidenced, for example, by a recent commitment from government in the UK to increase the 15 hours of funded early education for 3- and 4-year-olds from working families, which even featured in the Queen's Speech and earlier speeches given by the prime minister to the House of Commons. Disconcertingly, however, the report also concluded that whilst outcomes for children from disadvantaged backgrounds have improved, there are few, if any, indications that the gap is narrowing in any significant way. Early education, it was emphasised, can make a real difference to children's future life chances but only when children are in receipt of education that is of a high quality. Interestingly, it was also noted that whilst some 113,000 2-year-olds (approximating to 42 per cent of all eligible children) were eligible for 15 hours of free early education, their parents/carers did not in fact avail themselves of this offering. Responding to this limited take-up, the report proposed that health visitors could play a more central role in helping families to take up eligible places for their children when conducting the 'one-year check' on their children where important assessments of social, cognitive, emotional and physical development could take place, in addition to the monitoring of speech and language development. In doing so, parents could be alerted to the need to avail themselves of the additional support on offer through this government initiative and to how their children's learning might be advanced.

Crucially, the report also proposed that a significant factor accounting for why some children commencing school find themselves disadvantaged is because their school does not have a good enough relationship with its feeder nurseries, pre-schools and childminders. Schools, the report stressed, need to do more in supporting transitions and confronting, managing and removing the artificial barriers that prevent this. Difficulties with transition can be avoided when children attend school nurseries where it is possible to progress directly to their primary school without having to change provider. Interestingly, fewer than 5,000 schools were found to take in 2-year-olds and where they did, the children were, disproportionately, from families that were better off. The report noted that the quality of all early years providers would be judged against the EYFS, emphasising that 'the way that children learn at this stage in their lives is in the context of play'. Interestingly, the report also proposed that 'A child cannot learn if they are not well cared for. A child will not learn if they are not provided with experiences that help them learn through imitation and play'. This assertion that 'A child cannot learn if they are not well cared for' needs to be treated with caution and challenged in its interpretation of the term 'learn' (Gray and MacBlain, 2015; MacBlain, 2014; MacBlain et al., 2015). Gray and MacBlain (2015, pp. 106–7) have commented on how 'Learning is a difficult word to define … Arguably, it is one of the most misunderstood words in popular usage … within the field of education'. Children do in fact learn, even when they are not 'well cared for'. What caring does impact on is the quality of children's learning.

PRIMARY YEARS

 —— CASE STUDY 4.1 ——————————————

Miss Jones currently teaches David who is 8 years of age. She finds his behaviour difficult to manage and his literacy and numeracy skills are significantly lower than most of his class peers. She recently referred him to the school's educational psychologist. In her first meeting with the psychologist, she reported her views about David as follows:

> I really like David, basically he's a nice child but his behaviour is at times quite terrible. He constantly disrupts the other children and his reading and spelling are way behind all the others. His maths are almost non-existent and I am really worried about him. I have tried everything with him but nothing seems to make much of a difference. His concentration is really poor and he doesn't seem to stick with any work I give him for more than a few minutes before he starts doing something else.

What becomes clear from Miss Jones' account of David is that it tells the psychologist very little about David and even less about his learning. It tells the psychologist more about Miss Jones' emotional reactions to David's behaviour. Such phrases as 'I have tried everything', 'nothing seems to make much of a difference' and 'he constantly disrupts the other children' are vague, over-generalised, descriptive and emotive.

Now, consider the case below where a different teacher, Miss Brown, who is newly qualified, is reporting to the educational psychologist her views about a different child, Jason, also aged 8 years, who has caused her concerns relating to his poor progress in literacy and numeracy and his poor concentration.

— ⌕ —— CASE STUDY 4.2 ———————————————————

'Jason is intellectually very able and this becomes very evident when he is talking with other children. He has a large vocabulary and initiates conversations during group activities with confidence. He appears to have a very weak working memory, especially his auditory sequential memory – I know this because he has problems recalling more than a few instructions and he really struggles with his times tables and spelling. I have taken time to sit and observe him working on a number of tasks and he appears to be very easily distracted by those around him. He also seems to process visual information much slower than the others in his class, and especially when he is copying written information from the board.'

In the second case, Miss Brown is much more precise and objective in how she talks to the educational psychologist. She is drawing on specific and intentional observations she has made of Jason and basing her interpretations on actual evidence gained from these observations. She is also attempting to understand Jason's thinking and those specific factors that cause him to behave the way he does in particular learning situations. She is, therefore, able to have a much more informed and accurate conversation with the psychologist about Jason's learning than was the case with Miss Jones.

FOCUS ON THEORY

Central to the accurate identification and assessment of children's learning is the need for children to have effective teaching and learning which take into account such key factors as learning styles and strategies, current levels of intellectual ability, prior knowledge, status of language development, and so on. The identification and assessment of learning need to go far beyond simply 'looking' for what might be 'wrong' with children; it must also focus on the learning environments that are created by teachers. Failing to do so is to limit identification and assessment to an erroneous assumption that when children fail it is due entirely to factors within the child. Such a view is, of course, controversial and challenges teachers and practitioners to not only assess their pupils' learning but also to look closely and in an objective way at their own knowledge, abilities and skills, the environments they create in the classroom and the effectiveness of their own pedagogical practice (MacBlain et al., 2015).

In an attempt to understand what constitutes effective teaching and learning in school and thereby accurate identification and assessment, Hattie (2008) recently synthesised findings

(Continued)

(Continued)

from research spanning ten years, which involved thousands of children. Specifically, he examined six areas that play a major part in learning, namely: the *children themselves*, their *homes* and *teachers*, their *schools*, the *curricula* they received, and the *teaching* and *learning approaches* that took place in their schools. Hattie proposed that key to making a real difference in children's learning is the need to make teaching and learning 'visible', i.e. where teachers engage in critical and reflective evaluation of their own teaching and actively seek to view and understand learning through the eyes of the children they teach (Hattie, 2012; Hattie and Yates, 2014). Hattie also found that the expectations teachers have of their pupils is crucial and that these expectations and perceptions of their pupils' abilities and potential are based on their beliefs about what the pupils can achieve as learners (Hohnen and Murphy, 2016). By engaging more objectively with their pupils and 'freeing' themselves from existing and rigid perceptions of pupils' abilities, teachers can connect with the type of learning approaches being used by their pupils, and in doing so can engage in more effective identification and assessment of their pupils' needs, in particular how they approach new and unfamiliar learning situations and material. Failing to do so can often mean that the individual learning needs of children are not identified, effective assessment does not take place and children are subjected to yet more of the same:

> It is the case that we reinvent schooling every year. Despite any successes we may have had with this year's cohort of students, teachers have to start again next year with a new cohort. The greatest change that most students experience is the level of competence of the teacher ... It is surely easy to see how it is tempting for teachers to re-do the successes of the previous year, to judge students in terms of last year's cohort, and to insist on orderly progression through that which has worked before. (Hattie, 2008, p. 1)

Additional insights into effective and purposeful identification and assessment can also be located in the work of Marzano (Marzano, 2005, 2007; Marzano and Kendall, 2006). Marzano has emphasised that 'good' teachers set clear goals and offer clear feedback. They actively support pupils in their interactions with knowledge and new learning and set clear rules, which they insist on being observed and followed. Most importantly, 'good' teachers, he asserts, establish and maintain positive relationships with their pupils and purposely communicate high expectations of them. By working like this, teachers get to really 'know' their pupils and in doing so build up their own repertoire of pedagogical knowledge, which becomes exercised again and again on many different children and in many different learning situations.

Here, it is worth considering Marzano's notion of a new taxonomy, which is comprised of three systems: the *self-system*, the *metacognitive system* and the *cognitive system*; these are in addition to a separate *knowledge domain* and are key to purposeful and effective thinking and learning. As children are tasked with commencing an activity that is new to them, their *self-system* engages in a process whereby they must decide whether to engage actively with the new activity or instead just continue with the activity they are already engaged in. Once engaged with the new activity, the child's *metacognitive system* sets goals and then monitors the progress made with these goals. Once this is under way, the child's *cognitive system* then engages in processing the new information with existing information, whilst the child's *knowledge domain* provides the content, based on what the child already knows. Adopting Marzano's ideas, teachers and early years practitioners can use this structure to observe and interpret children's behaviour when they are working on particular tasks, as could have been the case with Miss Jones in the first study of David.

With regard to the knowledge domain, Marzano proposed three sub-sets, which he conceptualised as *information*, *mental* and *physical*. The *information* sub-set can be conceptualised as the organisation of ideas and principles, such as when children generalise about phenomena through their use of vocabulary. This sub-set is of course very important as it facilitates children in their ability to store greater quantities of information through allotting ideas and new concepts to categories. Consider, for example, the case of Peter who has been introduced to a new piece of vocabulary by his teacher – the word '*trumpet*'. When Peter questions his teacher as to what a '*trumpet*' is, for the word is new to him, his teacher explains that it is a musical instrument. Peter then 'knows' that, already, he has 'existing knowledge' about trumpets because he already 'knows' a great deal about musical instruments. The *mental* sub-set involves complicated processes, for example writing an essay or solving a mathematical computation, in addition to more simple processes such as following instructions in a newly acquired children's game. With the *physical* sub-set, the extent to which this appears within learning situations can vary considerably and will depend on the type of material being learned.

Now consider the views put forward by Reuven Feuerstein (Feuerstein et al., 1980) who draws attention to the learning environments that teachers create for children. Central to Feuerstein's ideas is the notion that it is not for teachers to originate and structure children's responses but rather to apply themselves to developing those processes whereby children may engage in problem solving and manage their own thinking through to completion of any tasks they are given. Feuerstein suggests that teachers act as *mediators* and engage their pupils in processes that actually develop their thinking on a much deeper level.

Feuerstein has proposed that the belief systems we hold about children's learning should see their potential as having almost no limits, though accepting that there are artificial barriers that inhibit positive change in children. Feuerstein also proposed that all children, no matter what their level of difficulty, can, with accurate identification and assessment and the correct type of intervention, develop into effective learners. Through adopting such belief systems, teachers and practitioners working in the early years can be freed from that type of constrained thinking that has limited them in the past; instead, such beliefs offer an ambitious but realistic vision of what is actually possible for all children. When practitioners think and act like this, certain consequences take place within children's thinking, the most notable of which

(Continued)

(Continued)

is what Feuerstein termed as *structural cognitive modifiability*. This refers to the idea that the cognitive structure of children's brains becomes altered through an enabling process through which children learn how to learn. In practice, learning becomes cumulative and impacts positively on children's functioning throughout their lives (Burden, 1987). This approach is directed at altering the structure of children's cognitive development, which is the way children act on and then respond to sources of information. Central to learning how to learn is mediated learning experience (MLE) and it is this concept of MLE that lies at the very heart of Feuerstein's Social Interactionist Theory of learning. Feuerstein et al. (1980, p. 16) have referred to MLE as:

> the way in which stimuli emitted by the environment are transferred by a 'mediating' agent, usually a parent, sibling or other caregiver. This mediated agent, guided by his intentions, culture, and emotional investment, selects and organises the world of stimuli for the child … Through this process of mediation, the cognitive structure of the child is affected.

The principal features of MLE are that teachers or mediators need to be aware, make known and ensure that children have understood what is intended of them (*intentionality and reciprocity*), that teachers explain to children why they will be working on particular tasks (*investment of meaning*) and that the activities the children will be undertaking are understood as having value over and above the here and now and can lead to further generalisation in their existing learning and knowledge (*transcendence*) (Burden, 1987). In this way, teachers can engage in the truly effective identification and assessment of children's learning, and create optimum learning environments that permit children to realise their potential.

 — **POINTS FOR DISCUSSION** ————————————————

1. View the YouTube video entitled 'The Art & Science of Teaching: Dr Robert Marzano', which gives an accessible introduction to Marzano's ideas on teaching and children's learning and the effective means by which teachers can maximise the impact on children's learning: www.youtube.com/watch?v=YhB_R_FT9y4. Then reflect on some of your own encounters when working with children. What type of verbal strategies did you employ to develop and extend their learning – for example, what type of questioning did you use that had the greatest impact on their learning?
2. View the following two YouTube videos: 'Feuerstein Method' at www.youtube.com/watch?v=dSGEMrOKHVI; and the Down Syndrome film 'Looking Up On Down' (Glow Films/Feuerstein Institute film by David Goodwin) at www.youtube.com/watch?v=IqSQI6VJgLk. Then consider how children's learning might be adversely affected by artificial barriers and how such barriers might be managed by the adults working with them.

ETHICAL ISSUES IN THE IDENTIFICATION AND ASSESSMENT OF CHILDREN

Any identification and assessment of young children must pay full attention to agreed and properly researched ethical guidelines. Such guidelines need to be firmly in place in any setting where children are to be assessed and they should be properly adhered to with close, careful and transparent monitoring by senior managers. It is now recognised that children have rights and the need to be heard. Attention needs to be given by all professionals to this important factor, which was commonly not the case in previous decades. Children may not, for example, wish to be assessed and identified as having a particular 'label'. Children may also come to feel resentful as they grow older that they have been identified, when younger, as having a particular problem; some children, for example, may have been identified and then formally recorded as having a 'behaviour problem' and being 'not very able' when in fact they have significant specific learning difficulties that professionals have failed to recognise.

LOW ACHIEVEMENT AND UNDERACHIEVEMENT

In 2009, the Office for Standards in Education (Ofsted) undertook a comprehensive review of provision for children and young people with special educational needs and disability in England (Ofsted, 2010). Following the review, it reported on how the term 'special educational needs' (SEN) was being far too widely used by practitioners, with 50 per cent of the schools and early years providers they visited employing the concept of 'low attainment' and 'relatively slow progress' as the two key indicators for deciding if children had a special educational need. Ofsted also reported on how some schools identified children as having SEN when their needs were not significantly different to those of their peers; though underachieving, these children's lack of progress could, in part, be accounted for by having provision offered to them that was 'not good enough', and with expectations of these children being 'too low'. In some cases, provision made to schools, which had required additional funding, was, in fact, being used 'to make up for day-to-day teaching and pastoral support', rather than being targeted at those children with SEN. In the case of children who needed complex and specialist support from health and other services to enable them to thrive and develop, the term 'educational needs' was frequently used but did not always offer an accurate reflection of their situation. Such findings are worrying and point to a mismatch between the actual abilities and potential of many children presenting with behavioural patterns construed as troublesome and the mistaken perceptions and subsequent categorisations of children made by some teachers and early years practitioners (MacBlain, 2014).

Ofsted also identified key factors which underpin best practice in all children's learning, and, thereby, effective identification, assessment and intervention. They found that where teaching and learning were of a high quality, 'assessment was secure, continuous and acted upon'. In addition:

- teachers planned opportunities for pupils to collaborate, work things out for themselves and apply what they had learnt to different situations
- teachers' subject knowledge was good, as was their understanding of pupils' needs and how to help them
- lesson structures were clear and familiar but allowed for adaptation and flexibility … presented information in different ways
- [teachers] understood … adjusted the pace of the lesson to reflect how children … were learning … understood clearly the difference between ensuring that children … were learning and keeping them occupied
- [teachers'] respect for individuals was reflected in high expectations … the effectiveness of specific types of support was understood and the right support was put in place at the right time. (Ofsted, 2010, p. 47)

CHILDREN WHOSE FIRST LANGUAGE IS NOT ENGLISH

Addressing the needs of children whose first language is not English typically requires careful and reflective thinking on the part of teachers and early years practitioners, as well as specific expertise and knowledge not only of the cultural aspects of the pupils themselves but also of the nature of pedagogies that evidence has suggested work effectively (MacBlain, 2014). Meeting the needs of these children brings with it a number of challenges and should be a whole school responsibility, led by senior management, and not the responsibility of one single member of staff. Schools and early years settings should seek to embrace the child's culture and that of their family as part of the whole school community. These children should not be viewed as a separate homogenous group but as having differing individual needs, and should not be 'lumped' together with children with SEN (MacBlain, 2014). Assessment should be child-centred and include children's strengths as well as weaknesses. Aspects of functioning in their own first language should, where possible, be assessed and recorded – this may require involvement by parents or a friend of the family to translate or, where possible, a translator. Offering advice to teachers in secondary schools, Brooks et al. (2004, p. 275) comment that we are likely to come across two main categories of pupils learning EAL:

- those who were born in Britain and who have progressed through the education system; some of these pupils may have entered school with little or no English

- those who have recently arrived in this country either because their families are seeking asylum or because one or both of their parents is studying or working in the UK.

Just a decade ago, Kenner (2006, p. 75) quoted Saxena (1994) who described a typical day experienced by a young 4-year-old child from a Punjabi family living in Southall, London:

> This boy observes his parents and grandparents reading newspapers and novels, and writing letters and shopping lists in Punjabi, Hindi and English. As a result, he can distinguish between three different types of script, although his school literacy experience is restricted to English only.

The above example demonstrates the complex nature of communication facing many young children whose first language is not English; the number of these children now arriving in the UK is much greater than in 1994 when Saxena made his observations. Teachers may not always be fully aware of the range of language and literacies that many children use and there may be scarce opportunities for children to use or even develop the range of literacies they have acquired within their school settings. Brooks et al. (2004) also make the point that the acquisition of EAL depends, amongst other factors, on the child's proficiency in their own first language. As in the case of children with EAL, it has been considered increasingly important to ensure that practice in schools and early years settings is of high quality and meets the needs of children. This has brought about a significant increase within the UK, and especially England, in inspection services tasked with the monitoring and evaluation of how practitioners work with children.

MONITORING AND EVALUATING PRACTICE

Inspection permeates almost every aspect of learning and teaching in the UK. Few teachers and early years practitioners, especially in England, would admit to paying little regard to monitoring and evaluation by Ofsted. In reality, much of the practice experienced by children in schools and early years settings is directly or indirectly influenced by the prospect of an inspection. In worst case scenarios, inspections can result in the downgrading of a school with very serious consequences for senior managers. Equally, schools and early years settings can find themselves upgraded following a positive outcome from an inspection, resulting in greater numbers of parents applying to have their children admitted. Though there has been a substantial growth in inspection services across the UK with frequent changes to the frameworks by which they are carried out, there have also been many criticisms of the role of inspection and its effectiveness.

In March 2014, Harriet Waldegrave and Jonathan Simons authored a report entitled 'Watching the watchmen: the future of school inspections in England' for Policy Exchange, a leading UK think tank. Their report (2014, pp. 10–11) made a number of recommendations aimed at reforming Ofsted, amongst which were the following:

- Inspectors should only be allowed to inspect a school when they have relevant and recent teaching experience in Special, Primary or Secondary Schools, or a high knowledge of assessment and pedagogical practice in that area.
- Inspectors should have to pass a data interpretation test.
- Ofsted should consider how to introduce additional methods to test the reliability and validity of their inspections.
- Schools' internal assessment procedures should be validated by Ofsted as to their rigour and frequency, to ensure moderation is reliable.
- Ofsted should pilot a survey of students' school experiences.
- Ofsted should ... exercise more caution in publications which seem to endorse certain teaching methods.
- Ofsted should consider carefully whether it retenders its contracts for Additional Inspectors when the contracts are re-let in 2015. Should Ofsted retender the contracts, it should place a condition that AIs work full time for the contractor so as to ensure organisational loyalty and mechanisms for development and information flow.

Perhaps as a result of such apparent criticism, Ofsted (2015a) produced the document, 'The future of education inspection: understanding the changes', which introduced the common inspection framework in England. In this document, Sir Michael Wilshaw (Her Majesty's Chief Inspector of Schools) drew particular attention to the importance of leadership as one of the primary means of raising standards. In his foreword to this new document, he commented as follows:

> If education is the key to unlocking the well-being and prosperity of our nation, then our future success rests in the hands of great leaders. Such leaders know how to use increased freedoms to bring about the transformation that children and learners need.

Sir Michael went on to stress how leadership would be at the centre of the new inspection framework when inspectors will:

> look at leaders' vision and ambition for all children and learners. They will want to see how leaders set the culture of their school or provider and how they ensure that all learners - particularly the most disadvantaged - make strong progress from their different starting points.

It is of course particularly heartening to see the clear emphasis that Ofsted will now place on the ambition that leaders should have for all children and learners, and this comes at a time when there is greater recognition that too many children are continuing to fail in our schools and early years settings (MacBlain, 2014; MacBlain, et al., 2015).

Sir Michael emphasised that new 'short' inspections for good schools and further education and skills providers will be designed with a particular focus on the quality of leadership as well as the capacity of leaders to 'drive improvement':

> Finally ... hundreds of serving leaders will join forces with HMI to deliver new inspections. Seven in 10 of our Ofsted Inspectors will be current practitioners leading good or outstanding institutions. These proven leaders will help to improve the quality and consistency of inspection ... These reforms reflect our determination to work much more closely with the sectors we inspect ... we will listen to professionals, reduce the burden of inspection on good schools and providers, and continually improve the way we carry out inspection.

The document went on to emphasise how the common inspection framework will build on previous changes but with a greater focus on leaders developing and sustaining ambitious cultures and visions in their schools, offering broad and balanced curricula, safeguarding and outcomes for all children where, importantly, inspectors will now place much greater weight on the progress of pupils in their schools rather than on comparisons with nationally published data.

 POINTS FOR DISCUSSION ——————

View the video clip on YouTube entitled 'Matthew Purves, Ofsted's Head of Education Inspection, Introduces Upcoming Changes', at www.youtube.com/watch?v=ttvAojAaO_E, uploaded on 15 June 2015, in which Matthew Purves offers an overview of the changes to the way Ofsted will inspect schools, further education and skills and early years provision from September 2015. Then consider what specific challenges you anticipate for those in management positions in schools and early years settings over the next decade.

SUMMARY

It is crucial that all young children entering early years or school settings have access to environments that not only optimise their learning but also actively develop their well-being. Practitioners working with children need to continually reflect on what makes for such positive environments and the processes by which these can be created, managed and sustained.

 EXTENDED AND RECOMMENDED READING

Noddings, N. (2002) *Starting at Home: Caring and Social Care*. London: University of California Press.

Ofsted (2015a) *The Future of Education Inspection: Understanding the Changes*. Manchester: Ofsted.

Ofsted (2015b) *The Report of Her Majesty's Chief Inspector of Education, Children's Services and Skills 2015: Early Years*. London: Ofsted.

Wyse, D. and Rodgers, S. (2016) *A Guide to Early Years and Primary Teaching*. London: Sage.

 Don't forget to visit **https://study.sagepub.com/contemporarychildhood** for a selection of free SAGE journal articles, web links, additional case studies, activities, and PowerPoints to help you revise.

REFERENCES

Association of Teachers and Lecturers (ATL) (2005) *An Intelligent Look at Emotional Intelligence*. London: Association of Teachers and Lecturers.

Beckley, P. (2012) *Learning in Early Childhood*. London: Sage.

Brooks, V., Abbott, I. and Bills, L. (2004) *Preparing to Teach in Secondary Schools*. Maidenhead: Open University Press.

Burden, R.L. (1987) 'Feuerstein's instrumental enrichment programme: important issues in research and evaluation', *European Journal of Psychology of Education*, 2(1): 3–16.

Cowie, H. (2012) *From Birth to Sixteen: Children's Health, Social, Emotional and Linguistic Development*. London: Routledge.

Department for Education (DfE) (2015a) *Special Educational Needs and Disability Code of Practice: 0 to 25 Years – Statutory guidance for organisations which work with and support children and young people who have special educational needs or disabilities*. London: DfE.

Department for Education (DfE) (2015b) *Reception Baseline Comparability Study*. London: DfE.

Department for Education and Skills (DfES) (2008) *Statutory Framework for the Early Years Foundation Stage*. Nottingham: DfES Publications.

Feuerstein, R., Rand, Y., Hoffman, M. and Miller, R. (1980) *Instrumental Enrichment*. Baltimore, MD: University Park Press.

Gray, C. and MacBlain, S.F. (2015) *Learning Theories in Childhood* (2nd edn). London: Sage.

Hattie, J. (2008) *Visible Learning: A Synthesis of Over 800 Meta-Analyses Relating to Achievement*. London: Routledge.

Hattie, J. (2012) *Visible Learning for Teachers: Maximising Impact on Learning*. London: Routledge.

Hattie, J. and Yates, G.C.R. (2014) *Visible Learning and the Science of How We Learn*. London: Sage.

Hohnen, B. and Murphy, T. (2016) 'The optimum context for learning: drawing on neuroscience to inform best practice in the classroom', *Educational & Child Psychology*, 33(1): 75–90.

Kenner, C. (2006) Using home texts to promote L1 and L2 literacy learning in the classroom. In T.M. Hickey (ed.), *Literacy and Language Learning: Reading in a First or Second Language*. Dublin: Reading Association of Ireland.

Kuczera, M., Field Hendrickje, S. and Windisch, C. (2016) *Building Skills for All: A Review of England – Policy insights from the survey of adult skills*. OECD Skills Studies. Available at: www.oecd.org/unitedkingdom/building-skills-for-all-review-of-england.pdf (accessed 6 February 2016).

Lancaster, Y. and Kirby, P. (2014) '"Seen and heard": exploring assumptions, beliefs and values underpinning young children's participation', in G. Pugh and B. Duffy (eds), *Contemporary Issues in the Early Years* (6th edn). London: Sage.

Lansdown, G. (2005) *The Evolving Capacities of the Child*. Innocenti Insight. Florence: UNICEF Innocenti Research Centre.

MacBlain, S.F. (2014) *How Children Learn*. London: Sage.

MacBlain, S.F. and Bowman, H. (2016) 'Teaching and learning', in D. Wyse and S. Rodgers (eds), *A Guide to Early Years and Primary Teaching*. London: Sage.

MacBlain, S.F., Long, L. and Dunn, J. (2015) *Dyslexia, Literacy and Inclusion: Child-centred Perspectives*. London: Sage.

Marzano, R. (2005) *School Leadership that Works: From Research to Results*. Alexandria, VA: ASCD.

Marzano, R. (2007) *The Art and Science of Teaching: A Comprehensive Framework for Effective Instruction*. Alexandria, VA: ASCD.

Marzano, R. and Kendall, J.S. (2006) *The New Taxonomy of Educational Objectives* (2nd edn). Thousand Oaks, CA: Sage.

Mathers, S., Ranns, H., Karemaker, A.M., Moody, A., Sylva, K., Graham, J. and Siraj-Blatchford, I. (2011) *Evaluation of the Graduate Leader Fund: Final Report*. DFE-RB144. London: DfE.

Miller, L. and Pound, L. (2011) *Theories and Approaches to Learning in the Early Years*. London: Sage.

Noddings, N. (2002) *Starting at Home: Caring and Social Care*. London: University of California Press.

Nutbrown, C. (2012) *Foundations for Quality: The Independent Review of Early Education and Childcare Qualifications – Final report* (www.gov.uk/government/uploads/system/uploads/attachment_data/file/175463/Nutbrown-Review.pdf).

Office for Standards in Education (Ofsted) (2010) *The Special Educational Needs and Disability Review*. London: Ofsted.

Office for Standards in Education (Ofsted) (2011) *Removing Barriers to Literacy*. London: Ofsted.

Office for Standards in Education (Ofsted) (2013) *The Most Able Students: Are they Doing as Well as they should in our Non-selective Secondary Schools*? London: Ofsted.

Ofsted (2015a) *The Future of Education Inspection: Understanding the Changes*. Manchester: Ofsted.

Ofsted (2015b) *The Report of Her Majesty's Chief Inspector of Education, Children's Services and Skills 2015: Early Years*. London: Ofsted.

Palmer, S. (2006) *Toxic Childhood*. London: Orion Books.

Saxena, M. (1994) 'Literacies among Panjabis in Southall', in M. Hamilton, D. Barton and R. Ivanic (eds), *Worlds of Literacy*. Clevedon, OH: Multilingual Matters.

Snelling, C.B. (2016) Is the 2014 Early Years Foundation Stage Framework Meeting the Social and Emotional Needs of Preschool Children who have Additional Learning Needs? Unpublished Master's dissertation, University of St Mark & St John, Plymouth.

Waldegrave, H. and Simons, J. (2014) *Policy Exchange 2014: Watching the Watchmen – The future of school inspections in England*. London: Policy Exchange (www.policyexchange. org.uk/images/publications/watching%20the%20watchmen.pdf).

Welsh, J. (2014) Promoting Young Children's School Readiness: What Parents Can Do. Available at: http://childencyclopedia.com/Pages/PDF/WelshANGxp1.pdf (accessed 22 April 2016).

Wood, E. (2014) 'Free choice and free play in early childhood education: troubling the discourse', *International Journal of Early Years Education*, 22(1): 4–18.

Woodhead, M. (2005) 'Early childhood development: a question of rights', *International Journal of Early Childhood*, 37(3): 79–98.

PART 2
THE CHILD AND THE FAMILY

5

THE CHANGING NATURE OF FAMILIES

Why you should read this chapter

Many people enter their chosen profession because they want to work with children. However, children are also part of families and if your profession involves children then working with families will become part of your job on a daily basis. It is widely acknowledged that parents are children's first and most enduring educators (QCA, 2000) and there has also been substantial research evidence on the benefits of parental involvement in their children's education. Indeed, Tekin (2016) states that involving parents in their children's education is inevitable and beyond dispute. However, there is still a gap in the rhetoric and reality of working with parents. As professionals, we need to understand how we can work with increasingly complex and diverse families.

By the end of this chapter you should:

- have an understanding of the increasing diversity of families
- appreciate the benefits and challenges for practitioners in working with families
- be aware of some examples of best practice in working with families.

DIVORCE, SEPARATION AND STEP-FAMILIES

The family lives of children and adults have become increasingly complicated in the last 30 years. This complexity is due to a number of changes such as high rates of children born outside of marriage, the growth in cohabitation, delays in the timing of marriage, high rates of divorce and high levels of re-partnering and the birth of children from multiple partners. In particular, it is the high levels of separation and re-partnering in society which produce multi-fold configurations of family relationships (Castrén and Widmer, 2015). Manning, Brown and Stykes (2014) provide a definition of complex families as those where a child's biological parents do not reside together, they may or may not have re-partnered (forming step- or blended families) and half or step-siblings may be present who do not share the same parents.

The most recent statistics indicate that 42 per cent of marriages in England and Wales end in divorce (ONS, 2013). However, since 2000, the divorce rate in England and Wales has appeared to be falling (ONS, 2013). Recent statistics for Scotland indicate a similar trend with a drop of 14 per cent in the number of divorces granted over the last four years (Scottish Government, 2014), and in Northern Ireland the divorce rate in 2013 was 18 per cent lower than in 2007 (NISRA, 2014). Of the constituent UK countries, Wales has the highest proportion of its population divorced at 9.7 per cent, whilst Northern Ireland has the lowest at 5.5 per cent. Nine per cent of England's population and 8.2 per cent of Scotland's population are divorced (ONS, 2014). There are lots of statistics on divorce that can be accessed but where do children fit into these figures? Nearly half of couples divorcing had at least one child under 16 living with the family (ONS, 2014). In 2014, 25 per cent of all families in the UK were lone-parent families and 11 per cent were step-families (ONS, 2015a).

WHAT IS MEANT BY STEP-FAMILIES?

The prevalence of separation and re-partnering in contemporary society has resulted in different family configurations. Knowles (2013) suggests that step-family refers to those in a family relationship because of marriage rather than because there is a biological connection. One or both of the adults in the family are parenting a child, or children, of whom they are not the birth parent but because they have married one of the parents of the child(ren). Both adults may have children from prior relationships and therefore the children in the family may have step-siblings.

Adults in step-families may try to maintain a large number of family ties originating from previous marriages, or they may limit the recognition of their family to the members of their new household (Castrén and Widmer, 2015). This has implications for children where they may have limited contact with relatives involved in the previous marriage such as grandparents, aunts, uncles and cousins, and this can impact on children emotionally and on their feelings of security in their new family arrangement.

There have been numerous studies which show that children who experience parental divorce generally report lower psychological well-being than children from intact families. It is alarming to note that recent research reports that this association has not decreased over time, even though divorce and separation have become more common and the social stigma of divorce has changed. The economic hardship and family dissension that result from divorce still appear to impact negatively on children (Gähler and Garriga, 2012).

From the child's perspective, divorce has come to mean a transition to a family divided into two households (Castrén and Widmer, 2015). Sadowski and McIntosh (2016) refer to this as living in 'shared time'. In their study of children's experiences of shared-time parenting, they reported that children had a sense of longing for the absent parent and this impacted on their ability to adjust to their parents' separation and the shared parenting arrangement. Indeed, in extreme cases they suggested that shared time appeared to create two 'absent' parents and left the child in what they termed 'a perpetual state of longing' (p. 69).

 —— POINTS FOR DISCUSSION ————————————————

Consider the range of families that you know. Manning, Brown and Stykes (2014) report that the family lives of both children and adults have become increasingly complicated, with children and adults moving across household boundaries and being members of several households:

Do you see this in your own experiences of a range of families you know?

How does this impact on the professional who is working with children?

Why is it important for the professional to have an awareness of the family structures of the children with whom they work?

In a recent report by the Centre for Social Justice (CSJ, 2014), it is claimed that it is more likely that a teenager sitting their GCSEs will own a smartphone than live with their father. The report maintains that strong and stable families are indispensable to a strong and stable society and it suggests that high levels of family breakdown threaten to undermine hard-won gains in education and welfare. It warns that the government is sleepwalking into a family breakdown crisis and that family breakdown has led to dysfunction and 'dadlessness' (p. 1).

THE IMPORTANCE OF FATHERS IN FAMILIES

There is a substantial body of research which highlights the very important role that fathers have in enhancing and facilitating the lives of children across all domains of development and well-being (Ihmeideh, 2014). Research suggests that children with involved fathers have better cognitive development, more positive attitudes to school, better language development, higher self-esteem and fewer behavioural problems (Keown and Palmer, 2014). It is sometimes suggested that fathers are particularly important in boys' development, yet research suggests that father involvement is important for both boys and girls and has been shown to influence different factors in the different genders. For example, a study by Sarkadi et al. (2008) found that fathers' involvement reduced psychological problems in young women and behavioural problems in boys. What is clear from the huge body of research is that the involvement of dads with their children delivers many benefits to children's development.

FATHERS' AND MOTHERS' INTERACTIONS WITH THEIR CHILDREN

Despite the research evidence of the significant benefits in involving fathers with their children, the role of fathers has been a much less studied subject than the role of mothers until more recent times. Consequently, Ihmeideh (2014) reports that fathers were often referred to as the 'invisible parents' or the 'hidden parents' in any document on parenting. Yet a father is a significant and important member of the family.

Fathers and mothers have been shown to interact with their children in different ways. Traditionally, we have the nurturing role of the mother versus the father's family provider role, but such views have been changing over the last 50 years as more mothers have joined the workforce and parenting roles have become shared. The modern-day father has moved beyond the breadwinner's role to be much more involved. Instead, the modern father will assume multiple roles, including breadwinner, carer and educator (Morgan et al., 2009). Recent research shows that mothers and fathers have unique but complementary roles. Mothers are involved in care-giving, socialisation and leisure, communication and educational activities and they foster a sense of security in the child, whereas fathers are more involved in physical play and exploration as well as outdoor games and sports. So they are operating more as an 'exploration partner', encouraging children in risk-taking and physical challenge (Newland et al., 2013).

Conversations that parents have with their children are also rich sources of involvement and research has shown that both mothers and fathers have frequent conversations with their children on shared activities and interests, relationships with friends and family and everyday activities. However, fathers are still more likely to talk about sport, physical activity and computer-based topics than mothers (Keown and Palmer, 2014). Hence, the main message from the studies on the influence of mothers and fathers on their children's development and achievement is that both mothers' and fathers' input is important, separately from each other and together (Pleck, 2010).

WHAT IS FATHER INVOLVEMENT?

Father involvement is often perceived as direct interaction with the child. However, a widely recognised framework by Pleck et al. (1985) suggests that real involvement also includes accessibility (the time that the parent is accessible to the child but not interacting with them directly) and responsibility for planning and arranging activities for their child and taking care of the child's needs. Various researchers have devised very detailed taxonomies to try to capture all of the dimensions of father involvement, but many of them fall short of capturing the depth and complexity of the fathering role in a diverse range of social contexts.

There have been conflicting views of fathers in policy and in the media. Many of these views have positioned fathers as unwilling or unable to support and nurture their children, and Hawkins and Dollahite (1997) presented this as a deficit approach to fathering. The media have supported this approach, showing men and women in very stereotyped parenting roles in advertising. However, more recently this deficit approach has been replaced with a generative discourse which sees men as both willing and able to be involved in nurturing their children (Potter et al., 2013), and advertising in the media has picked up on this capable and nurturing modern father.

The role of fathers in the family in the twenty-first century has changed, with men being encouraged to be much more involved in the home and this includes childcare. In 2015, new legislation on parental leave came into effect in the UK which allows fathers to take on the same caring role as mothers. Fathers had been entitled to two weeks of paid paternity leave in the UK since 2003, but now parents can share parental leave following the birth or adoption of a child.

YOUNG FATHERS

Young fathers are usually defined as males aged between 16 and 24 years old and they are often the most invisible and vulnerable parents in the UK. Research has shown that many young fathers come from low socio-economic backgrounds, have poorer educational attainment and fewer employment opportunities than their childless peers, and may experience emotional difficulties and have a history of delinquent behaviour (Ross et al., 2012).

The occurrence of the birth of a child before adulthood is reached can be a serious life stressor, especially for young men who do not have effective social support in place. Becoming a father at a young age can serve as a catalyst for triggering aggressive or deviant behaviour (Wilkinson et al., 2009). However, it is also argued in the literature that teenage pregnancy can offer young people a route into adulthood and a positive role identity of being a parent (Graham and McDermott, 2006). Having a child can be an accomplishment, a source of pride and, potentially, of giving and receiving love (Wilkinson et al., 2009). There is growing focus on young parents both in research and in policy and there is emerging evidence which justifies a more positive view of young fathers (Braye and McDonnell, 2012). Feelings of exclusion and marginalisation are commonly reported by young fathers in their experience of being involved in their children's birth and upbringing, and young men are conscious of negative attitudes from professionals (Ross et al., 2012). This stereotypical view of young fathers as feckless and unconcerned about their responsibilities has been challenged by numerous studies and many report that young fathers want to be more present in the lives of their children. Indeed, their fathering ideals are strikingly similar to those of typical older, middle-class fathers. However, they have much less chance of achieving them because of the disadvantages they experience (Wilkinson et al., 2009). Considering the research evidence that highlights the important role that fathers play in the lives of families, there is considerable work to be done in both policy and practice to ensure that young fathers are made visible, supported and encouraged to fulfil their fathering role for the benefit of their children.

EFFECTIVE INVOLVEMENT OF FATHERS

Based on the research evidence that suggests that fathers' involvement with their children is linked to higher educational achievement, it is therefore important to encourage fathers' engagement in early years settings and school. However, in a study on fathers' involvement in young children's literacy development, Morgan et al. (2009) cautioned that fathers are often much more involved with their children than they are given credit for, and just because their participation is not highly visible does not mean that it does not happen.

 CASE STUDY 5.1

School X decided to use a dad-friendly hook of combining a practical activity with a competitive event as a means of getting dads both more involved with the school and in spending some focused time with their children. The starting point was inviting dads into school one evening to hear about a go-kart competition. Over coffee and buns, there was informal discussion about making a go-kart with children, during which there was the opportunity for teachers and fathers to get to know each other and for some fathers this was their first time in the school building. Fathers then worked with their children in their own time to build any sort of device that ran on wheels without an engine. The go-karts were raced at a family-themed evening at the school that included a local band, ice-cream and fish and chip vans, and a sense of community as extended family members and friends came along for the race. This event developed stronger relationships between the school and dads, and encouraged some dads to have confidence in being more involved in their child's school.

The Fatherhood Institute is a registered UK charity which works to promote the role of fathers in policy, research and practice. It promotes Fathers Reading Every Day (FRED), which is a supported reading programme in some schools and early years centres which involves fathers reading with their children. It also runs Fathers' Story Week during the week of Fathers' Day in June, which promotes fathers and children spending time together in support of children's learning and development. More information and practical ideas are available at the website (www.fatherhoodinstitute.org).

 POINTS FOR DISCUSSION

Every early years setting and school is different as are the families with whom they work, and activities which might be successful in one setting might not work in another. Consider some settings you are familiar with and discuss some activities which might engage fathers of children in those settings to become more involved in their child's development and/or education.

GRANDPARENTS AND FAMILIES

There are 14 million grandparents in the UK today. Half of these grandparents are under the age of 65 and 10 per cent are aged under 50. Recent studies have shown that the average 10-year-old child has three living grandparents (Grandparents Plus, 2011). Whilst the contribution of grandparents to families has been largely absent in the numerous studies on the importance of parental involvement in children's learning and well-being, this has been changing over the last 20 years. Grandparenting has become a more researched area as the role of grandparents in the family and society has become more visible, as populations age and life spans become longer and grandparents are being recognised as having a variety of functions within their intergenerational families. Grandparents often live in three-generational households which comprise of grandparents, grandchildren and at least one of the children's parents. They can also live in skipped generational households which consist of grandparents and grandchildren but not the children's parents (Glaser et al., 2014). In the USA, census data shows that 4.9 million children are being raised solely by their grandparents. In Canada, 2011 census statistics show that 75,000 children were being raised by their grandparents without any parental involvement. It is estimated that 200,000 to 300,000 children in the UK are being brought up by grandparents as a result of serious difficulties, such as parental death, drug or alcohol abuse, or imprisonment (Gautier et al., 2013).

The role of grandparents is valued in many cultures. In China, for example, families have been challenged by industrialisation with over 120 million people relocating from rural communities to cities. However, children have remained in the countryside under the care of grandparents out of necessity (Nyland et al., 2009). Grandparents are seen as 'family maximisers' in this role and it is estimated that 58 million Chinese children are 'left behind' and raised by grandparents, thus creating greater economic security for the whole family (Baker and Silverstein, 2012).

ROLE OF GRANDPARENTS IN FAMILIES

Research indicates that grandparents have a variety of functions within families and in the lives of their grandchildren. They are referred to as family watchdogs, protectors, confidantes, valued elders, connectors, mediators and benefactors. All of these terms suggest an instrumental role in providing physical, financial or emotional support as an additional layer to that provided by parents. Kornhaber (1996) suggests that grandparents act as a mentor, role model and nurturer as well as playing the role of historian, where they are able to provide first-hand accounts of family history, practices and rituals of the past. This role of historian is seen as especially important in families that have migrated from their country of origin. In a study on intergenerational learning between children and grandparents in families of Bangladeshi origin who were living in London (Kenner et al., 2007), grandparents had a key part to play in passing on cultural knowledge to their grandchildren. This included knowledge of family history, language and heritage. In a recent study on grandparenting in Tonga (Vakalahi, 2010), it is even claimed that the preservation and perpetuation of cultural customs and traditions, and the ultimate survival of Tongan culture, is dependent on grandparents teaching these cultural values, beliefs and practices to their grandchildren.

Grandparents are also very important at times of family crisis and can play a significant role during family breakdown where there is separation, divorce or remarriage (Tan et al., 2010). The time and attention that they can give to their grandchildren allows for a relationship which can provide security and potentially fill the parenting gap.

 —— POINTS FOR DISCUSSION ———————————

Discuss with your peers what you remember about your own grandparents:

Were they involved in your early care and upbringing and, if so, in what ways?

How would you describe your relationship with your grandparents?

Has this relationship changed as you have grown older?

GRANDPARENTS AND CHILDCARE

We have already discussed how grandparents are central in many families in the support they provide in a myriad of ways and there is also evidence that grandparents are playing an increasing role in rearing the next generation (Tan et al., 2010). In a recent report, the Institute for Public Policy Research claims that, across Europe, nearly one in three mothers in working families with dependent children is either the sole or main 'breadwinner'. This is particularly common in lower-income families, with older or more educated mothers and mothers of older children (IPPR, 2015). The UK Government has published plans to encourage up to half a million more women into work by the start of 2016 and claims that it wants to support women who want to work by increasing access to childcare. The employment rate for women is already at its highest since comparable records began, with over 68 per cent of women aged 16–64 in work (ONS, 2015b). With more mothers working, grandparents are playing an increasingly prominent role in providing childcare and this is especially true for low-income families. Grandparents are reported to be the main childcare arrangement for 35 per cent of families (Statham, 2011). However, research shows that few grandparents provide full-time care, with the majority providing 10 hours of care or less per week. Until relatively recently, the role of grandparents in caring for their grandchildren, and thereby assisting mothers to work, has been almost invisible in government policy. Other European countries, such as Germany, Hungary and Portugal, have allowed parents to transfer parental leave to a grandparent and even allow grandparents paid leave to look after a grandchild in an emergency. The UK Government is beginning to recognise the economic potential of grandparents providing childcare and has recently announced plans to similarly share leave and statutory parental pay. It recognises that this policy will particularly benefit single mothers who, without a partner to share leave with, will now be able to do so with one of their child's grandparents (BBC, 2015).

IMPACT OF CARING FOR GRANDCHILDREN ON THE HEALTH AND WELL-BEING OF GRANDPARENTS

There have been debates within the literature on increasing pressures on older people in society. They are being forced to remain in the workplace for longer as state pensions are being delayed. Many also provide care at home for frail or ill spouses and they are also under pressure to provide childcare as rates of family breakdown, single motherhood and financial pressures challenge their children's families. However, in a recent study on grandparenting in Europe, the impact of providing childcare on grandparents' health was found to be positive. Grandparents who provided childcare were more likely to report good health, even after their previous health status was taken into account, and, for many grandparents, looking after their grandchildren was a positively affirming and rewarding experience (Glaser et al., 2014).

Findler (2007) suggests that professionals working in the early years need to be aware of this increasing role of grandparents in providing assistance and support within families. She advocates providing possibilities for involving grandparents in activities within early years settings and schools to empower them in their role. The website www.grandparentsplus.org.uk is a very useful resource for more information on many of the issues we have addressed regarding grandparents.

— 🔍 —— CASE STUDY 5.2 ─────────────────────

Nursery School X recognised that many grandparents were dropping children off and collecting them from nursery and also providing childcare for significant periods of time during the week. Many of these grandparents had no experience of pre-school education and were unsure about what went on in the nursery setting and what their grandchildren were learning from 'playing all day'. A Grandparents' Week was initiated and grandparents were invited to come in and to volunteer their particular skills. Many grandparents were keen to take up the offer and were encouraged by their grandchildren to do so! One grandmother brought in a basket of wool and knitted at a table; another played the piano in the background; and another baked scones with a group. One grandfather gardened with a group of children, while another brought in a range of simple wooden boats he had made and the children experimented with sailing them in a paddling pool outside. The nursery staff reported the mutual appreciation between grandparents and grandchildren of the range of skills each other had and the shared enjoyment and respect they showed to each other.

FOCUS ON THEORY

The Russian-born American psychologist Urie Bronfenbrenner developed the Ecological Systems Theory (1979) to explain how a child's development is affected by everything in their surrounding environment. He presented the environment on five different levels: the microsystem, the mesosystem, the exosystem, the macrosystem and the chronosystem. You can read more about the complete model in other texts (see Gray and MacBlain, 2015), but we will look at the first two levels here in relation to the previous case study. The microsystem is closest to the child as are the elements of the environment with which they have direct contact, such as home, childcare and school. Children are influenced by people in the microsystem, including family members, caregivers, teachers and peers, and their interactions with them will have an effect on the child's development. The second level of Bronfenbrenner's model, the mesosystem, describes how the different parts of the microsystem work together and interact, which can have an indirect impact on the child's development. In the example above, the nursery setting is an important element of the child's microsystem as are the nursery teachers and assistants who work there. Home and the wider family circle such as grandparents are also part of the microsystem. The mesosystem is where the nursery has taken the opportunity to invite grandparents into the setting to see the children's learning environment and activities. So the different elements of the microsystem are working together and this can have a positive impact on the child's development.

WORKING WITH REFUGEE AND ASYLUM-SEEKING FAMILIES

In recent times, the media has been dominated by unforgettable images of people crossing the Mediterranean Sea in overcrowded boats trying to escape the war in Syria. It is claimed by the UN Refugee Agency that more people now than at any other time have been forced to flee their homes and seek refuge elsewhere due to war, conflict and persecution. There were 59.5 million people forcibly displaced by the end of 2014 compared to 37.5 million a decade ago. The war in Syria is the world's single largest driver of displacement and the UN High Commissioner for Refugees claims we are witnessing a paradigm shift and an unchecked slide into an era in which the scale of global forced displacement is dwarfing anything seen before.

DEFINITIONS OF TERMS

The terms immigrant, asylum seeker and refugee are used frequently in the media and there can be confusion over their meaning and what the similarities and differences are. The definition of a refugee can be found in the 1951 United Nations Convention Relating to the Status of Refugees, which is the centrepiece of international refugee protection today:

> A person who owing to a well-founded fear of being persecuted for reasons of race, religion, nationality, membership of a particular social group or political opinion, is outside the country of his nationality and is unable or, owing to such fear, is unwilling to avail himself of the protection of that country; or who, not having a nationality and being outside the country of his former habitual residence as a result of such events, is unable or, owing to such fear, is unwilling to return to it. (United Nations Refugee Agency [UNHCR], 2011, p. 14)

Refugees are fleeing from war and persecution in their own countries and can cross borders into other countries to seek sanctuary and assistance from those countries and other organisations. The UNHCR states that refugees are defined and protected in international law covering a wide range of aspects, such as safety from being returned to the danger from which they have left; access to fair asylum procedures; and respect for their basic human rights to allow them to live in dignity and safety, while helping them to find a longer-term solution.

An asylum seeker is someone who says he or she is a refugee, but whose claim has not yet been evaluated. Countries have their own asylum systems to determine which asylum seekers qualify for international protection. Those who don't qualify can be sent back to their own countries (UNHCR, 2015). In the UK, a person is officially a refugee when they have their claim for asylum accepted by the government (The Refugee Council, 2015).

Immigrants are people who have citizenship in one country but who come to another country with the intention of living there. They are not moving because of persecution or armed conflict, but rather they choose to move for a variety of reasons, including to find work, seek education or join family members. They are different from asylum seekers and refugees in that they have the necessary visas, paperwork and clearance to enter and live in the new country. They also have the choice to return home without any fear of death or persecution. The UNHCR states that blurring the terms immigrant and refugee can have very serious consequences for the lives and safety of refugees, as it takes attention away from the legal protection that refugees require and undermines public support for them. At the end of 2014, there were 117,161 refugees and 36,383 pending asylum cases in the UK, and the UK Government has announced that 20,000 refugees from Syria will be brought into the UK by 2020.

SUPPORTING REFUGEE AND ASYLUM-SEEKING FAMILIES AND CHILDREN

Refugees are one of the most marginalised groups in society and there is still huge ground to cover in understanding the best ways to support these families. Refugee families cannot be considered as an homogenous group and have very complex lives. This can be understood better by considering a range of pre-migration, trans-migration and post-migration factors (Hamilton and Moore, 2004). Pre-migration factors relate to the experiences of the family before leaving the home country such as parents' educational status and profession, housing, health and well-being. Trans-migration factors include traumatic journeys to escape conflict, border crossings and time spent in temporary refugee camps with inadequate shelter, food, water, medical aid or education. Post-migration factors include time spent in holding centres, being sent to unknown areas to live, separation from or bereavement of family members, poverty and adaption to the new environment which includes home, school and culture (Whitmarsh, 2011).

Many refugees will have physical and psychological problems as a result of the aforementioned factors. Post-traumatic stress disorder (PTSD) is the most researched mental health difficulty in war-affected children but other consequences can include depression, aggressive behaviour and social difficulties (McMullen et al., 2013). Children's parents also experience trauma, mental health issues and stress over the lack of control in their children's lives and parents' mental health has been found to affect their children's mental and behavioural health (Tanaka, 2013).

Many refugees living in the UK experience problems of social exclusion, including poverty, poor housing, poor access to health and social welfare services, limited language support and discrimination (Spicer, 2008). The media and society's attitudes to refugees contribute to barriers to inclusion and integration. However, educational settings are important places for promoting children's integration (Rutter, 2003) and it is children rather than their parents who are often the primary agents of integration within the new country (Olwig, 2003).

--- —— POINTS FOR DISCUSSION ————————

Think, pair and share potential barriers to inclusion that refugee families face. Then consider Olwig's claim that children can be the main helpers in assisting families to integrate into their new country. Why might this be?

IMPORTANCE OF EDUCATION AND THE SCHOOL ENVIRONMENT FOR REFUGEE CHILDREN

Much has been written about the important role of education and the school environment in the successful integration of refugee families and it is clear that they are crucial in facilitating both refugee children and adults in a new society (Bačáková, 2011). In a recent study focusing on an ethnic minority group who had experienced a prolonged state of exile in a refugee camp in Thailand, nursery schools were set up in the camp with a view to creating child-centred, creative, learning-friendly environments. The results showed that those children who attended the nursery schools for more than a year were better at playing cooperatively with other children and were more aware of their own and others' feelings. Therefore, nursery schools were seen to be making a positive difference in the development of young children in refugee camps (Tanaka, 2013).

The main points put forward to support the importance of educational environments in assisting with social inclusion are that schools facilitate contact with the local community; reintroduce a sense of normality and routine; provide a safe environment; increase self-reliance; and foster social and intellectual development (Bačáková, 2011). However, research has identified key barriers to this happening in practice. The first barrier is schools' lack of information about the children, including knowledge of their previous educational history. Insufficient teacher experience of teaching children from different cultural backgrounds is another recognised barrier. For example, diverse cultural beliefs and practices will impact on whether parents will shake hands, hug or bow when they meet teachers and whether they will offer teachers gifts (McBrien, 2011). The cultural differences between children's home environments and their early years or school settings can also be difficult for children to navigate and can impact on their behaviour, and yet teachers can be totally unaware of these differences (Haines et al., 2015). Insufficient cooperation between schools, parents and social workers is also a problem and this can be because of language barriers and lack of time. Insufficient funding, support provision and resources in schools are also barriers where many teachers feel they are left to sink or swim without the necessary support (Bačáková, 2011).

— —— POINTS FOR DISCUSSION ─────────────

McBrien (2011) presents some of the cultural differences she found when working with a range of refugee families. Consider the following:

Vietnamese and Cambodian refugee parents honour the role of teachers and feel it is disrespectful to ask the teacher questions about their children.

Many Sudanese children adopt the culturally appropriate stance of avoiding eye contact with adults.

Vietnamese mothers spoon-feed their young children rather than expecting them to eat by themselves.

How might some of these cultural differences present possible misunderstandings between refugee families and early years professionals or teachers?

THE WAY FORWARD

Research would indicate that schools and early years settings need much more support in working with refugee families in terms of finance, translation and resources. There is also a pressing need for more in-service training programmes that address innovative pedagogies in the light of linguistic and cultural diversity (McBrien, 2011).

WORKING WITH LESBIAN, GAY, BISEXUAL AND TRANSGENDER FAMILIES

Definitions and images of 'family' are continually changing. As we have seen in this chapter, real-life experiences of families can include a whole range of parenting structures and these can include lesbian, gay, bisexual and transgender (LGBT) parents. Families where children are being raised by LGBT parents are increasingly common due to recent changes in the law.

LEGAL CHANGES REGARDING LGBT ISSUES

The last 50 years have seen huge changes in both the legal system and the social acceptance of homosexuality in the UK. Homosexuality was illegal in England and Wales until 1967. In Scotland and Northern Ireland, it was illegal until 1980 and 1982 respectively. The Civil Partnership Act came into force in the UK in 2005, allowing same-sex couples to form civil partnerships, giving them greater rights and responsibilities within a relationship and also greater recognition in society. More recently, the Marriage (Same Sex Couples) Act 2013 in the UK allowed the first same-sex marriages to take place in England and Wales in March 2014. Scotland followed closely behind with its first same-sex marriages taking place in December 2014. However, while civil partnerships are legal within Northern Ireland, no legislation has been passed for same-sex marriage in Northern Ireland, despite a recent survey showing that the majority of the sample (58 per cent) were in favour of it (ARK, 2014). A referendum on same-sex marriage in the Republic of Ireland in 2015 led to it being the first country in the world to legalise same-sex marriage by popular vote.

Same-sex couples have had the right to adopt children since the introduction of the Adoption and Children Act 2002 in England and Wales, and the Adoption and Children (Scotland) Act 2007. In 2014, there were an estimated 84,000 families consisting of same-sex parents and 11 per cent of these families had dependent children (ONS, 2015a). Indeed, the government reported in March 2015 that the number of children adopted by gay and lesbian families had reached record highs, with 480 children placed in such families in the 12 months from March 2014 to March 2015 (GOV.UK, 2015).

Attitudes to transgender are also changing and, in the last decade, transgender people have been accorded greater protection in law from discrimination. The terminology around transgender is constantly shifting. Gender dysphoria describes the discomfort felt by people whose innate gender identity (their sense of being a man or a woman) conflicts with their visible sex characteristics, and the term transsexual applies to people whose gender dysphoria is so severe that they deal with it by transitioning, with medical assistance, to a different gender role than that assigned at birth. The term transgender is broader and includes all who experience some degree of gender variance (Reed et al., 2009). However, it is very difficult to obtain figures for families with transgender members as many do not reveal their gender variance nor seek any medical treatment, and some who choose to have medical treatment do so privately. However, a recent BBC report highlighted that the number of young people referred to England's only gender identity clinic for under-18s had doubled in the last year to nearly 1,400 (BBC, 2016).

Until recently, there has been very little research on LGBT families but this has been a growing area of interest within policy and practice.

 — POINTS FOR DISCUSSION

Discuss with a peer what you think are some of the issues that might arise in an early years or classroom setting when working with LGBT families. Consider the professionals who work there, the parent body and the children who attend the setting. How do you think some of these issues might be addressed effectively?

WHAT RESEARCH TELLS US ABOUT LGBT FAMILIES

A recent study by researchers at Cambridge University (Mellish et al., 2013) focused on the adoption of children in early childhood by families who were headed by gay fathers, lesbian mothers or heterosexual parents. It investigated parent–child relationships and also parent and child well-being and it found more similarities than differences between family types. Some interesting findings showed that gay fathers were significantly less likely to report having depressive symptoms than lesbian women or heterosexual parents. Gay fathers also appeared to have more interaction with their children and their children had particularly busy social lives. However, overall the study argues that children of gay or lesbian parents are no more likely to suffer from differences in gender behaviour, stigma and teasing from peers or psychological disorder than children from families headed by heterosexual parents.

Other studies on work with LGBT families suggest that many early childhood settings produce and reproduce understandings of family that favour heterosexual households and silence other set-ups such as those with gay and lesbian parents (Fox, 2007). Indeed, it is suggested that the privileging of heteronormativity, where heterosexuality is taken for granted, means that children with parents who identify as being LGBT may never see their families acknowledged, as neither pedagogy nor the curriculum resources reflect positive images of homosexuality or gender variance. This culture of heteronormativity can result in LGBT parents and their children feeling marginalised, ignored and silenced as their identity is not given any focus (Hegde et al., 2014).

Cultural acceptance of LGBT-headed families has been slowly increasing and it is clear that the attitudes of early years professionals and teachers is crucial in regard to the well-being of children from these families. There is limited research evidence in this area, although it is a growing one within research. In one such study in the USA (Hegde et al., 2014), it was shown that, overall, teachers hold a positive attitude to homosexuality yet they are not always comfortable, nor do they feel prepared, to work with families with LGBT parents. Early childhood students have also been shown to hold positive attitudes to homosexuality but, similarly, they do not feel comfortable interacting directly with LGBT parents; they were willing, however, to take action in their school or early years setting to help children and parents feel more accepted (Averett and Hegde, 2012).

HOW EARLY YEARS SETTINGS AND SCHOOLS MIGHT DEVELOP EFFECTIVE PRACTICE IN INCLUDING LGBT FAMILIES

There is a legal obligation to recognise increasingly complex families and to work with a wide range of families without discrimination. The Equality Act 2010 makes it illegal in England, Scotland and Wales to discriminate against anyone because of their sexual orientation. Under this Act, it is also illegal to discriminate against or harass a person because they are undergoing or have undergone gender reassignment. In Northern Ireland, the Equality Act (Sexual Orientation) Regulations (NI) 2006 and the Sex Discrimination (Gender Reassignment) Regulations (NI)

1999 provide similar legal protection against discrimination and harassment. It has been suggested that there is a pressing need for much more research on how resources and programmes that reflect LGBT families can create the right space and opportunity in early years settings to develop diverse understandings of these families (Cloughessy and Waniganayake, 2014). It is also suggested that there is a clear need for training programmes for early years professionals and teachers to enable them to feel more comfortable and prepared to work with these families (Hegde et al., 2014). Some researchers go further and suggest that teachers need to unlearn stereotypes and biases in their move towards more inclusive ways of teaching (Kintner-Duffy et al., 2012).

There is a small body of work addressing how picture books can be used to develop an understanding of diverse families. Many people find discussing sexuality and sexual identity very difficult and it is particularly challenging to do so with younger children. The use of picture books and stories has been shown to actively promote understanding around diversity and, in one study (Kelly, 2012), picture books which introduced alternative families were shown to be beneficial in helping children to understand families from multiple and diverse perspectives. Whilst this study suggested that the use of picture books in this way does not have to be difficult or dangerous, other projects using such books led to unwanted media attention, the books being withdrawn from schools and the project finishing early (Depalma, 2011).

Hence, it is clear that whilst attitudes to LGBT families are changing there are still challenges in ensuring that these families feel accepted and that children can be assisted in their understanding about more diverse families. Attitudes of professionals are a potential barrier and training on appropriate pedagogy and resources is essential in the way forward.

SUMMARY

This chapter has addressed how many modern families do not fit into the popularised notion of the 'nuclear family' which is seen as comprising a father, a mother and several children. As one recent newspaper article stated, 'one thing is clear: the nuclear family has been nuked' (Costello and Barham, 2014). Professor Edmund Leach in his lecture on A Runaway World in 1967 (see http://downloads. bbc.co.uk/rm; http/radio4/transcripts/1967_reith3.pdf for the full transcript of this speech) called the notion of the nuclear family the 'cereal packet image' of family and he criticised the 'soppy propaganda about the virtue of a united family life', instead arguing that human beings have managed to invent all sorts of different styles of domestic living and that we will have to invent more in the future. Nearly 50 years later, we can see that Professor Leach's thoughts on the changing family still hold true. Whilst the media still promotes this image of the nuclear family, there has been an explosion of diverse and new family structures around the globe. For those who are working with children and their families, it is essential to understand the diversity of the modern family, the challenges and opportunities in working with a range of families, and to be responsive in engaging appropriately with all families.

— EXTENDED AND RECOMMENDED READING —

Castrén, A, and Widmer, E. (2015) 'Insiders and outsiders in stepfamilies: adults' and children's views on family boundaries', *Current Sociology*, 63(1): 36–56.

Provides challenging insights into children's experiences of divorce and separation.

Cloughessy, K. and Waniganayake, M. (2014) 'Early childhood educators working with children who have lesbian, gay, bisexual and transgender parents: what does the literature tell us?', *Early Child Development and Care*, 184(8): 1267–80.

Provides an interesting analysis of the literature on working with LGBT parents in early years settings.

Haines, S.J., Summers, J.A., Turnbull, A.P., Turnbull, H.R. and Palmer, S. (2015) 'Fostering Habib's engagement and self-regulation: a case study of a child from a refugee family at home and preschool', *Topics in Early Childhood Special Education*, 35(1): 28–39.

Provides an interesting case study of one child from a refugee family in pre-school.

Ihmeideh, F.M. (2014) 'Giving fathers a voice: towards father involvement in early years settings', *Early Child Development and Care*, 184(7): 1048–62.

Investigates the beliefs and practices of Jordanian fathers with regards to young children.

Don't forget to visit **https://study.sagepub.com/contemporarychildhood** for a selection of free SAGE journal articles, web links, additional case studies, activities, and PowerPoints to help you revise.

REFERENCES

ARK (2014) *Queering the Family: Attitudes towards Lesbian and Gay Relationships and Families in Northern Ireland.* Belfast: NILT.

Averett, P.E. and Hegde, A. (2012) 'School social work and early childhood students' attitudes towards gay and lesbian families', *Teaching in Higher Education*, 17(5): 537–49.

Bačáková, M. (2011) 'Developing inclusive educational practices for refugee children in the Czech Republic', *Intercultural Education*, 22(2): 163–75.

Baker, L. and Silverstein, M. (2012) 'The well-being of grandparents caring for grandchildren in rural China and the United States', in S. Arber and V. Timonen (eds), *Contemporary Grandparenting*. Bristol: Policy Press. pp. 51–70.

BBC (2015) *Working Grandparents to Share Parental Leave and Pay* (www.bbc.co.uk/news/uk-politics-34437405).

BBC (2016) *Gender Identity Clinic for Young People Sees Referrals Double* (www.bbc.co.uk/news/uk-36010664).

Braye, S. and McDonnell, L. (2012) 'Balancing powers: university researchers thinking critically about participatory research with young fathers', *Qualitative Research*, 13(3): 265–84.

Bronfenbrenner, U. (1979) *The Ecology of Human Development*. Cambridge, MA: Harvard University Press.

Castrén, A. and Widmer, E. (2015) 'Insiders and outsiders in stepfamilies: adults' and children's views on family boundaries', *Current Sociology*, 63(1): 36–56.

Centre for Social Justice (CSJ) (2014) *Fully Committed? How a Government Could Reverse Family Breakdown*. London: CSJ.

Cloughessy, K. and Waniganayake, M. (2014) 'Early childhood educators working with children who have lesbian, gay, bisexual and transgender parents: what does the literature tell us?', *Early Child Development and Care*, 184(8): 1267–80.

Costello, J. and Barham, N. (2014) 'Modern family: can marketers catch up with culture?', *The Guardian*, 2 June (www.theguardian.com/media-network/media-network-blog/2014/jun/02/modern-family-television-marketers-diversity).

Depalma, R. (2011) 'The No Outsiders Project: in search of queer primary pedagogies', *Transformations*, 21(2): 47–58.

Findler, L. (2007) 'Grandparents: the overlooked potential partners – perceptions and practice of teachers in special and regular education', *European Journal of Special Needs Education*, 22(2): 199–216.

Fox, R. (2007) 'One of the hidden diversities in schools: families with parents who are lesbian or gay', *Childhood Education*, 83(5): 277–81.

Gähler, M. and Garriga, A. (2012) 'Has the association between parental divorce and young adults' psychological problems changed over time? Evidence from Sweden, 1968–2000', *Journal of Family Issues*, 34(6): 784–808.

Gautier, A., Wellard, S. and Cardy, S. (2013) *Forgotten Children: Children Growing up in Kinship Care*. London: Grandparents Plus.

Glaser, K., Gessa, G. and Tinker, A. (2014) *Grandparenting in Europe*. London: Grandparents Plus.

GOV.UK (2015) Record Number of Children Adopted by LGBT Families (www.gov.uk/government/news/record-number-of-children-adopted-by-lgbt-families).

Graham, H. and McDermott, E. (2006) 'Qualitative research and the evidence base of policy: insights from studies of teenage mothers in the UK', *Journal of Social Policy*, 35(1): 21–37.

Grandparents Plus (2011) Policy Briefing Paper 01 (www.grandparentsplus.org.uk/wp-content/uploads/2011/03/Policy-Briefing-01-paper-statistics-Feb-2011.pdf).

Gray, C. and MacBlain, S. (2015) *Learning Theories in Childhood* (2nd edn). London: Sage.

Haines, S.J., Summers, J.A., Turnbull, A.P., Turnbull, H.R. and Palmer, S. (2015) 'Fostering Habib's engagement and self-regulation: a case study of a child from a refugee family at home and preschool', *Topics in Early Childhood Special Education*, 35(1): 28–39.

Hamilton, R. and Moore, D. (eds) (2004) *Educational Interventions for Refugee Children: Theoretical Perspectives and Implementing Best Practice*. London: Routledge.

Hawkins, A.J. and Dollahite, D.C. (1997) *Generative Fathering: Beyond Deficit Perspectives*. Thousand Oaks, CA: Sage.

Hegde, A.V., Averett, P., White, C.P. and Deese, S. (2014) 'Examining preschool teachers' attitudes, comfort, action orientation and preparation to work with children reared by gay and lesbian parents', *Early Child Development and Care*, 184(7): 963–76.

Ihmeideh, F.M. (2014) 'Giving fathers a voice: towards father involvement in early years settings', *Early Child Development and Care*, 184(7): 1048–62.

IPPR (2015) Who's Breadwinning in Europe? A comparative analysis of maternal breadwinning in GB and Germany (www.ippr.org/publications/whos-breadwinning-in-europe).

Kelly, J. (2012) 'Two daddy tigers and a baby tiger: promoting understandings about same gender parented families using picture books', *Early Years*, 32(3): 288–300.

Kenner, C., Ruby, M., Jessel, J., Gregory, E. and Arju, T. (2007) 'Intergenerational learning between children and grandparents in east London', *Journal of Early Childhood Research*, 5(3): 219–43.

Keown, L.J. and Palmer, M. (2014) 'Comparisons between paternal and maternal involvement with sons: early to middle childhood', *Early Child Development and Care*, 184(1): 99–117.

Kintner-Duffy, V.L., Vardell, R., Lower, J.K. and Cassidy, D. (2012) 'The changers and the changed: preparing early childhood teachers to work with lesbian, gay, bisexual and transgender families', *Journal of Early Childhood Teacher Education*, 33(3): 208–23.

Knowles, G. (2013) 'Step-families and step-parenting', in G. Knowles and R. Holmström (eds), *Understanding Family Diversity and Home–School Relations*. London: Routledge. pp. 73–87.

Kornhaber, A. (1996) *Contemporary Grandparenting*. Thousand Oaks, CA: Sage.

McBrien, J.L. (2011) 'The importance of context: Vietnamese, Somali, and Iranian refugee mothers discuss their resettled lives and involvement in their children's school', *Compare: A Journal of Comparative and International Education*, 41(1): 75–90.

McMullen, J., O'Callaghan, P., Shannon, C., Black, A. and Eakin, J. (2013) 'Group trauma-focused cognitive-behavioural therapy with former child soldiers and other war-affected boys in the DR Congo: a randomised control trial', *Journal of Child Psychology and Psychiatry*, 54(11): 1231–41.

Manning, W., Brown, S. and Stykes, J.B. (2014) 'Family complexity among children in the United States', *The Annals of the American Academy of Political and Social Science*, 654(1): 48–65.

Mellish, L., Jennings, S., Tasker, F., Lamb, M. and Golombok, S. (2013) *Gay, Lesbian and Heterosexual Adoptive Families*. London: BAAF.

Morgan, A., Nutbrown, C. and Hannon, P. (2009) 'Fathers' involvement in young children's literacy development: implications for family literacy programmes', *British Educational Research Journal*, 35(2): 167–85.

Newland, L.A., Chen, H., Coyl-Shepherd, D.D., Liang, Y., Carr, E.R., Dykstra, E. and Gapp, S.C. (2013) 'Parent and child perspectives on mothering and fathering: the influence of ecocultural niches', *Early Child Development and Care*, 183(3–4): 534–52.

NISRA (2014) Marriages, Divorces and Civil Partnerships in Northern Ireland 2013 (www. nisra.gov.uk/archive/demography/publications/marriages_divorces/MDCP2013.pdf).

Nyland, B., Zeng, X., Nyland, C. and Tran, L. (2009) 'Grandparents as educators and carers in China', *Journal of Early Childhood Research*, 7(1): 46–57.

Olwig, K. (2003) 'Children's places of belonging within immigrant families of Carribean background', in K. Olwig and E. Gulløv (eds), *Children's Places: Cross Cultural Perspectives*. London: Routledge. pp. 217–35.

ONS (2013) What Percentage of Marriages End in Divorce? (www.ons.gov.uk/ons/rel/ vsob1/divorces-in-england-and-wales/2011/sty-what-percentage-of-marriages-end-in-divorce.html).

ONS (2014) Stepfamilies in 2011 (www.ons.gov.uk/ons/dcp171776_360784.pdf).

ONS (2015a) Families and Households 2014 (www.ons.gov.uk/ons/dcp171778_393133. pdf).

ONS (2015b) UK Labour Market (www.ons.gov.uk/ons/rel/lms/labour-market-statistics/ january-2015/statistical-bulletin.html).

Pleck, J.H. (2010) 'Paternal involvement: revised conceptualisation and theoretical linkages with child outcomes', in M.E. Lamb (ed.), *The Role of the Father in Child Development* (5th edn). Hoboken, NJ: John Wiley & Sons. pp. 58–93.

Pleck, J.H., Lamb, M.E. and Levine, J.A. (1985) 'Facilitating future change in men's family roles', *Marriage and Family Review*, 9: 11–16.

Potter, C., Walker, G. and Keen, B. (2013) 'I am reading to her and she loves it: benefits of engaging fathers from disadvantaged areas in their children's early learning', *Early Years*, 33(1): 74–89.

QCA (2000) *Curriculum Guidance for the Foundation Stage*. London: QCA/DfEE.

Reed, B., Rhodes, S., Schofield, P. and Wylie, K. (2009) *Gender Variance in the UK: Prevalence, Incidence, Growth and Geographic Distribution*. London: Gender Identity Research and Education Society.

Ross, N.J., Church, S., Hill, M., Seaman, P. and Roberts, T. (2012) 'The perspectives of young men and their teenage partners on maternity and health services during pregnancy and early parenthood', *Children in Society*, 26: 304–15.

Rutter, J. (2003) *Working with Refugee Children*. York: Joseph Rowntree Foundation.

Sadowski, C. and McIntosh, J. (2016) 'On laughter and loss: children's views of shared time, parenting and security post separation', *Childhood*, 23(1): 69–86.

Sarkadi, A., Kristiansson, R., Oberklaid, F. and Bremberg, S. (2008) 'Fathers' involvement and children's developmental outcomes: a systematic review of longitudinal studies', *Acta Paediatrica*, 97(2): 153–8.

Scottish Government (2014) Civil Law Statistics in Scotland 2012–13 (www.gov.scot/ Resource/0044/00446819.pdf).

Spicer, N. (2008) 'Places of exclusion and inclusion: asylum-seeker and refugee experiences of neighbourhoods in the UK', *Journal of Ethnic and Migration Studies*, 34(30): 491–510.

Statham, J. (2011) *Grandparents Providing Child Care: Briefing Paper*. London: Childhood Well-being Research Centre.

Tan, J., Buchanan, A., Flouri, E., Attar-Schwartz, S. and Griggs, J. (2010) 'Filling the parenting gap? Grandparent involvement with UK adolescents', *Journal of Family Issues*, 31(7): 992–1015.

Tanaka, A. (2013) 'Assessment of the psychosocial development of children attending nursery schools in Karen refugee camps in Thailand', *International Journal of Early Childhood*, 45(3): 279–305.

Tekin, A.K. (2016) 'Parental perceptions of life context variables for involvement in their young children's education', *Education 3–13: International Journal of Primary, Elementary and Early Years Education*, 44(3): 353–66.

The Refugee Council (2015) Who's Who? (www.refugeecouncil.org.uk/policy_research/the_truth_about_asylum/the_facts_about_asylum).

United Nations Refugee Agency (UNHCR) (2011) The 1951 Convention Relating to the Status of Refugees and its 1967 Protocol (www.unhcr.org/4ec262df9.html).

UNHCR (2015) Asylum-Seekers (www.unhcr.org/pages/49c3646c137.html).

Vakalahi, H.F.O. (2010) 'Tongan grandparents and grandchildren: the impact of grandparenting', *International Social Work*, 54(4): 580–98.

Whitmarsh, J. (2011) 'Othered voices: asylum-seeking mothers and early years education', *European Early Childhood Education Research Journal*, 19(4): 535–51.

Wilkinson, D.L., Magora, A., Garcia, M. and Khurana, A. (2009) 'Fathering at the margins of society: reflections from young, minority, crime-involved fathers', *Journal of Family Issues*, 30(7): 945–67.

6

THE PARENT'S
VOICE

Why you should read this chapter

Practitioners working with children need to fully appreciate the importance of properly collaborating with parents, which means, in essence, hearing what parents have to say. All-too-often this has failed to be the case, with parents feeling ignored and even isolated. In some cases, parents may have felt removed from key decision-making processes that have been shaped and then taken by professionals.

By the end of this chapter you should be able to:

- demonstrate knowledge and understanding of the importance of listening to parents
- demonstrate knowledge and understanding of safeguarding procedures and processes
- reflect on your own practice in light of two high-profile cases and two illustrative case studies contained within this chapter.

LISTENING TO PARENTS

At times, parents may feel unheard and even isolated when key decisions are being made about their children (MacBlain et al., 2015). It is surprising that all-too-often this continues to be the case. Parents will undoubtedly know more about their children's needs than many of the professionals they come into contact with. They will, for example, have unique insights into their children's behaviour, their feelings and emotions (Jackson and Needham, 2014; Tekin, 2016), and crucially they will have detailed and important knowledge of those family and community cultures that their children have been born into.

It is important to recognise that, for many children, listening to and facilitating greater involvement by fathers is essential; doing so can provide deep insights into children's cognitive and emotional development that will be beneficial to professionals. This may frequently be the case where fathers from lone-parent households have been closely involved in the learning of their children (MacBlain and MacBlain, 2004). Involving fathers can also have an enormous positive impact on the future learning of children (Ihmeideh, 2014; Kucirkova and Sakr, 2015; Potter et al., 2013). There will be fathers, however, who may need guidance in supporting their children, especially where their children have experienced difficulties in their first stages of life, as with children, for example, who have special needs or who have been affected by trauma (MacBlain, 2014). Fathers will also need to feel that their contributions are appreciated and welcomed by teachers and other professionals. Such views are very much in keeping with recent trends by governments over the last few decades towards recognising the voice of children and their rights (Konstantoni, 2013; Meehan, 2016; Merewether and Fleet, 2014).

It is also important for parents to feel assured that adults working with their children are properly qualified; this has been more of an issue in the early years sector where it has been proposed in recent years that practitioners should be better qualified (Nutbrown, 2012). Citing the work of Rodd (2012), Nicholson (2016, p. 97) has commented as follows:

> the early childhood sector is currently operating in a disjointed way, with conflicting ideologies and no real understanding of a way to unite the sector and move forward, thus making practitioners ineffective in supporting and promoting children's rights.

Parents need to feel assured that teachers are maintaining and developing their own professional development (Coleman et al., 2012). Though the situation has improved in recent years (Gray and MacBlain, 2015, pp. 195–6), it is still worth noting that just over a decade ago Jarvis (2005, p. 4) felt able to comment on how:

> Education differs from comparable professions, such as medicine and psychology, in that although there is a thriving field of professional research, it takes place largely in isolation from professional practice. It is a rare doctor that does not peruse the medical

research literature at least occasionally, and it would be unusual for a psychologist not to at least dip into current psychological literature – this is a requirement if they have chartered status ... but teachers largely ignore education research.

As all parents know, childhood can bring enormous challenges and with these challenges there often come significant levels of stress. There will be many parents, for example, who find themselves at different stages of their children's lives, having to deal with issues that may be health related, of an educational nature or in some cases driven by more complex factors of a psychological nature (Mas et al., 2016). In such instances, parents may feel confused, misinformed and vulnerable. They may even feel alone and unheard and, in more extreme cases, experience a sense of losing control to professionals, systems and processes that are unfamiliar to them and even frightening. It is at times like these that parents need to be listened to and supported in ways that take into account their own personal needs as adults, as well as those of their children (Dunn, 2015; Hornby and Lafaele, 2011). In addition to support mechanisms within the child's school and/or early years setting, there is also a range of external support mechanisms, such as social services, educational psychology services, the Child and Adolescent Mental Health Service (CAMHS), Kidscape and Mumsnet, that are available to parents. The quality and available access to these can, however, differ significantly, depending on what part of the country parents live in.

One recent and openly proactive attempt at supporting parents has been that of 'Parent View', which was set up a number of years ago by Ofsted (https://parentview.ofsted.gov.uk/). This initiative now provides parents with opportunities to feed back to Ofsted their views about the school their children attends and, more particularly, their estimations of the quality of teaching, how the school deals with such issues as bullying and, importantly, how the school manages poor behaviour. Parents now have a facility and a direct conduit through to Ofsted for offering information at any time online, as opposed to, as in the past, waiting for their child's school to be inspected. Ofsted then uses this information from parents when making decisions about those schools it feels are in need of an inspection. It is important, however, to reflect on the lack of access that some parents in very low-income families will have to computers in the home and, thereby, to online feedback mechanisms.

It should also be recognised that there are many parents who will have had difficult experiences when they, themselves, were at school. They may, for example, lack the confidence to comment on their children's experiences at school and how the school or early years setting is managing their child's learning and/or behaviour. They may also lack the confidence to make an appointment with teachers whom they may see as authority figures. To such parents, schools may be perceived as forbidding and unwelcoming places. It is essential, therefore, that these parents are supported and encouraged in developing positive and affirming relationships with their child's school that actively break down such barriers and facilitate opportunities for them to openly discuss any concerns they might have about their children (Arnold, 2003; Feiler, 2010; MacBlain, 2014; Ward, 2013).

One particularly helpful means of overcoming potential barriers between anxious parents and their children's school or early years setting is when the child's teacher or early years practitioner agrees with parents to visit them at their home and to meet with the child (Thornton and Brunton, 2007). This can, for example, be done before children enter primary school. One of the authors of this text (SM) had direct experience of this where a school that he worked with allowed its Special Educational Need Co-ordinator (SENCo) time at the end of each academic year to visit children in their homes prior to transition. The SENCo would take a small easel and crayons and work with the child in their home for an hour or two along with the child's parent. In this way, she could start to form a positive working relationship with the parents and break down any potential barriers that the parents might have developed. The school found this to be an excellent use of the SENCo's time as it reduced significantly any potential difficulties and/or problems they had with parents.

This can be enormously powerful and have a highly positive effect on the levels of support and continuity that the child feels are available to them. Indirectly, this will almost certainly lead to improvements in the child's learning and, more particularly, their emotional development.

— 🔍 —— CASE STUDY 6.1 ————————————————

THE CASE OF ADAM - AN ILLUSTRATIVE STUDY

Adam is 11 years of age and is due shortly to transfer to his local secondary school. He only recently started at his primary school, having moved to the area with his mother and step-father and two younger sisters. The head teacher has just referred Adam to the educational psychologist following growing concerns about his behaviour and attitude to adults and other children in the school. Adam's behaviour in school is characterised by extremely high levels of inattentiveness, hyperactivity, distraction of the other children and abusive language. His literacy and numeracy skills are very poor and he currently reads at around the same level as a child in Key Stage 1. The head teacher has found her dealings with Adam's mother to be extremely difficult and it has now reached the stage where Adam's mother is refusing to speak with the head teacher. The head teacher has found Adam's mother to be very aggressive and reluctant to talk about Adam's home situation and about his development prior to moving to the local area. Adam's father left the family home when he was very young and his mother has struggled to support Adam and herself financially after she was made redundant from the factory where she had worked for years, following a downturn in the international market for the goods her factory makes. Since then, she has had to accept handouts from neighbours and every week visits a foodbank to get extra food when she runs out of money. She has tried unsuccessfully to gain employment but lives in an area with extremely high levels of unemployment. At the same time that the educational psychologist became involved, the head teacher also made a referral to social services because of concerns relating to Adam's dishevelled appearance when he comes to school, his acknowledgement that he has little to eat at home, and several bruises on his neck. When she or Adam's teacher move physically very close to him, he flinches and, on occasion, has run and hidden under the teacher's desk, refusing to come out when asked. He presents as being very defiant, aggressive and even cruel to other children and as showing little remorse for his actions, even when he has hit other children or been very callous towards them. Adam's head teacher has heard rumours from other children that Adam is engaging in substance abuse. On occasion, Adam's teacher has expressed concerns that she feels he is very depressed and showing unusual signs of heightened anxiety.

Following her referral to the educational psychologist, a multi-professional meeting was set up, which included the school social worker and educational psychologist, the head teacher and class teacher and the school's SENCo, with Adam's mother being present throughout the meeting. Adam was also invited into the meeting for a while in order to allow him to express his own feelings and perceptions of his behaviour. The meeting went well and it was agreed that the school social worker would visit the home on a weekly basis over the next three months, and that the educational psychologist would work with the class teacher and SENCo to implement a behaviour modification programme, which the psychologist would then review on a monthly basis when she visited the school. It was also agreed that a referral should be made to the Child and Adolescent Mental Health Service (CAMHS) for an assessment of Adam's emotional well-being, and that following that assessment a further meeting would be held when an Education Health Care (EHC) plan would be created. At the centre of the plan was Adam's well-being and it was recognised at the outset that there were many factors in his life that were affecting his progress. It was also acknowledged that his mother required a range of interventions and that she herself was struggling with many factors beyond her control. Also at the heart of the EHC plan was the need to support Adam's mother in addressing her own personal issues, which it was considered would then impact positively on Adam.

FOCUS ON THEORY

It is important, at the outset, to consider the wider context in which Adam was growing up and the external influences that impacted on his early learning and development. The theoretical perspectives offered by Bronfenbrenner (1979, cited in Gray and MacBlain, 2015) can be useful here. Bronfenbrenner noted that external factors influence children's learning, and he was

(Continued)

(Continued)

notable in his emphasis on adopting a holistic view when studying children. Bronfenbrenner developed an 'ecological' model of human development (see Figure 6.1) in which he proposed a number of interrelated systems (presented as layers), each of which contained factors that shaped children's development (see Gray and MacBlain, 2015, Chapter 7 for a detailed discussion of Bronfenbrenner's ideas).

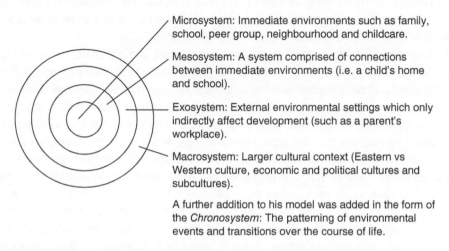

Microsystem: Immediate environments such as family, school, peer group, neighbourhood and childcare.

Mesosystem: A system comprised of connections between immediate environments (i.e. a child's home and school).

Exosystem: External environmental settings which only indirectly affect development (such as a parent's workplace).

Macrosystem: Larger cultural context (Eastern vs Western culture, economic and political cultures and subcultures).

A further addition to his model was added in the form of the *Chronosystem*: The patterning of environmental events and transitions over the course of life.

Figure 6.1   Bronfenbrenner's ecological model of individual development

Bronfenbrenner's theoretical perspective offers much to help us in our understanding of Adam. From birth, Adam was directly and indirectly influenced by many external factors – for example, when his father left home he became a child growing up in a lone-parent household, his mother was made redundant and the community he lives in is one where unemployment is very high, there is a visible and significant drug culture and examples of poverty are everywhere around him. His mother has been unable to afford to buy books and there is no computer in the home. Most weeks, they run out of electricity and on quite a few occasions Adam has been unable to complete homework. Adam's level of nutrition is poor and since early childhood he has been used to a very poor diet, which impacts on his energy level; sleep has also been an issue for Adam as he is frequently extremely cold at night. Due to lack of income, his mother rarely socialises and, as a consequence, Adam spends most evenings and weekends alone with his mother.

Quite clearly, Adam needed a proper assessment with an accurate and objective identification of problems affecting his progress. Gaining accurate information is essential in any assessment and this can be done through sensitive discussions with parents, in addition to gaining information gained from teachers and other professionals. It is important for parents to understand that interventions by professionals will have been informed by clear guidance accumulated over many years from research and professional practice, though this may vary depending on levels of training, expertise and resourcing; the time that professionals can give to particular cases can vary considerably. One example of a very effective intervention was a guide published by the Children and Young People's Mental Health Coalition (CYPMHC, 2012), which sought to support head teachers in preventing emotional and behavioural difficulties in children. The guide brought to the attention of head teachers the fact that pupils with conduct disorder and severe Attention Deficit Hyperactivity Disorder (ADHD), as in the case of Adam, are more likely to experience marked difficulties in the acquisition of literacy and numeracy skills, which would work against them accessing the curriculum and may lead to them coming to see themselves as failing (MacBlain, 2014). The CYPMHC also drew attention to an important distinction between *conduct disorder*, which they defined as 'a repetitive and persistent behaviour problem, where major age-appropriate societal norms or the basic rights of others are violated', and *emotional disorder*, which, they proposed, refers to 'conditions such as depression and anxiety' (p. 4). The guide also offered the following rather disturbing facts in relation to children in their post-primary phase of education, suggesting that without proper support Adam's future is likely to be an unhappy one, unless he receives effective and purposeful interventions:

> 1 in 10 or at least 3 young people in every class has a behavioural or emotional difficulty ... Almost half of young people with fewer than five GCSEs graded A to C said they 'always' or 'often' feel down or depressed compared with 30 per cent of young people who are more qualified ... and 7 will have been bullied ... 1 in 4 young people of secondary school age will have been severely neglected, physically attacked or even sexually abused at some point in their lives.

It is now accepted by most, if not all, practitioners working with children of all ages that behavioural and emotional difficulties can impact detrimentally on academic achievement. This is a crucial point, for it is typically the case that children with persisting conduct or emotional disorders, as in the case of Adam, are most likely to have special educational needs, find themselves excluded from school, and even acquiring a police and criminal record due to unlawful acts, most typically carried out under the influence of older children and young adults. Recently, Kring et al. (2013) have referred to the Diagnostic and Statistical Manual of Mental Disorders (DSM-5) in their discussion of conduct disorder, which they suggest focuses on those acts that are illegal and that are construed as violating the rights of other individuals and breaking the consensus of agreed social norms. Kring et al. proposed that in order to meet the criteria for conduct disorder, acts need to be characterised by such elements as aggression and cruelty, lack of remorse, a degree of callousness and high rates of frequency (in the case of Adam, he meets all of these criteria). They also suggest that:

> A related but less well understood externalizing disorder in the DSM-IV-TR is oppositional defiant disorder (ODD). There is some debate as to whether ODD is distinct from conduct disorder, a precursor to it, or an earlier and milder manifestation of it ... Commonly comorbid with ODD are ADHD, learning disorders, communication disorders, but ODD is different from ADHD in that the defiant behavior is not thought to arise from attentional deficits or sheer impulsiveness. (p. 407)

Worryingly, it is also frequently the case that children and young people with conduct disorders engage in substance abuse and may demonstrate much higher levels of anxiety and depression than would be typical of their peers.

 **CASE STUDY 6.2**

THE CASE OF TONY – AN ILLUSTRATIVE STUDY

Tony's parents have been very concerned about his progress since he commenced school at 5 years of age. Before that, they also expressed their concerns on a frequent basis to staff at the nursery because of worries about his language development. They feel they have been fobbed off by staff who have assured them that Tony will improve as he gets older. Tony is now 10 years and six months old and due to transfer to secondary school next year. His reading and spelling are very poor and to date he is still unable to master and remember his times tables. He has only recently learned to tell the time and gets very anxious when asked to engage in even simple numerical operations. His handwriting is almost impossible to read and he has developed a whole range of strategies for avoiding any work that requires writing. He is extremely disorganised, and planning and then writing stories present him with enormous challenges. His verbal articulation is poor and he presents as having difficulties, at times, in understanding what his teacher is asking of him, frequently ending up giving the wrong responses. He frequently struggles at home with homework as he cannot remember what he is supposed to do. His class teacher has always been concerned about his poor coordination and describes him as a 'lovely little boy who is always bumping into things and being in the wrong place at the wrong time'. She gets cross with Tony when he is changing for PE lessons as he is always the last child to be ready and frequently loses items of clothing. Tony is, however, very creative and enjoys art and technology. He loves to make things, but since he was very young gets extremely frustrated if he cannot complete a task or put things back together again.

Tony is due to transfer to secondary school at the end of this academic year and his parents are now insisting on an assessment by an educational psychologist. Tony's greatest fear about going to secondary school is being asked to read aloud in front of his peers. Though Tony's parents have frequently spoken with his teachers over the years and expressed concerns about his lack of progress, they have always been told that whilst Tony generally struggles with work he is, nevertheless, making progress. Following assessment, the educational psychologist discussed her findings with Tony's parents and sent a copy of her report to the school and Tony's parents. An extract from her report read as follows:

Current level of intellectual functioning

In order to gain additional information in regard to Tony's cognitive functioning I administered the Wechsler Intelligence Scale for Children. On this occasion, Tony achieved the following scores [Table 6. 1].

Table 6.1 Tony (Intellectual functioning)

Index	Centile
Working Memory	1
Processing Speed	5
Verbal Comprehension	47
Perceptual Reasoning	45

Two thirds of children are considered to function within the average range of ability, which is represented between the 16th and 84th centiles, with the 16th centile lying at the lowest end of the average range and the 84th centile at the highest. The 85th centile upwards represents increasingly higher ability where the 95th centile represents the top 1% of ability. The 1st centile represents the lowest 1% of ability.

Discussion of statistical results

The above results taken together with my discussion with Tony's parents suggest to me that Tony has the specific learning difficulty dyslexia with elements of dyspraxia that are significant. Of particular note, are Tony's centile scores on Working Memory and Processing Speed Indexes, which are well below the average range and stand in contrast to his other scores...

Literacy

Tony was assessed on his Reading Accuracy (Word Recognition), Reading Comprehension and Spelling. He achieved the following reading and spelling results [Table 6.2].

(Continued)

(Continued)

Table 6.2   Tony (Literacy scores)

Test	Centile
Basic Reading	25
Reading Comprehension	50
Spelling	04

It is clear from [Table 6.2] that Tony experiences marked difficulties with literacy. In particular, he experiences significant difficulties with individual word recognition and decoding as well as with spelling ... I formed the opinion that Tony finds the whole process of spelling to be quite confusing. This, combined with his use of very poor strategies, underpinned by extremely weak working memory and slow processing speed, has caused him to experience marked difficulties in his acquisition of literacy.

Summary and recommendations

In summary, Tony's difficulties in the areas of Working Memory and Processing Speed are significant and, in my opinion, may mask underlying abilities. I have agreed with Tony's parents that I will refer him to the Speech and Language Therapy Service and to the Occupational Therapist in order to gain further information in regard to the possibility of developmental co-ordination disorder/dyspraxia. I have also suggested to Tony's parents that they arrange for his GP to arrange for Tony to have a hearing test in order to check his current hearing status. I have also requested that the head teacher arranges a multi-professional meeting at the end of term when those professionals who have been involved in the assessment of Tony can attend or, if not, forward their written reports for consideration. I have also suggested to Tony's head teacher that a representative from Tony's future secondary school attend the meeting when interventions can be planned to meet his needs. That meeting can also form a starting point for putting into place an Education Health Care (EHC) plan for Tony.

FOCUS ON THEORY

It is clear that Tony is presenting with significant problems in the areas of working memory and processing speed, in addition to difficulties in the area of speech and language. It is also clear that Tony's parents have felt excluded from any real decision making, with even their earliest concerns about his poor progress in literacy and numeracy not being properly recognised and addressed. In fact, it was not until the educational psychologist assessed Tony that crucial underlying factors affecting his progress were identified, namely problems in the areas of working memory and processing speed. Up to this point, Tony's parents had been left feeling that they were not being listened to and that his teachers were of the opinion that, intellectually, Tony was not very able.

It is now recognised that poor progress in literacy (and numeracy) is, for many children, due, in large part, to problems in the area of short-term memory, or, as it is more commonly referred to, working memory. Whitebread (2012, pp. 98–9) has suggested that working memory has three distinctive features: rehearsal and the articulatory loop, multi-sensory representations and limited capacity. When a child's capacity to store information in working memory is very limited and information that is held quickly decays (after about 30 seconds), as is the case with Tony, children require another means of holding information for longer periods. This is done through rehearsal. Through rehearsing information in working memory, it is possible to store it for longer. Rehearsal also facilitates the transfer of information into the long-term memory where it can then be stored for considerably longer. Not only do children begin to develop their ability to engage in rehearsal from a very early age and throughout primary and post-primary education, but, importantly, they also improve the quality of this process and, as they grow older, their use of working memory typically, but not in all cases, improves. The second feature of working memory identified by Whitebread is its multi-sensory nature or, more specifically, the 'visuo-spatial scratch pad', which facilitates the storing and subsequent manipulation of visual images. Having the capacity to represent sensory information in working memory in different ways increases the strength of the memory trace. Though this appears at first hand to be an obvious assertion, it can, nevertheless, be crucially important to the learning of many children. This is so often the case with children who have specific learning difficulties such as dyslexia and who, like Tony, typically present in classrooms as struggling to retain information such as spellings and calculations in working memory long enough, and in a way that the information can be transferred to the long-term memory where it has to be recalled at a later date. Being taught to use different senses together and in unison can be a most effective means of improving the memory capacity of children with the type of difficulties presented by Tony. Whitebread's third feature is limited capacity. It has been known for many years that adults can typically hold around seven bits of information in their short-term memory. However, as new bits of information flow into short-term memory, other bits already stored there are pushed out. Children have a smaller capacity than adults and, therefore, can hold fewer bits of information in short-term storage. These factors, in addition to his weak skills in language processing, were impacting on Tony's learning and leading his teachers to conclude that he had poor concentration and attention, was unmotivated and even lazy when, in fact, his problems had been of a very specific nature. His parents' intuition had, in effect, been accurate.

WORKING WITH PARENTS

In the study *Schools and Parents*, Ofsted (2011) reported how Her Majesty's Inspectors had visited 47 different types of schools between September 2009 and March 2010, with the aim of meeting with teachers and parent groups and evaluating the developing effectiveness of parent–school partnerships. The inspections demonstrated a successful picture of schools working in partnership with parents. A fundamental difference reported between school phases was that whilst in those primary and special schools visited, parents often worked directly with teachers and children, this was much rarer in secondary schools with parents having less of an understanding of their children's learning. This may not come as a surprise given the more complex nature of the curriculum in secondary schools where children learn a much wider range of subjects and in much greater depth than in primary or special schools. The report offered a number of key findings, which included the following:

> All the schools visited valued the key role of parents ... but ... with very varied quality and outcomes ... In the best cases seen, joint working between the home and the school led to much better outcomes for pupils; in particular, this helped pupils with special educational needs and/or disabilities, those with low attendance or who were potentially vulnerable in other ways ... All the schools visited were using, or experimenting with, new technology in their communications with parents ... In the best practice, complaints were used as an opportunity to improve services and understand better the wishes and views of parents ... Although parents often worked helpfully alongside staff ... the various skills, qualifications, experience and insights of parents were underused ... The schools' evaluation of the impact of their work with parents was poor ... Home-school agreements had a low profile.

The above findings are very useful and, in addition to highlighting strengths and weaknesses, clearly point to ways in which schools and early years settings can work to develop effective partnerships with parents. One important factor that influences the nature of such partnerships is the difficulty that many parents have in being able to give time to them because of work commitments.

PARENTS' WORKING PATTERNS

A further change that has impacted on the lives of many children has been the increase in hours worked by their parents. This has led to growing demands on many parents and, arguably, mothers who are expected to manage busy lives and the increasing demands made on them. Few parents have the means to express their voice at a national level and to seek practical and economic support in their lives, support that will help them manage the education and learning of their children. Less than a decade ago, James (2007, p. 273) recognised that since 1998 the number of adults in Britain who work more than 60 hours a week has more than doubled from 10 to 26 per cent, with British adults working on a full-time basis at an average of 44 hours per week, which is the highest in the European Union. Since then, the working patterns of parents, which have traditionally defined many aspects of family life, have continued to change, and though such emerging patterns may present difficulties they also offer opportunities, especially for many women. Today, women in western industrialised countries have, for example, far more opportunities to work and follow a career path than was the case in previous generations. Many have come to experience much greater freedom and liberty and have acquired rights that, previously, were simply unattainable. Importantly, increased opportunities in education have brought to women and men new opportunities for engaging in work that allows them to improve their economic standing as well as that of their families. It must be recognised of course that some mothers choose to work for reasons other than financial gain, such as meeting personal aspirations. Whatever the reasons, it is now most often the case that working patterns for many families result in time being spent by one or both parents away from the family home. It is increasingly the case that working patterns are changing the nature of family life and in many cases their children's learning. This may be considered to be a good or bad thing, depending on the nature and quality of the experiences at home. A recent study in the USA (Vittrup et al., 2016), which sought to explore parents' attitudes to media and the perceptions they had of their children's knowledge and engagement with different media technologies, in addition to their children's knowledge and experience of technologies, revealed, unsurprisingly, that there was heavy media consumption. More surprisingly, however, the study found that less than half of the parents they surveyed (n = 101) could identify their children's technological proficiency with accuracy, even though their children engaged in heavy usage of media. Though parents demonstrated positive attitudes to media many disagreed with recommendations offered by expert sources regarding the age-appropriateness of screen time.

Families in the UK have, over the last few decades, found themselves needing to earn higher incomes to meet the rising costs of living and, most notably, those expenses associated with much higher mortgages. The cost of housing in some parts of the UK is now, for many young people, too expensive and frequently beyond their financial means, which was less the case in previous decades. This often leads to both parents having fewer options in regard to working patterns, especially where there are additional costs relating to children; in many cases, parents now find themselves having to work significantly long hours. Household incomes vary enormously and there are many factors that impact on a parent's ability to add to their income. A two-parent household, where both parents are working and in good health, will be at an advantage to a lone-parent household or a household where there is poor health (both mental and/or physical) or a disability. An increasing polarisation is being witnessed between such families and their income. The Office for National Statistics (ONS) offered insights into the changing nature of working patterns in the UK, as follows:

Over the past 40 years there has been a rise in the percentage of women aged 16 to 64 in employment and a fall in the percentage of men. In April to June 2013 around 67 per cent of women aged 16 to 64 were in work, an increase from 53 per cent in 1971. For men the percentage fell to 76 per cent in 2013 from 92 per cent in 1971. In April to June 2013, looking at the not seasonally adjusted series, around 13.4 million women aged 16 to 64 were in work (42 per cent part-time) and 15.3 million men (12 per cent part-time). For those who worked full-time there were differences in the average hours worked per week. For example, full-time men worked on average 44 hours per week whilst full-time women worked 40 hours per week. While there have been increases in the number of women in work, the percentage of them doing a part-time role has fluctuated between 42–45 per cent over the past 30 years. (2013, p. 1)

The UK falls significantly behind most of the industrialised world in regard to maternal employment rates, reporting that with British mothers whose youngest child is aged 3–5 years, average employment rates are around 58 per cent compared to that of 64 per cent across the industrialised world (Fitzgerald and Kay, 2016). When compared with Finland, the situation in the UK can appear wanting. Following as much as a year's maternity leave, the majority of women in Finland return to work after giving birth. Fitzgerald and Kay (2016, p. 121) have detailed some of the high levels of provision available to mothers in Finland and, importantly, emphasise how children themselves are accorded an entitlement to provision. They note, for example, how every child has a right to 'Early Childhood Education and Care' (ECEC) from birth until the age of 7, and parents have this as an entitlement from within two weeks of commencing work or undertaking a programme of study. In addition, children are given access to day care from birth until the age of 6, usually within publically subsidised private care or publically funded day care settings. From the age of 6, children then attend pre-school for one year, during which they have a half day of early education followed by the remainder of the day in day care.

Traditionally, many parents in the UK have relied on relatives to look after their children while they work; this continues to remain the case in other countries such as Ireland where a recent downturn in the economy has led to some parents struggling with the affordability of childcare and having to rely on relatives (Palaiologou et al., 2016, p. 61). Increasingly, however, parents have grown to rely on the services of childminders. However, the nature of childminding in the UK has been changing quite dramatically over recent years, with much greater emphasis now being placed on the need to gain relevant qualifications, increased monitoring of practice through inspection and a growing accountability and requirement to work more multi-professionally, which often involves working with other agencies and stakeholders (Brooker, 2016). The result has been a marked decline in registered childminders, which appears to offer few signs of slowing down. The level of decrease in numbers of registered childminders can be seen by the fact that in 2006 there were 71,500, whilst in 2010 there were 57,900, and more recently in 2014 fewer than 52,000 (Brind et al., 2011; Ofsted, 2014, cited in Fitzgerald and Kay, 2016).

SUMMARY

For too long, many parents have felt isolated and unheard when they have expressed concerns about their children's progress and even about health-related issues. Misguided perceptions of parents being 'fussy' or 'over-anxious' have grown up over the years and this has often led to some parents feeling that they should not speak to professionals about their children as they may be 'wasting' their time. Such notions, in addition to professionals failing to properly identify children's needs through appropriate, effective and purposeful assessment and interventions, and then listen carefully and objectively to parents, have meant that many children have fallen through the net.

 EXTENDED AND RECOMMENDED READING

Jackson, D. and Needham, M. (2014) *Engaging with Parents in Early Years Settings*. London: Sage.

> A useful and very readable text that offers readers many relevant insights into the practical implications of working in partnership with parents.

Ward, U. (2013) *Working with Parents in Early Years* (2nd edn). London: Sage.

> A useful text that focuses on important implications, practices and processes central to working with parents of young children.

Don't forget to visit **https://study.sagepub.com/contemporarychildhood** for a selection of free SAGE journal articles, web links, additional case studies, activities, and PowerPoints to help you revise.

REFERENCES

Arnold, C. (2003) *Observing Harry: Child Development and Learning 0–5*. Maidenhead: Open University Press.

Brind, R., Norden, O., McGinigal, S., Garnett, E., Oseman, D., La Valle, I. and Jelicic, H. (2011) *Childcare and Early Years Providers*. London: DfE.

Bronfenbrenner, U. (1979) *The Ecology of Human Development*. Cambridge, MA: Harvard University Press.

Brooker, L. (2016) 'Childminders, parents and policy: testing the triangle of care', *Journal of Early Childhood Research*, 14(1): 69–83.

Children and Young People's Mental Health Coalition (CYPMHC) (2012) Resilience and Results: How to Improve the Emotional and Mental Well-being of Children and Young People in Your School (www.cypmhc.org.uk/media/common/uploads/Final_pdf.pdf).

Coleman, M.R., Gallagher, J.J. and Job, J. (2012) 'Developing and sustaining professionalism within gifted children', *Gifted Child Today*, 35(1): 27–37.

Dunn, J. (2015) 'Insiders' perspectives: a children's rights approach to involving children in advising on adult-initiated research', *International Journal of Early Years Education*, 23(4): 394–408.

Feiler, A. (2010) *Engaging 'Hard to Reach' Parents*. Chichester: Wiley-Blackwell.

Fitzgerald, D. and Kay, J. (2016) *Understanding Early Years Policy* (4th edn). London: Sage.

Gray, C. and MacBlain, S.F. (2015) *Learning Theories in Childhood* (2nd edn). London: Sage.

Hornby, G. and Lafaele, R. (2011) 'Barriers to parental involvement in education: an explanatory model', *Educational Review*, 63(1): 37–52.

Ihmeideh, F.M. (2014) 'Giving fathers a voice: towards father involvement in early years settings', *Early Child Development and Care*, 18(7): 1048–62.

Jackson, D. and Needham, M. (2014) *Engaging with Parents in Early Years Settings*. London: Sage.

James, O. (2007) *Affluenza*. London: Vermillion.

Jarvis, M. (2005) *The Psychology of Effective Learning and Teaching*. Cheltenham: Nelson Thornes.

Konstantoni, K. (2013) 'Children's rights-based approaches: the challenges of listening to taboo/discriminatory issues and moving beyond children's participation', *International Journal of Early Years Education*, 21(4): 362–74.

Kring, A., Johnson, S., Davison, G., Neale, J., Edelstyn, N. and Brown, D. (2013) *Abnormal Psychology* (12th edn). Singapore: John Wiley & Sons.

Kucirkova, N. and Sakr, M. (2015) 'Child–father creative text-making at home with crayons, iPad collage and PC', *Thinking Skills and Creativity*, 17: 59–73.

MacBlain, S.F. (2014) *How Children Learn*. London: Sage.

MacBlain, S.F. and MacBlain, M.S. (2004) 'Addressing the needs of lone-parent families', *Academic Exchange Quarterly*, 8(2): 221–5.

MacBlain, S.F., Long, L. and Dunn, J. (2015) *Dyslexia, Literacy and Inclusion: Child-centred Perspectives*. London: Sage.

Mas, J.M., Baqués, N., Balcells-Balcells, A., Dalmau, M., Giné, C., Gràcia, M. and Vilaseca, R. (2016) 'Family quality of life for families in early intervention in Spain', *Journal of Early Intervention*, 38: 59–74.

Meehan, C. (2016) 'Every child mattered in England: but what matters to children?', *Early Child Development and Care*, 186(3): 382–402.

Merewether, J. and Fleet, A. (2014) 'Seeking children's perspectives: a respectful layered approach', *Early Child Development and Care*, 184(6): 897–914.

Nicholson, N. (2016) 'The issue of professionalism', in I. Palaiologou (ed.), *The Early Years Foundation Stage: Theory and Practice*. London: Sage.

Nutbrown, C. (2012) *Foundations for Quality: The Independent Review of Early Education and Childcare Qualifications – Final report*. Runcorn: Department for Education (DfE).

Office for National Statistics (ONS) (2013) *Women in the Labour Market*. London: ONS. Available at: www.ons.gov.uk/ons/dcp171776_328352.pdf (accessed 20 January 2015).

Office for Standards in Education (Ofsted) (2011) *Schools and Parents*. London: Ofsted.

Ofsted (2014) *Registered Childcare Providers and Places in England, August 2014: Key Findings*. London: Ofsted.

Palaiologou, I., Walsh, G., MacQuarrie, S., Waters, J., Macdonald, N. and Dunphy, E. (2016) 'The national picture', in I. Palaiologou (ed.), *The Early Years Foundation Stage: Theory and Practice*. London: Sage.

Potter, C., Walker, G. and Keen, B. (2013) 'I am reading to her and she loves it: benefits of engaging fathers from disadvantaged areas in their children's learning', *Early Years*, 33(1): 74–89.

Rodd, J. (2012) *Leadership in Early Childhood* (4th edn). Maidenhead: McGraw-Hill International.

Tekin, A.K. (2016) 'Parental perceptions of life context variables for involvement in their young children's education', *Education 3–13: International Journal of Primary, Elementary and Early Years Education*, 44(3): 353–66.

Thornton, L. and Brunton, P. (2007) *Bringing the Reggio Approach to Your Early Years Practice*. Abingdon: Routledge.

Vittrup, B., Snider, S., Rose, K.K. and Rippy, J. (2016) 'Parental perceptions of the role of media and technology in their young children's lives', *Journal of Early Childhood Research*, 14(1): 43–54.

Ward, U. (2013) *Working with Parents in Early Years* (2nd edn). London: Sage.

Whitebread, D. (2012) *Developmental Psychology and Early Childhood Education*. London: Sage.

7

MULTI-PROFESSIONAL PERSPECTIVES

Why you should read this chapter

Practitioners working with children will inevitably find themselves having to work with other professionals. Understanding how other professionals work, therefore, and how practice across different professions can inform our work with children is now seen as fundamental to supporting children and especially those children who present, at some stage in their childhood, with needs, complex or otherwise.

By the end of this chapter you should be able to:

- demonstrate knowledge and understanding of how professionals work together
- consider the challenges facing professionals working together
- reflect on the importance of professional working with parents and keeping the child at the centre of any interventions and decisions
- reflect on recent initiatives that will impact on inter-agency work with young children.

EVOLVING PERSPECTIVES

Multi-professional perspectives have evolved largely in isolation of one another and it has only been in recent decades that professionals have gradually, though not entirely, come to work more closely together. This has largely come about as a result of the *Victoria Climbié* case and subsequent cases such as those of *Baby P*, which brought about a raft of new legislation and new initiatives, most notably 'Every Child Matters' (DfES, 2003), and heralded the urgency of professionals working more closely together in ways that are purposeful, effective and transparent (Laming, 2003). More recently, Senior (2016) has brought to the public attention the circumstances surrounding the recent harrowing accounts of young girls in the English town of Rotherham, who had been subjected to abuse over a period of years.

SAFEGUARDING

Safeguarding is everyone's responsibility (DfE, 2015). All those who work with children – be they teachers, GPs, nurses, midwives, health visitors, early years professionals, youth workers, police, accident and emergency staff, paediatricians, voluntary and community workers and social workers – have a responsibility for keeping children safe. No single professional can have a full picture of a child's needs and circumstances, and if children and families are to receive the right help at the right time, everyone who comes into contact with them has a role to play in identifying concerns, sharing information and taking prompt action – in effect, working together. In order for organisations and practitioners to collaborate effectively, it is vital that practitioners working with children and families are very clear about the functions and parameters of their own roles as well as those of other professionals with whom they are working. Recently, Nikiforidou and Anderson (2016, p. 274), in making reference to Adams (2007), commented as follows:

> No system can fully eliminate risk ... everyone is a risk *'expert'* in the sense of being trained by practice and experience on the management of risk and risky situations. Risks and dangers are part of our lives ... Safeguarding and promoting the welfare of children can be achieved through critical reflection, high-quality assessments, decision and review points with a clear analysis, timeliness and systematic investigation of the child's needs, parents' or carers' capacity to respond to those needs, and the broader impact of the family, community and environmental circumstances.

One of the most important features of multi-agency work with children has been that of Local Safeguarding Children Boards (LSCBs). An LSCB must be established for every local authority area. The LSCB has a range of roles and statutory functions, including developing local safeguarding policy and procedures and scrutinising local arrangements. Section 14 of the Children Act 2004 sets out the objectives of the LSCBs, which are: (1) to coordinate what is done by each person or body represented on the Board for the purposes of safeguarding and promoting the welfare of children in the area, and (2) to ensure the effectiveness of what is done by each person or body for those purposes. Regulation 5 of the Local Safeguarding Children's Boards Regulations 2006 sets out the functions of the LSCB in relation to the above objectives under section 14 of the Children Act 2004, as follows:

(a) developing policies and procedures for safeguarding and promoting the welfare of children in the area of the authority, including policies and procedures;

(b) communicating to relevant persons and bodies the need to safeguard and promote the welfare of children, raising their awareness of how this can best be done and encouraging them to do so;

(c) monitoring and evaluating the effectiveness of what is done by the authority and their Board partners, and advising them on ways to improve;

(d) participating in the planning of services for children in the area of the authority;

(e) undertaking reviews of serious cases and advising the authority and their Board partners on lessons to be learned.

As an ongoing means of ensuring standards and quality, the Office for Standards in Education (Ofsted) undertakes reviews of LSCBs in England under the terms of the single inspection framework, in order to determine the effectiveness of LSCBs in carrying out their statutory functions (this is also the case in other parts of the UK). In addition, they monitor the quality of work undertaken by partner agencies in protecting and caring for children and young people. It was of particular note that, recently, Ofsted (2015) found just over 25 per cent of LSCBs to be 'good overall' and reported on how their evidence, gained from reviews, indicated that effective boards were typically characterised by 'mature partnerships', which had formed the foundations on which resources could be shared and priorities agreed on. In those boards considered to be good overall, responsibilities were 'clearly articulated' among the director of children's services, the chief executive for the local authority and the chair of the LSCB. Effective and purposeful strategic links could be identified between the objectives and priorities of key partners, as well as those of key decision-making groups, for example local health and well-being boards. These LSCBs and their partners characteristically demonstrated high levels of determination for improving the quality of frontline practice and for undertaking regular audits and actively working to identify weaknesses, in addition to challenging each other to improve their practice.

Ofsted also found that LSCBs requiring improvement did not regularly and robustly examine the quality of their practice, with progress against improvement priorities being much slower than their 'good overall' counterparts. Partners, and in particular, schools were found to be 'generally less engaged in the boards' work'. Of concern was the finding that less effective LSCBs were not sharing transparent and clear performance data relating to children and young people who were missing or who were 'subject to or at risk of child sexual exploitation', even though this was a requirement of statutory guidance. Weaker Boards were found less able to challenge how services were being delivered and as a result were not effective enough (2015, p. 20). In its report, Ofsted drew particular attention to the fact that when services for the safeguarding of children and young people were determined to be inadequate, then 'the weight of that judgement' and the 'necessary improvement action' fell most heavily on the local authority and the director of children's services as opposed to the LSCB or its partners. It also drew attention to the important fact that whilst local authorities held most of the accountability, they did, in fact, have limited powers to make others take action. Rather worryingly, Ofsted concluded that whilst accountability for services was fundamental to improving the care and protection of children, the current framework of accountabilities was not working. The report recommended that 'government needs to review where responsibility lies locally for protecting children and who should have the power to take decisive action if the needs of children are being compromised' (2015, p. 21). In summary, procedures produced by LSCBs are there to ensure effective inter-agency communication and safeguarding practice, in addition to providing a framework within which safeguarding decisions can be made.

 POINTS FOR DISCUSSION ────────────

View the following two YouTube video clips: 'Wandsworth Safeguarding Children and Young People Board', at www.youtube.com/watch?v=_mdjk_k8j50, which gives an excellent introduction to the nature of Safeguarding Children Boards; and 'Leeds Safeguarding Children Board: The Early Help Approach', at www.youtube.com/watch?v=L2r5g9EigCA, which looks closely at an approach used across the city of Leeds and focuses on assessing the needs of children and/or families early on, in order that needs can be quickly addressed to ensure effective and timely responses and with the appropriate provision of services. The approach highlights the importance of professionals, parents and children having effective and purposeful dialogues. Then consider what practical support early years practitioners and primary school teachers can offer that will remove barriers preventing children in neglectful families from making progress.

In the Green Paper *Every Child Matters* (DfES, 2003), it was proposed that there should be a Common Assessment Framework (CAF). This was due to concerns at the time that arrangements for identifying and responding to children's needs were failing to achieve the outcomes detailed in the Every Child Matters proposal. The CAF is a tool that enables early and effective assessment of children who need additional services or support from more than one agency. It offers a basis for early identification of children's additional needs, the sharing of this information between organisations and coordinated service provision. It is a four-step process whereby practitioners can identify a child or young person's needs early, assess those needs holistically, deliver coordinated services and review progress.

The CAF is designed to be used where practitioners are worried about how well a child or young person is progressing, i.e. where concerns exist in regard to their health and welfare, development and behaviour and learning, or any other aspect of their well-being. It is also used where a child or young person or, indeed, their parent/carer raises a concern with a practitioner or where a child or young person's needs are unclear or broader than the practitioner's services can manage. The process is voluntary and informed consent is mandatory; families do not have to engage and if they do, they may then choose what information they wish to share. Importantly, children and their families should not, in any way, feel stigmatised by the CAF; it is not a referral process but, rather, a request for services. Findings from the CAF may, however, give rise to concerns about a child's safety and welfare, especially where parents or carers are experiencing difficulties in meeting their children's needs because of such factors as domestic violence, substance misuse, mental illness and/or learning disability (Munro, 2011). Effective early help relies on local agencies working together to identify children and families who would benefit from early help and undertake an assessment of need for early help. It also provides targeted services which focus on activity to significantly improve the outcomes for the child. The key task is to understand the child's world and use the information to promote their welfare. The early help on offer should draw on intervention services and high quality support in universal services and may typically include family and parenting programmes, assisting with health issues and help for problems relating to drugs, alcohol and domestic violence.

It is important that there are clear criteria for taking action and that effective support can be provided by all the relevant agencies. Effective sharing of information between professionals and local agencies is, of course, essential for effective identification, assessment and service provision. Early sharing of information is key to the provision of effective early help where problems are arising. Sharing information can be essential to putting in place effective child protection services. Serious case reviews (SCRs) have, for example, highlighted how poor information sharing has contributed to serious injuries in children and even, in some cases, death, as was the case with *Victoria Climbié* (Laming, 2003). Fears about information must not prevent the promotion of children's welfare and their protection. The issue of consent, however, can be a complex one; in worst case scenarios, lack of understanding on the part of professionals could mean that they may assume, incorrectly, that no information can be shared.

— 🔍 —— **CASE STUDY 7.1** ————————————————

THE CASE OF VICTORIA CLIMBIÉ

In 2001, Victoria Climbié, then aged 8, was killed by her aunt and her aunt's boyfriend. Fitzgerald and Kay (2016, p. 55) have indicated that this case 'highlighted existing flaws in the management of child welfare, deficits in communication between key responsible agencies, poor-quality training and the lack of ability of staff to work effectively in protecting children'. The following extract from the Laming report (2003, p. 1) indicates the extent of the harrowing and deeply disturbing events experienced by Victoria:

> The purpose of this Inquiry has been to find out why this once happy, smiling, enthusiastic little girl – brought to this country by a relative for 'a better life' – ended her days the victim of almost unimaginable cruelty. The horror of what happened to her during her last months was captured by Counsel to the Inquiry ... who told the Inquiry: 'The food would be cold and would be given to her on a piece of plastic while she was tied up in the bath. She would eat it like a dog, pushing her face to the plate. Except, of course that a dog is not usually tied up in a plastic bag full of its excrement ... Victoria spent much of her last days, in the winter of 1999–2000, living and sleeping in a bath in an unheated bathroom, bound hand and foot inside a bin bag, lying in her own urine and faeces. It is not surprising then that towards the end of her short life, Victoria was stooped like an old lady and could walk only with great difficulty.

———

— 🔍 —— **CASE STUDY 7.2** ————————————————

THE CASE OF BABY P

Writing for the popular UK newspaper the *Daily Mail*, Allen and Fernandez (2008) revealed how, as a very young child, *Baby P's* smiles had masked his terrible pain and fear brought about by those adults who should have been protecting and caring for him and how he had been used 'as a punchbag' and 'trained like a dog'. Allen and Fernandez gave graphic details of Baby P's horrific abuse, revealing that the child's fingernails had been 'pinched – and possibly ripped by pliers – until they fell off'. They reported how, when searching his home, police had discovered dog mess as well as human faeces on the floor, the remains of bodies of dead chicks and mice 'and a dismembered rabbit' lying around in addition to 'items of pornography'. They were reported in the same article as finding Baby P's cot and the walls in his bedroom stained with blood. The police also found evidence that he had, as Allen and Fernandez reported, 'been inflicting pain on himself by headbutting walls and floors'. Baby P was 17 months of age when he died in London following many injuries over a period of 8 months, during which he had been known to professionals working for children's services and health professionals. The case shocked the British public, particularly because of the extent of the injuries and because this was happening only years after the Victoria Climbié case and subsequent Laming report in 2003. Child protection services along with other agencies were heavily criticised.

Referring to a number of studies (Anning, 2005; Anning et al., 2010; Warmington et al., 2004), Palaiologou (2012, p. 116) has offered different definitions regarding the type of structures and practice that are evident today in terms of multi-agency working:

- *inter-agency* working: involving more than one agency, working together in a planned and formal manner rather than simply through informal channels of communication
- *multi-agency working*: joint planning or, possibly, a form of replication, resulting from the lack of a coherent policy
- *joined-up working*: policy or thinking referring to deliberately conceptualised and coordinated planning that takes account of multiple policies and varying agency practices.

Palaiologou goes on to identify three models of multi-agency working: the *multi-agency panel*, where members meet regularly though they are not permanent and remain with their own agencies; *multi-agency teams*, where members are more permanent and where there is more of a sense of team identity with a team leader; and *integrated services*, where 'the team is co-located, usually part of a community-based service providing inter-disciplinary services to children and families' (2012, p. 117).

Historically, different professions have evolved their own unique ways of working, their own traditions and values and even their own professional use of language (Barr et al., 2005) – for example, children presenting with difficulties may be described by teachers and educational psychologists as children with special educational needs, but by social workers as children with a disability. Effective and easy collaboration between professional agencies and groups may even be marred by a lack of 'basic trust and mutual goodwill … organisational policies, bureaucratic professionals and codes of confidentiality' (Aubrey, 2014, p. 275). Worryingly, Aubrey went on to comment in rather stark terms on how 'rivalry fed by differences in professional power, status and esteem may exacerbate territorialism and raise concerns about protecting vested interests' (p. 275). Sadly, it remains the case that, all too often, agencies continue to work separately from one another and in ways that fail to demonstrate joined-up thinking and practice.

To this end, the very purpose of inter-professional practice amongst agencies has, in the past, often been affected by perverse factors beyond the control of the agencies themselves. Roaf (2002, pp. 36–7) has, for example, commented as follows:

> In general terms agency purpose consists of a core of responsibilities, translated in a range of services decreed by government and tradition. The exact nature of the brief is an evolving one and in some instances arbitrary … Services thus develop and become differentiated over time in response to a range of political, organisational and societal needs.

Following the Laming Inquiry in 2003 and the subsequent Children Act 2004, *Children's Trusts*, which had been tasked with overseeing the welfare of children, were instructed to:

> Co-locate services … establish multi-disciplinary teams … implement a Common Assessment Framework (CAF) [see below] for identifying additional needs of children and young people (CYP) and their families … set up information-sharing systems … and provide joint training and efficient arrangements for safeguarding children. (Aubrey, 2014, p. 276)

However, it must be acknowledged that an increasingly noticeable feature of professional organisations over the last few decades has been the growth in levels of specific expertise in their workforce, which again sets professions apart.

CHALLENGES OF MULTI-AGENCY WORKING

The case studies referred to earlier illustrate a number of issues relating to multi-agency working, in particular an unwillingness on the part of some professionals to make referrals, often due to a perception that other professional bodies, in particular health professionals, are over-worked and over-stretched, and that some children's difficulties are not severe enough to warrant more formal assessment (MacBlain, 2014). Recently, the Office for Standards in Education, Children's Services and Skills (Ofsted) (2015) published *The Report of Her Majesty's Chief Inspector of Education, Children's Services and Skills 2013–14 Social Care*, in which it commented on how the demand for children's services has been continually rising over the last seven years. In 2013–14, for example, the number of referrals to children's social care services made by someone who had concerns about a child increased by over 10 per cent, with the number of child protection investigations rising by 12 per cent and the number of children and young people being classified as 'looked after' rising by 1 per cent.

The report emphasised that most of the resources available to local authorities that were allocated for spending on the social care of children, were in fact spent on high-cost services, helping children and young people and their families when concerns about their safety and welfare had risen to such a point that the statutory duty to assess and then investigate had been triggered. It was estimated that for each £1 spent on preventative early intervention services by local authorities, a further £4 was being spent on 'reactive child prevention work'. Of concern, however, was the finding by Ofsted that its inspections of early interventions and neglect had found compelling evidence that children and young people growing up in complex and damaging circumstances were frequently having to wait far too long for support. Even more concerning was the finding by Ofsted of evidence indicating that when high thresholds for further investigation into concerns failed to be met, it was frequently the case that families received no help at all.

The report also acknowledged how a number of local authorities were continuing to experience difficulties in the recruitment and retention of experienced social workers, which resulted in high caseloads and limitations in 'frontline practice'. Worryingly, Ofsted also indicated in the report how there has been an increasing turnover of directors of children's services and that these individuals are viewed as having a critical role in maintaining stability amongst the social care workforce, as well as offering inspirational leadership and vision. Indeed, strong leadership was viewed as being extremely important in motivating and helping key social care staff to improve services for children and young people (2015, pp. 13–14).

PROFESSIONALS AND PARENTS: WORKING TOGETHER

Ward and Brown (2014, cited in Pugh and Duffy, 2014, pp. 246–7) have offered a very harrowing example of a case that shocked the public and which clearly illustrated the importance of professionals working more closely and more effectively with parents and in ways that are transparent and accountable (Case Study 7.3).

 **CASE STUDY 7.3**

In 2009, a female member of staff, 'K', at Nursery 'Z' in Plymouth [England] was found guilty on seven counts of sexual assault and six counts of making and distributing indecent pictures of children ... The Serious Case Review found a number of factors at individual, agency and strategic levels that might have prevented abuse from happening at the nursery or led to its early identification ... At an individual level K had been demonstrating increasingly sexualised behaviour over the previous 6 months ... These

(Continued)

(Continued)

behaviours were evidently inappropriate, yet no one felt able to challenge her ... At an agency level it became evident that the nursery was run very informally, with boundaries between staff and parents blurred by friendship networks, and with senior staff forming a clique that made it difficult to question them. Lax recruitment procedures, a lack of supervision, poor access to safeguarding training, and a failure to provide clear procedures for intimate care of children or for complaints about individual members of staff had all led to a situation where risks were not identified ... At a strategic level, Nursery Z's status as an unincorporated institution had led to insufficient arrangements for governance and accountability; there was also insufficient integration with other services.

Case Study 7.3, offered by Ward and Brown, illustrates, quite clearly, the problems that can arise when agencies are not working closely together and where there is a lack of transparency and accountability. This is in spite of the lessons that had been learned from the cases of Victoria Climbié and Baby P, and subsequent legislation and shifts in policy and working practices. When Case Study 7.3 is examined at the *individual*, *agency* and *strategic* levels, it can be seen that problems occurred at all levels. Had agencies been working much more closely together, then it is almost certain that these events would not have taken place and problems would have been identified at an early stage and dealt with in the correct manner. More recently, the insights offered by Senior (2016) into the Rotherham scandal (referred to earlier) have indicated that there is still much to do in regard to multi-agency working.

— —— POINTS FOR DISCUSSION ———————————

1. View the following link to *Plymouth Safeguarding Children Board: Serious Case Review: Overview Report - Executive Summary in Respect of Nursery Z, March*: www.plymouth. gov.uk/serious_case_review_nursery_z.pdf. Then consider what factors at each of the *individual*, *agency* and *strategic* levels prevented staff expressing concerns.
2. View the following two YouTube videos: (1) 'Using Multi Agency Collaboration to Help Families', at www.youtube.com/watch?v=ZMlEVzl2g40 (National College for School Leadership), in which Claire Murdoch shows the necessity of working with other agencies to provide the best possible support for families; and (2) 'Every Child Matters & Multi-Agency Working', at www.youtube.com/watch?v=sGRYCC6lFRg, which gives an excellent account of how professionals can work together to support children, young people and their families. Then consider how health visitors work with early years practitioners and primary school teachers to support families.

It is essential that families and professionals work closely together. By doing so, they can create and sustain more effective environments for children, which work to improve well-being (Colverd and Hodgkin, 2011; Cowie, 2012; MacBlain, 2014). This, however, is not always the case, as can be seen from the example above. There may be families, for example, who perceive professional involvement in their lives as intrusive, especially if they feel the way they care for their children is being called into question. Some parents may, as children themselves, have witnessed their own parents having difficult experiences with professional agencies and, as such, grown up with a mistrust of professionals.

Parents have a right to know what is being said about them. Indeed, it is so often the case that parents will know more about the problems facing their children than professionals do. Any interventions and decisions being made about children should draw on as much knowledge from parents as possible, whilst keeping the child at the centre of any proposed actions. It is important, therefore, that professional agencies work closely with families and in a transparent way. This said, it also needs to be recognised that there may be circumstances where decisions have to be made without parents or other members of the family being present, such as when children are at risk within the family. Professionals ought never to lose sight of the principle that they are acting in the best interests of the child.

Normally, personal information about children and families is subject to a legal duty of confidentiality and should only be disclosed to third parties (including other agencies) with the consent of the subject of that information. Wherever possible, consent should be obtained before sharing information with third parties. However, in some circumstances consent may not be possible or desirable as it may compromise the safety and welfare of the child. There may be occasions, therefore, when it is appropriate and necessary for professionals to meet together without parents being present, to reflect on their own practice in a particular case and to develop a multi-agency strategy and action plan for dealing with complex issues and difficulties; this may be the case where there are problems of professional engagement with a family or where a situation involving a child and/or their family may lead to criminal enquiries.

It is now generally accepted by professionals that interventions which involve parents or primary caregivers as well as immediate family members have greater prospects for positive outcomes, especially if these interventions take place early in the lives of children, as indicated earlier where it was acknowledged that children's needs should be carefully identified with appropriate interventions during the Integrated Review at 2 to 2½. Kring et al. (2013, p. 412) made reference to the ideas of Gerald Patterson and his colleagues who developed and evaluated a behavioural programme called 'Parent Management Training' (PMT), in which parents of very young children are introduced to methods for modifying their own responses to their children. Parents, for example, were encouraged to reward 'prosocial' as opposed to 'antisocial' behaviours in a consistent way or, as Kring et al. suggested:

'Parents are taught to use techniques such as positive reinforcement when the child exhibits positive behaviours and time-out and loss of privileges for aggressive or antisocial behaviours' (2013, p. 412).

Kring et al. have gone on to suggest that whilst this type of programme may have been modified by others over the years, it remains the 'most efficacious intervention' for children who present with symptoms of conduct disorder and oppositional defiance disorder (ODD). Children, for example, who attend nurture groups are far more likely to benefit from their experiences and even go on to be better learners. In particular, children's emotional intelligence (see Chapter 3) would be more likely to develop as they come to establish more secure attachments. One further initiative that has been used increasingly in schools is the *Social and Emotional Aspects of Learning* (SEAL) programme (see http://webarchive. nationalarchives.gov.uk/20110809101133/nsonline.org.uk/node/87009), which promotes those social and emotional skills believed to contribute to positive behaviour and good emotional health and well-being in children.

RECENT INITIATIVES

The UK and especially England is not short on initiatives. In fact, a raft of successive initiatives over the last few decades have, in many respects, come to determine and even define the practice of all those who work with children (MacBlain, 2014). Practitioners working with children across the UK have had to adjust how they work with children as a result of changes in government, shifting and emerging ideologies that are, all-too-often, politically driven, and, more recently, economic factors. There are a number of recent initiatives, some of which are still in the process of being formulated, that are worth considering in detail because of the potential they have to alter practice significantly, and in ways that some practitioners will view as very positive but others will view as potentially detrimental to children's learning. The first of these relates to practice amongst different professionals working with children prior to entering primary school.

INTEGRATED REVIEW AT 2–2½ YEARS

Recently, the UK Department of Health (DoH) commissioned the National Children's Bureau (NCB) to undertake a review – the 'Integrated Review' (NCB, 2015) into early childhood. The purpose of the review was to identify children's progress at age 2 to 2½, in particular their strengths and needs, as a means of promoting positive outcomes for children in later years, in terms of their health and well-being, their learning and behaviour. The rational underpinning of the review was to change thinking and practice for the better.

The review was introduced against a background of other developments for children in this age range. It was proposed, for example, that its introduction should be supported by the Health Visitor Implementation Plan (see www.gov.uk/government/publications/health-visitor-implementation-plan-2011-to-2015). This was a four-year programme which was to focus on increased recruitment and retention of health visitors as well as their professional development. An increase in the commissioning of services was also viewed as desirable. In addition to this development, much greater entitlement to free early education for 2-year-olds was also proposed. For example, from September 2010, every 3- and 4-year-old became entitled to 15 hours per week of funded early education. This was later increased to embrace 2-year-olds considered to be 'disadvantaged'. This was gradually phased in, with some 20 per cent of 2-year-olds becoming eligible in September 2013 and some 40 per cent becoming eligible in September 2014. The increase in children attending early years settings would then mean that far more children could benefit from an integrated review of their health and early education.

In addition to the above, it was proposed that there would be a measure of public health for children at this young age, which would then inform policy decisions in regard to shaping services. It was proposed that data be gained through the *Integrated Review*, in addition to the *Healthy Child Programme Review* (see www.gov.uk/government/publications/healthy-child-programme-rapid-review-to-update-evidence, also at 2 years of age for children who are not in early education). Questionnaires were to be completed by parents along with their health visitors and were to focus on communication, gross and fine motor coordination, problem solving, and children's personal and social development. Importantly, it was considered that a separate questionnaire, encompassing children's social and emotional development, would be introduced at a later date.

In 2014, the Children and Families Act became law and set out new requirements for those organisations involved in working with children with special educational needs and/or disabilities. This Act covers the age range 0–25 years and emphasises early identification and assessment that are coordinated and carefully planned, resulting, for many children, in the creation of new 0–25 Education, Health and Care (EHC) plans (see www.legislation.gov.uk/ukpga/2014/6/contents/enacted).

From October 2015, the responsibility for commissioning public health services for children aged 0–5 was transferred to local authorities, which included health visiting, the *Healthy Child Programme* and the review at 2 to 2½ years. Importantly, whilst health visitors, for example, were to continue being employed by their providers, which is, typically, the NHS, responsibility for the actual planning of and payment for services was to lie with local authorities (see The King's Fund website for further information regarding the new NHS health and well-being boards: www.kingsfund.org.uk/projects/new-nhs/health-and-wellbeing-boards).

The government planned to 'mandate' particular elements of the Healthy Child Programme from October 2015, in order to facilitate a process whereby local authorities come to provide universal services, which offer parents and their infants the very best start to their lives. The mandated elements were to be the five universal health visitor assessments, which included the review at 2 to 2½ years and focused on the health development and well-being of children at this young age. The review was tasked with exploring appropriate interventions for children and their families, and particularly those for whom progress was considered to be below that which might be expected of them. In addition, the review was tasked with generating information which could be used to plan services in the future, in order to reduce inequalities in the outcomes of children later in their lives. As an outcome of the review, local authorities, health visiting services and early years providers were, from September 2015, expected to pull together health and early education reviews for young children reaching the age of 2 to 2½.

A key rationale for this review was that it has been acknowledged for a long time that this stage in the lives of young children is hugely important (Dyson et al., 2009; Marmot, 2010; Sylva et al., 2008). Children at this age typically go through very fast growth in development and learning. It is important, therefore, that children's needs are carefully identified, especially those who might require additional support from health professionals – for example, health visitors, speech and language therapists, physiotherapists and/or professionals working in the field of education such as early years practitioners and educational psychologists. It is now accepted that purposeful and effective interventions at this stage of a child's life can have a significant and positive impact on their later lives and their realisation of potential (MacBlain, 2014). Combining health and education reviews at this age supports professionals, parents and carers in effective identification and intervention. It is almost certain that interventions for those children who require additional support will be much more effective at this early stage in their cognitive, social and emotional development. All too frequently, children have, in the past, been left to develop and learn in ways that have failed to identify problems, which cause later and more acute and entrenched difficulties, as is the case, for example, with children who have underlying processing problems that affect their language and access to literacy (MacBlain et al., 2015).

Key principles underpinning the review were that parents should be involved, especially those who are disadvantaged, that they should be active participants where decisions are to be made about their children's learning and emotional development, and that the children should also be actively involved and, crucially, be at the centre of the review itself and demonstrating what they are capable of, in addition to information gained from the professionals' observations. Crucially, also, professionals, practitioners and parents should respect one another's viewpoints and work together when making decisions that are realistic and obtainable, and in such a way that they support children's well-being.

SUMMARY

Practitioners working with young children will, from time to time, find themselves working with other professionals from health and educational backgrounds and even social services. Knowing how other professionals work and how inter-agency work can promote the well-being of children is now an essential factor in managing the education and learning of children. It is crucial that professionals work as closely as is possible with parents and seek to involve parents in any decision making. It is clear that whilst multi-agency working has improved greatly over the years, there is still some way to go.

 EXTENDED AND RECOMMENDED READING

Batty, D. (2001) 'Timeline for the Climbié case', *The Guardian*, 24 March. Available at: www.theguardian.com/society/2001/sep/24/childrensservices (accessed 30 March 2016).

> Offers an account of the events leading up to the death of Victoria Climbié and, though very harrowing, indicates the extent to which services failed to work together.

Fabian, H. and Mould, C. (2009) *Development and Learning for Very Young Children*. London: Sage.

> A very useful resource, focusing on children in the 0–3 years age range. This text covers a great deal of material, including stages of child development, development and learning, in addition to looking at policy and practice.

National Children's Bureau, Early Childhood Unit (NCB) (2015) *The Integrated Review: Bringing Together Health and Early Education Reviews at Age Two to Two-and-a-Half*. London: NCB.

> An excellent insight into assessment at age 2 years and how different agencies can be involved.

Office for Standards in Education, Children's Services and Skills (Ofsted) (2015) *The Report of Her Majesty's Chief Inspector of Education, Children's Services and Skills 2013–14 Social Care*. Manchester: Ofsted.

> A thorough and informative study into the social aspects of children's development and learning.

REFERENCES

Adams, J. (2007) *Risk*. London: Taylor & Francis/Routledge.

Allen, V. and Fernandez, C. (2008) 'Treated like a dog, used as a punchbag: the life and death of a baby boy called "Smiley"', *Daily Mail*. Available at: www.dailymail.co.uk/news/article-1084972/Treated-like-dog-used-punchbag-The-life-death-baby-boy-called-Smiley.html (accessed 27 February 2016).

Anning, A. (2005) 'Investigating the impact of working in multi-agency service delivery settings in the UK on early years practitioners' beliefs and practices', *Journal of Early Childhood Research*, 3(1): 19–50.

Anning, A., Cortell, D., Frost, N., Green, J. and Robinson, M. (2010) *Developing Multi-professional Teamwork for Integrated Children's Services*. Maidenhead: Open University Press.

Aubrey, C. (2014) 'Leading and working in multi-agency teams', in G. Pugh and B. Duffy (eds), *Contemporary Issues in the Early Years* (6th edn). London: Sage.

Barr, H., Koppel, I., Reeves, S., Hammick, M. and Freeth, D. (2005) *Effective Interprofessional Education: Argument, Assumption and Evidence*. Oxford: Blackwell.

Colverd, S. and Hodgkin, B. (2011) *Developing Emotional Intelligence in the Primary School*. London: Routledge.

Cowie, H. (2012) *From Birth to Sixteen: Children's Health, Social, Emotional and Linguistic Development*. London: Routledge.

Department for Education (DfE) (2015) *Working Together to Safeguard Children: A Guide to Inter-agency Working to Safeguard and Promote the Welfare of Children*. London: DfE.

Department for Education and Skills (DfES) (2003) *Every Child Matters*. London: DfES.

Dyson, A., Hertzman, C., Roberts, H., Tunstill, J. and Vaghri, Z. (2009) *Childhood Development, Education and Health Inequalities: Report of Task Group – Submission to the Marmot Review*. London: The Marmot Review.

Fitzgerald, D. and Kay, J. (2016) *Understanding Early Years Policy* (4th edn). London: Sage.

Kring, A., Johnson, S., Davison, G., Neale, J., Edelstyn, N. and Brown, D. (2013) *Abnormal Psychology* (12th edn). Singapore: John Wiley & Sons.

Laming, Lord (2003) *The Victoria Climbié Inquiry: Report of an Inquiry by Lord Laming*. London: TSO.

MacBlain, S.F. (2014) *How Children Learn*. London: Sage.

MacBlain, S.F., Long, L. and Dunn, J. (2015) *Dyslexia, Literacy and Inclusion: Child-centred Perspectives*. London: Sage.

Marmot, M. (2010) *Fair Society, Healthy Lives: Strategic Review of Health Inequalities in England Post 2010*. London: The Marmot Review.

Munro, E. (2011) *The Munro Review of Child Protection: Final Report – A child-centred system*. London: DfE.

National Children's Bureau (NCB), Early Childhood Unit (2015) *The Integrated Review: Bringing Together Health and Early Education Reviews at Age Two to Two-and-a-Half*. London: NCB.

Nikiforidou, Z. and Anderson, B. (2016) 'Working together to safeguard children', in I. Palaiologou (ed.), *The Early Years Foundation Stage: Theory and Practice*. London: Sage.

Office for Standards in Education, Children's Services and Skills (Ofsted) (2015) *The Report of Her Majesty's Chief Inspector of Education, Children's Services and Skills 2013–14 Social Care*. Manchester: Ofsted.

Palaiologou, I. (2012) *Ethical Practice in Early Childhood*. London: Sage.

Pugh, G. and Duffy, B. (2014) *Contemporary Issues in the Early Years* (6th edn). London: Sage.

Roaf, C. (2002) *Coordinating Services for Included Children: Joined up Action*. Buckingham: Open University Press.

Senior, J. (2016) *Broken and Betrayed: The True Story of the Rotherham Abuse Scandal by the Woman Who Fought to Expose it*. London: Pan Books.

Sylva, K., Melhuish, E., Sammons, P., Siraj-Blatchford, I. and Taggart, B. (2008) 'Effective Pre-school and Primary Education 3–11 Project (EPPE 3–11)', *Report from the Primary Phase: Pre-school, School and Family Influences on Children's Development during Key Stage 2 (Age 7–11)*. DCSF Research Report 061. London: DCSF.

Ward, H. and Brown, R. (2014) 'Safeguarding children in the early years, in G. Pugh and B. Duffy (eds), *Contemporary Issues in the Early Years* (6th edn). London: Sage. pp. 246–7.

Warmington, P., Daniels, H., Edwards, A., Leadbetter, J., Martin, D., Brown, S. and Middleton, D. (2004) Conceptualizing Professional Learning for Multi-agency Working and User Engagements. Paper presented at British Educational Research Association annual conference, University of Manchester, 16–18 September.

PART 3
MODERN AND EMERGING CHILDHOODS

8
POLICY, DISCOURSE AND IDENTITY

Why you should read this chapter

It is clear that the dominant political discourse, and the policy that emanates from such discourse, will impact on children and those involved in childhood education. Political interest in childhood education is increasing across the globe, with this interest seemingly grounded in a neo-liberal ideology. Parameters of practice, or controls for practice, are being drawn based on a discourse of enabling children to be *ready* for the next stage of their development and ultimately *ready* for work – practice that childhood educators will be accountable for.

By the end of this chapter, you should be able to:

- reflect on the ideology underpinning childhood education policy and consider how this is evident in political discourse
- reflect on how both childhood education and the professional identity of childhood educators is influenced by policy and political discourse
- examine potential forms of professionalism within childhood education
- reflect on personal values for childhood education and how childhood educators can position themselves within policy and practice.

POLICY AND PRACTICE

Whilst policy, on a superficial level, is simply documentation, it is documentation that regulates practice. Policy aims to *modify* practice; it aims to align practice with the values of governmental ideology. All childhood practitioners are required to translate and interpret policy, in order to enable them to either fully embrace intended practice or locate themselves in a position whereby they can balance policy intentions with their own potentially differing values. Practitioners can be positioned by policy or position themselves within policy (Lea, 2013). Either way, we cannot ignore that there is an 'interplay between policy and teaching that directly impact[s] children' (Heimer and Klefstad, 2015, p. 241).

It is important that there is an understanding of how policy can regulate or, indeed, is regulation. However, it is also important that this regulation is not, or does not have to be, all confining. Heimer and Klefstad (2015, pp. 240–1) helpfully utilise the analogy of a series of small cogs working within a larger cog. The smaller cogs represent the content and curriculum, and their movement around the outer cog represents pedagogy and the practitioner. The outer cog illustrates 'the power of the context binding the ability for teachers to teach in natural ways to support the unique needs of children' (2015, pp. 240–1). The key is that whilst policy regulates content, curriculum, pedagogy and practitioners, there is the potential for movement within policy; there is an opportunity to interpret and position practice within the confines of policy.

This *movement* within the confines of policy parameters is important because there is a reciprocal relationship between policy and the dominant political discourse; put simply, this means policy is far from neutral. Once policy is established, it is 'intimately and deliberately woven into the fabric of professional identity and practice' (Lea, 2013, p. 21), Therefore, policy, and the ideology underpinning it, will influence what is seen to be professional and good practice in childhood education.

As such, childhood educators are required to work or *perform* within a context that defines what *quality* looks like. Individual policy decisions may seem discrete but there is an intersectionality that exists whereby the holistic result is one of data-driven, high-stakes accountability and performativity for educators. It is interesting to see how some childhood educators are responding to this and are seemingly finding approaches or strategies to work within this educational landscape, becoming *tempered radicals* (Carlone et al., 2010) or *policy entrepreneurs* (Lea, 2013), so as to mediate the potential negative effects of the dominant, but superficial, discourse that may threaten the values they hold for childhood education. These are understandable reactions because educators face a difficult challenge; whilst *quality* is rightly viewed as incredibly important in childhood education, and particularly in early childhood education, it is a word that is frequently used but not clearly defined (Campbell-Barr and Leeson, 2016).

CONTEMPORARY POLITICAL IDEOLOGY AND PHILOSOPHY

Apple (2013, p. 6) argued that childhood education policies emanate from 'a vision that sees every sector of society as subject to the logics of commodification, marketization, competition and cost-benefit analysis'. Moss (2015) agrees and questions the appropriateness of this within education, emphasising his discomfort with the same neo-liberal philosophy that constructs specific *standards* that treat education as a commodity. Sachs (2001, p. 156) provides a clear example of such philosophy in action, noting how policies in education are aimed at:

> removing costs and responsibilities as a means of raising standards from the state and thus improving efficiency and responsiveness as a means of raising standards of performance. Putting education into the market place means making education appear more like a commodity so that parents are given access to a range of products from which they can select.

If we accept that the philosophy driving policy interventions is neo-liberal, then we need to acknowledge the potential threat to education for social justice, social capital and cooperation. A focus that only emphasises competition and economics may mean we are at risk of sacrificing 'the flourishing of the whole child' (Lea, 2013, p. 14). Of course, this could be labelled as an extreme viewpoint but, within the UK, Adams et al. (2015) have already argued that the more holistic education of a child is becoming threatened, and it would appear that 'economics' and 'education' are not far apart in political discourse; this is evident even in President Obama's 2016 State of the Union Address, where childhood education is woven explicitly into the economic discussion, identifying that children need to be 'job-ready' (Obama, 2016).

IS RECOGNITION POSITIVE?

There is no question that there has been greater worldwide government attention paid to childhood education in recent years and a significant increase in early childhood education registrations. As an example, Moss (2015, p. 226) noted how the English Government's attitude to childhood education has moved from 'indifference to high priority' and how this is mirrored worldwide, to the number of children being enrolled in education from early childhood increasing by 46 per cent between 1999 and 2010.

Of course, in principle, such recognition is positive, with both education practice and educators themselves benefiting in terms of support and resources. It may be that educators welcome a discourse of 'high priority', perceiving it as an enhancement of status (Ryan and Bourke, 2013). Unfortunately, the approach to

providing recognition will be controlled by the political reasoning behind the initial desire for it. Moss (2015, p. 227), for example, suggests that the increased attention given to childhood education is a result of governments' alarm 'at the persistence and increase in various social problems and at the threat to national survival arising from intensified global competition'. This view would seem to be supported by the UK Department of Education (2013, p. 6) in documentation that states that better childhood education and care are 'vital to ensuring we can compete in the global race' Worryingly, rather than an enhancement of status there is potentially a replacement of professional values with organisational values, and a replacement of collaboration and trust with managerial controls (Ryan and Bourke, 2013). There needs to be an acceptance that there is *hidden reasoning* behind a dominant discourse and this is particularly evident in childhood education. Discourses, according to Campbell-Barr and Leeson (2016), can mask assumptions and render political ideologies and objectives invisible. Worryingly, in this instance, such *hidden* reasons for the increase in recognition of childhood education can potentially be at odds with the values that a majority of educators hold regarding educational principles.

The question that needs to be answered is: how does *recognition* manifest itself? Recognition from a political perspective that wants to see impact on societal issues and the economy will inevitably come in the form of *algorithms of accountability* and performativity. Of course, in principle, accountability is not negative (Spencer-Woodley, 2013) and childhood education and childhood educators have a responsibility for high-quality provision. A debate emerges on what *quality* is or looks like, and what controls, in terms of curriculum, pedagogical approaches, organisational structures, professional development and inspection, emanate from those views. Whilst childhood educators may have fought for recognition and policy has, indeed, given childhood education a degree of *recognition*, this has not been through the pay or status of practitioners but through increased accountability and control being placed on these practitioners. Moss (2015, p. 231) bluntly states that 'the new policy priority given to early childhood education … has been accompanied by the dominance of one discourse, a discourse of control'.

 POINTS FOR DISCUSSION

It has been argued that there is a direct journey from philosophy and discourse to practice and control. Analyse some of the selected text utilised by UK Minister of State for Schools Nick Gibb as he addressed the London Thames Mathematics Hub Primary Conference (27 March 2015) and consider how or whether discourse influences practice (the full speech is available at: www.gov.uk/government/speeches/nick-gibb-speech-on-governments-maths-reforms):

Our approach to deliver greater autonomy for schools through academisation was based on clear evidence from around the world that in the most successful school systems schools are autonomous and accountable … few pupils at primary or secondary school knew their times tables. Long multiplication and long division were rarely taught, with inefficient methods such as the grid method for multiplication and chunking for long division commonplace in classrooms, neither of which are used in the Far East. When I showed visiting members of the Shanghai Municipal Education Commission they were bemused … This stagnation was reflected in our international performance in maths. Coming 24th in the PISA maths tables in 2012 was equivalent to a 3 year difference between the performance of our 15-year-olds and those at the top of the table – in Shanghai. And take up of the study of maths post-15 in England was among the lowest throughout the OECD … Here we are today talking about mastery – which embodies the idea that every pupil can do well and achieve high standards in maths. Mastery is the model of the high-performing Asian systems such as Shanghai, Singapore and South Korea. It delivers a meticulous approach to arithmetic, whole class teaching and focused 35 minute lessons. Frequent practice allows pupils to consolidate their understanding, and pupils are assisted through immediate and tailored in-class questioning and scaffolding techniques. Homework is frequent, and simply and quickly marked.

REGULATION, CONTROL AND ACCOUNTABILITY

Moss (2015, p. 226) states that as childhood education became a higher priority it led to a 'powerful discourse of control'. Government discourse, according to Moss (2014; 2015, p. 236), is all about quality and 'high returns' and is 'focused intently on predictability, certainty and closure of predetermined goals achieved'. There is a situation of multiple government-led initiatives combined with exceptional levels of political interference and regulation, which makes the childhood education landscape incredibly challenging (Heimer and Klefstad, 2015). This challenge includes maintaining or developing a professional identity that is not determined by political discourse; disconcertingly, Osgood (2010, p. 119) argues that political discourse is so dominant that it can effectively silence alternative debates around professionalism and what it means to be a professional, and posits that childhood educators must define professionalism 'from within'.

High-quality education is apparently becoming 'clearly' defined; it can be measured, inspected and is devoid of context. Political discourse will inevitably reinforce the notion that there is no alternative to this definition. As Sachs (2001, p. 156) notes, 'the efficient operation of the market is fostered through the combination of legislative controls and internal, institutional mechanisms, notably performance indicators and inspections'. Campbell-Barr and Leeson (2016) succinctly refer to such controls as *external surveillance systems*. Disconcertingly,

Campbell-Barr and Leeson (2016) continue to state that underpinning these systems, like all children's services, is a collective set of assumptions about childhood and child development that are presented as truths but never questioned. From a governmental perspective, there is no desire to debate emerging *truths* and it is very clear that the acknowledgement of different perspectives is uncommon amongst policy makers (Moss and Dahlberg, 2008). A point of irony is that, as there is greater understanding of the complexities of learning, there appears to be a desire to simplify *algorithms of accountability* and a desire for formalised standards of practice. As Moss (2015) implies, the more complex things become, the more policy makers seem to desire processes of reduction and control.

It is worthwhile considering the implications of this *simplification* process. As an example, whilst definitions of teacher effectiveness and thoughts on how to measure it are vastly inconsistent, policy makers have developed methods of measurement of effectiveness in inspection frameworks (Range et al., 2012). Indeed, Moss and Dahlberg (2008) note that despite Ofsted terminology including *efficiency* and *effectiveness*, as well as *performance* and *quality*, such terminology has not been freely defined. It would appear that quantitative methods are sought to evaluate quality and effectiveness in order to try and identify patterns and trends for the purposes of comparison. Such quantitative comparisons form the basis of the league tables and data dashboards that Lea (2013, p. 23) refers to as blunt instruments used to 'rank organisational compliance with policy objectives ... devised to assist consumers, not citizens, to choose their "preferred" educational service'.

 — POINTS FOR DISCUSSION —————————

Are league tables and openly available data dashboards a positive step for childhood education?

Following the previous example through, simplifying *effectiveness* to a series of quantitative data sets ignores much of the affective or emotional identity that underpins childhood educators' views of professionalism (Osgood, 2010). The data are flawed because of the simplification process but are presented as the universal truth in order to identify trends and create competition or 'consumer choice'. There is no consideration of the impact that these assumptions will have on childhood educators or the children within the educational setting. Any changes to practice to align with these accountability measures are automatically assumed to be positive. In addition, if parents assume the data are accurate then this may influence the choice of setting for their children, potentially influencing finance, resources and support for educators and children in specific settings. Despite all the simplification and all the assumptions, the resulting data feed a political discourse that is now deemed to have *evidence* that can be used to justify further policy decisions. Regulation and control remain.

The impact of control and regulation is felt directly in education settings as particular schedules, non-negotiable curricula, and practices aligned to inspection begin to emerge. As Heimer and Klefstad (2015, p. 241) note, a 'regulating curriculum policy is most often translated as standards and assessments, block schedules, and scripted curriculum that bind the context in which teachers teach and exist under the auspices of universally supporting all children to achieve developmentally appropriate goals'. Moss (2015, p. 232) refers to the situation as a 'counsel of despair', with education settings being 'reduced to institutions for regulating childhoods'.

The list of concerns is extensive as regulation and control do not sit comfortably with educators who view childhood as socially constructed, with children being active social agents in the construction of their own childhoods (James, 2010). As Moss and Dahlberg (2008) imply, by establishing norms against which performance is assessed, we are shaping policy and practice, but not necessarily those of our choice. Indeed, Moss and Dahlberg (2008) ponder whether quality can take into account context and values, subjectivity and plurality. If quality is 'neither neutral nor self-evident but saturated with values and assumptions' (Moss and Dahlberg, 2008, p. 5), it could be argued that quality should be viewed as a subjective concept, not as an objective data-prescribed one. Disconcertingly, despite all the questions around quality, it is very clear that quality is being defined by policy and regulation.

It is not unsurprising that it is the manifestation of the regulation and control that has raised concerns. Heimer and Klefstad (2015), for example, argue that the pressure that is created in attempting to achieve *imposed* standards can actually create additional constraints for teachers when interpreting and enacting curriculum with young children. The drive for high-stakes accountability that emerges from a performativity agenda can potentially harm the childhood education experience as well as the professional identity of childhood educators. A key concern for many educators in developed countries, such as the UK, the USA and Australia, is a move towards a system which focuses on standardised testing, the results of which are publicly available. This pressure to perform and demonstrate accountability gives rise to fears about negative impacts on children's well-being, learning, teaching and curriculum (Adams et al., 2015). 'Arguably, the high stakes inherent in the performativity discourse can mean the holistic takes second place in practice, even if it is held in high value by trainers, trainees and teachers alike. Yet the performativity culture in schools is unlikely to diminish' (Adams et al., 2015, p. 15). Indeed, Heimer and Klefstad (2015, p. 239) note the obvious growth and focus on accountability toward *proficiency* for all children in the USA, and they provide the examples of 'Race to the Top', 'Common Core Standards' and 'Danielson Teacher Effectiveness Evaluations' to emphasise their point.

— ⟋ —— POINTS FOR DISCUSSION ————————————

Parker (2015, p. 134) notes how contemporary politically driven policies in the UK associated with academy status ('unequivocally favoured by the government') and the new primary curriculum are being denigrated by some for reliance on weak data, and demanding too much from children who are too young, ignoring critical skills of thinking and creativity. Heimer and Klefstad (2015, p. 249) also ponder that whilst 'perhaps well intended, policy can have detrimental effects on children'. Select a recent government education policy and compare the *declared* intentions of the policy with how these intentions are practically applied and operated. Will practice enable the intentions to be achieved? What are the positive and negative effects of this policy, once in practice, on children?

The impact of control is evidently felt by educators. As regulation, control and accountability become the *norm*, this can have a significant impact on the motivation and professional identity of childhood educators. It should be stressed that accountability is not inherently *bad*; educators should have a sense of responsibility for ensuring that every child has a high-quality education. However, it should be remembered that the selected *algorithms of accountability* will be based on *organisational* values or perceptions, the desire for conformity and the desire for children to be *ready* to contribute to the 'global economic race'. These *algorithms of accountability* may contradict those of an individual educator and the associated discourse seemingly perceived 'as a disciplinary mechanism' (Ryan and Bourke, 2013, p. 412). Such perceptions would seem to be supported even in political circles; for example, in the UK, a Commons Education Select Committee report (2016, para. 23) points out that the 'landscape of oversight, intervention, inspection and accountability is now complex and difficult for many of those involved in education ... to navigate'.

Notably, Parker (2015) argued that it may seem that the government is promoting greater autonomy for educationalists as 'the government's clear intention to shift power to the frontline ... could suggest a good opportunity for schools to have a powerful impact on pupils' learning'. The same author responds, however, noting the major issue is that educators are expected to 'align their vision with centralised expectations' exemplified by high levels of accountability. In short, and as Ryan and Bourke (2013, p. 412) bluntly argue, educators have been subjected to 'accountability regimes', and they claim this is very obvious in the political discourse and political decisions that currently exist in America, Australia and the UK. Even discourse that seemingly has great value, such as professional standards, can have a *hidden* or ulterior focus; as Sachs (2001, p. 156) notes, 'the rise of a teacher professional standards movement in the UK, USA and Australia can be seen to be more concerned with standardisation of practice rather than quality, despite the public rhetoric for the latter'.

Standardisation, conformity and *norms* for educators and children are aimed at allowing measurement against externally imposed and politically driven targets. It is inevitable that the accountability and performativity agenda that emerges as part of a broader ideology will be economically driven, high stakes and competition-focused. The algorithms of accountability form part of the control of the *market*. As Sachs (2001, p. 156) succinctly notes, 'the efficient operation of the market is fostered through the combination of legislative controls and internal, institutional mechanisms, notably performance indicators and inspections'.

 — CASE STUDY 8.1 ———————————————————

Worryingly, in the *Times Education Supplement* (TES) Kaye Wiggins reported on a recent National Association of Schoolmasters Union of Women Teachers (NASUWT) survey [verified independently] that stated that 74 per cent of teachers had seriously thought about leaving the profession in the last 12 months (available at: www.tes.com/news/school-news/breaking-news/exclusive-three-quarters-teachers-are-thinking-quitting-and-moving). Wiggins (2016) also included a copy of a letter from a teacher to her parents, explaining why she was about to leave the profession for a while; some excerpts are provided here:

> To be honest I'm exhausted with teaching. You know what it is like – I still absolutely love my 8.45 to 3.30 contact with the students but there's no way I can find a work life balance and I've reached the conclusion that I never ever will.

> My commitment to my students prevents me from allowing myself to do anything but the best I can, and my commitment to my family means I'm trying to keep my weekends free from work.

> I am too shattered in the evenings to work efficiently so I am setting an alarm at 5am on my teaching days to try to find an extra hour to do marking.

> I'm perpetually tired and/or ill and never feel like I'm doing as good a job as I want to be doing.

> I'm trying desperately to keep my head above water, which is a ridiculous and soul-destroying way to live.

> When I'm at home, if I'm not working I feel guilty for the pile of work that's sitting in the hall that needs to be done and if I'm working I feel frustrated and angry that I'm not with [my partner] and [my son].

(Continued)

(Continued)

That is on top of working three days at school from 7.45 to 4.45/5.15, on two of which I don't take my morning break as I have five full sessions of teaching. I take a 15 minute lunch break as there's always just too much to do, and I want to minimise the amount I take home (ha ha, as if that ever happens - I'm laden like a packhorse daily just in case I magically find five or six hours overnight to clear the perpetual backlog).

My other issue is the emotional investment. I haven't got sufficient inner calm or emotional strength to cope with looking after my tutor group (most of whom are in a similarly exhausted state to me from their own self drive and pressure from themselves, their peers, parents' ambitions, the ridiculous aspirational targets that mean if they don't get an A the data system codes them as red for underperforming).

I need those emotional reserves for myself, for [my son, my partner] and for the rest of my family and friends.

Quite simply, the system is broken, which we all know, yet senior leaders continue to put pressure on middle leaders who perhaps inadvertently maintain pressure on the departmental staff to continue to work in the way I have just described. And because everyone is working in this way I've just described, at all levels within a school, then no one has the head space to address any of those issues so we all just collapse at the next holiday, regain some composure and do it all again the next term.

Whilst it upsets me to acknowledge that I'm no longer strong enough to continue in such a crazy system, and it upsets me that good teachers have to leave the profession, my stubborn streak is not quite resilient enough to sacrifice myself any more.

Case study 8.1 offers insight into how educators can feel *positioned* and pressured by accountability measures that can lead to an unsustainable situation; this educator is clearly struggling to balance personal views on professionalism and those that she perceives are being required by the political narrative and by the regulation that exists.

PROFESSIONALISM AND PROFESSIONAL IDENTITY

DEMOCRATIC VERSUS MANAGERIAL PROFESSIONALISM

Professionalism is generally seen as a sociocultural construction, developed within a cultural and historical context (Osgood, 2010). Murray (2013) also notes that there is a personal meaning to professionalism, with individuals associating emotional and cognitive experiences with it. Unfortunately, at present, Harwood and Tukonic

(2015) suggest that childhood educators, in particular early childhood educators, are beginning to perceive a 'glass ceiling' effect to their professionalism, with political narrative forming obstacles to the construction of a professional identity. Similarly, Osgood (2010, p. 122) noted that the regulatory and performativity agenda within early childhood education was imposing external 'normalising constructions of professionalism', lacking the *affective* nature that seemed to define most educators' conceptualisation of professionalism. Supporting this view that professionalism should have a broader nature, Goodson (2003) refers to *principled professionalism* – a professionalism that moves beyond practical perspectives, promotes reflectivity and acknowledges the emotional, moral and social purposes of education. Sachs (2001) would label this latter form of professionalism *democratic professionalism* and argues that at the heart of it is an emphasis on collaboration and cooperation between educators and educational stakeholders, and implies that 'child-centred pedagogy' is central. As such, the implication is that childhood education should strive for such *principled* or *democratic professionalism*, but instead educators are faced with a professionalism much more bound in competition and managerial principles, espoused both implicitly and explicitly through political discourse. Such professionalism has 'outcome-focused pedagogy' at its core (Ryan and Bourke, 2013). Sachs (2001, p. 151) refers to this professionalism as *managerial professionalism*, stating that recent government policies:

> promoting devolution and decentralisation have provided the conditions for an alternative form of teacher professionalism to emerge, one that gains its legitimacy through the promulgation of policies and the allocation of funds associated with those policies, namely managerial professionalism.

Ryan and Bourke (2013) imply that policies in Australia and the UK clearly signal the increasing development of a discourse that links professionalism with competition, *norms* and competence-based standards. The resulting structures and *algorithms of accountability* have, therefore, resulted in the legitimisation of a particular form of educator professional based around managerial principles. Through discourse analysis of both the Australian and UK professional standards frameworks, Ryan and Bourke (2013) argue that there is a move towards *performative professionalism* (Beck, 2008), where educators are expected to *demonstrate* or *perform* in order that the profession can be monitored and visible. It appears that there is little room for consideration of educators' thoughts, deliberations, motivation or satisfaction in this performance (Beck, 2008). They summarise by stating that governments in Australia and the UK are carefully attempting to shape the education profession 'through behavioural-heavy standards, with little regard for the attitudinal, emotional and intellectual dimensions of the trustworthy professional' (Ryan and Bourke, 2013, p. 421). The fear is that those educators who embrace, align with or simply fail to position themselves within this political discourse will become 'tick-box professionals who present a veneer of quality' (2013, p. 421).

If we accept that managerial professionalism is being encouraged, it is obviously important that we consider the principles underpinning it. Clarke (1995, cited in Sachs, 2001, p. 151) suggests that two themes or principles underpin the new managerialism: 'universalism' and 'isomorphism'. *Universalism* holds that all organisations are basically the same regardless of function or context, and should pursue efficiency. *Isomorphism* is the assumption that commercial organisations are the most naturally occurring form of coordination, and thus public sector systems are deemed to be misaligned at best, deviant at worst. As such, managerial professionalism has competition and 'blanket' standards at its core with little thought for context.

Managerial professionalism sees educators as unquestioning supporters of outcome-oriented pedagogy related to becoming *ready* for the world of work (Ryan and Bourke, 2013). Miller (2008) acknowledges the tensions between the development of professional roles in early childhood education and care whilst meeting accountability measures and regulation of practice; the suggestion is that professional autonomy could be threatened with technical conformity underpinning *desired* professionalism. Osgood (2006, p. 7) has argued a similar point previously, noting that regulation and control ('the regulatory gaze') can lead early childhood educators to 'conform to dominant constructions of professionalism'. As such, we can be left with what Casey (1995, cited in Sachs, 2001) refers to as 'designer employees' – employees that are encouraged through political discourse 'to demonstrate compliance to policy imperatives' (Sachs, 2001, p. 156). As Murray (2013, p. 537) argues, it is a *technician notion* of professionalism that views both learning and teaching quality as a product that can be tested at a specific moment in time.

 — **POINTS FOR DISCUSSION** —————————————

Whilst there is no consensus on what constitutes professionalism, there is no doubt that dominant discourses 'assert particular realities and priorities' (Sachs, 2001, p. 150). Consider the *journey* from neo-liberal discourse, through policy decisions that encourage competition and commercial engagement (e.g. academy sponsorship), to a new view of professionalism for childhood educators. What are the implications for current childhood educators and childhood education?

PROFESSIONAL IDENTITY

It has been argued that perceptions of what constitutes professionalism, and therefore self-perceptions of professional identity, are pivotal to the cognitive and emotional well-being of educators; Bolivar and Domingo (2006, p. 340) argued, for example, that during change and reform, particularly as a result of ideological change, there are 'serious consequences' for the previously accepted professional identities of educators. Worryingly, it can have short- and long-term effects on both identity and practice. Murray (2013) suggests, for example, that any challenge to personal identity will significantly influence educators' ability to innovate and deal with change. Obviously, in an educational landscape that changes rapidly, the need for resilience and the ability to adapt are crucial; any threat to professional identity requires serious focus. Unfortunately, ideological discussions regarding professionalism are 'noticeably absent' in the policy and framework literature often produced by governments (Harwood and Tukonic, 2015, p. 36). Interestingly, Sachs (2001) implies that this may be intentional as governments do not see it in their best interests to have an autonomous education service; a fixed view of professionalism can help provide the framework for *controls* that can serve the needs of the state. Murray (2013, p. 531) similarly notes that any professional role requires *social legitimacy* to have recognition and influence, the implication of which is that there is no benefit to government by encouraging a narrative that may threaten the standardised and imposed view of professionalism.

Notably, Sachs (2001) argues that identity must continually be *negotiated*, allowing us to remain autonomous in all contexts and to differentiate ourselves. Such negotiation would aim to prevent a harsh mismatch between external views of professional identity and those views held individually. The potential impact of such a mismatch between external and internal views of professional identity is important to consider. Murray (2013, p. 529) succinctly summarises the reason for this:

> The internal view of professional self is a vital component because it is based on what a person values in their role and informs their professional practice. These internal beliefs and perceptions need to be reconciled with a critical interpretation of external requirements and expectations to enable the individual to practise their profession with integrity.

A challenge to an educator's values can influence educator retention and success, and a challenge to personal values and ideals in education may mean educators feel unable to continue in the profession (Heimer and Klefstad, 2015). Notably, Bolivar and Domingo (2006) argue that the challenge or *split* in professional identity appears when a personal identity for an individual ('identity for himself or herself') is not consistent with the attributed or perceived required identity ('identity for others'). The authors continue to suggest that whilst political rhetoric often praises the importance of educators, 'the controls of new educational policies' can easily de-professionalise them (Bolivar and Domingo, 2006, p. 352). Beck (2008) appears to agree, noting how neoliberal policies are initiating a process of de-professionalism masked as re-professionalism.

Self-perceptions of professional identity are pivotal to a number of aspects associated in an educational context and educational *eco-system*. There will be cognitive and emotional implications and reactions that are both rational and non-rational, explicit and implicit. Consider, for example, the potential impact on educators' self-efficacy and collective efficacy; we are already aware that there is a strong correlation between educators' beliefs about their capacity to face the challenges of contemporary educational reality and children's motivation and learning outcomes (Penninckx et al., 2015).

It would seem that educational reform that is imposed without consideration for the emotions and impact on the professional identity of educators may be doomed to failure. The reason for such *failure* may be the result of a 'crisis of professional identity' (Bolivar and Domingo, 2006, p. 344) that can cause resistance to change, drive educators away from a personal commitment to education towards '*escape* routes' (e.g. guilt, resistance, stress, demoralisation) or drive them to 'strategic redefinitions' of practice, as they adapt to an increasing lack of control (2006, p. 344). It would appear that educators can modify their practice in the face of a challenge to their professional identity or a desire to match what they perceive as the ideal professional identity. There is very clearly a strong link between educators' practice and their sense of identity (Sachs, 2001).

Disconcertingly, there is evidence that the emergence of *designer employees* (Casey, 1995, cited in Sachs, 2001) *or tick-box professionals* (Ryan and Bourke, 2013) – those who it can be assumed are basing their identity on what they perceive to be desired externally ('identity for others') – can lead to questionable practice. Take, for example, the suggestion that high-stakes testing in the USA (e.g. Criterion-Referenced Competency Tests [CRCT]), combined with high-stakes accountability, led teachers in both Chicago and Atlanta to cheat in order that pupils were perceived to be progressing and achieving certain grades (e.g. see *WXIA-TV,* '11 Atlanta educators convicted in cheating scandal', *USA Today,* 1 April 2015, at www.usatoday.com/story/news/nation/2015/04/01/atlanta-schools-cheating-scandal-verdict/70780606/).

Taking the discussion further, it is important to consider the impact of high-stakes inspection; Penninckx et al. (2015, p. 2) reviewed a range of research from across Europe and noted how inspections are associated with 'undesirable side-effects' such as *intended strategic behaviour* (e.g. window-dressing activities), *unintended strategic behaviour* (e.g. disturbing effects on normal school life) and *other side-effects* (e.g. increased stress). In addition, there was 'a decreased level of professional enthusiasm before and during the inspection' (2015, p. 13). So questions remain: how can childhood educators, and childhood education, achieve *principled* or *democratic professionalism* within a political discourse that encourages *performance* or *managerial professionalism*? How can educators maintain a sense of professional identity that considers attitudinal, cognitive and emotional values, and can resist or position itself within a context that is competition-focused and managerial in nature? Sachs (2001, p. 157) appears to argue that educators need to directly challenge or balance managerial discourses with democratic discourses that have emancipatory aims and are rooted in 'principles of equity and social justice'; by implication, there is a need to support a more 'activist identity' (p. 157).

TEMPERED RADICALS AND POLICY ENTREPRENEURS

Interestingly, there is evidence that childhood educators and others engaged in the childhood education system do wrestle with the potential clash between the practical application of political discourse and their own personal values and identity. As Lea (2013) would suggest, they position themselves to mediate the impact of political discourse on children and on themselves. Meyerson (2004) utilised the term 'tempered radical' to identify individuals who appreciated that any organisation or context is continually evolving, and as such it is possible to walk the fine line between remaining *corporate* and being a catalyst for challenge and change. These individuals 'are not heroic leaders of revolutionary action; rather they are cautious and committed catalysts that keep going and who slowly make a difference' (Meyerson, 2004, p. 16). The suggestion is that 'tempered radicals' take advantage of opportunities to question, they challenge assumptions and modify boundaries of inclusion and can do so because they are able to differentiate among views that they are willing to compromise on and those that are non-negotiable; they have positioned themselves. It is suggested that this clarity enables individuals to be resilient and confident in what they are – crucial characteristics in an education context, in particular within a context where professionalism and identity are being threatened by contemporary political discourse.

The term 'tempered radical' has appeared in education, and it is intriguing to note how a range of case studies, such as those in the USA researched by Carlone et al. (2010, p. 941), have highlighted that educators struggle with the 'many biases, contradictions and unintended consequences prevalent in education policy today' and therefore have to 'work as "tempered radicals", "working the system"' (p. 941), in order to feel true to their professional and pedagogical beliefs.

The concept of mediating policy and *declared* ideology is not new within education, and is evident across the globe. As an example, researching within Israeli schools, Tuval (2014, p. 1) noted how educators developed a range of 'camouflage strategies' in order to cope with the apparent incompatibility between declared institutional discourse and personal beliefs, without explicitly requiring them to choose one position over the other. A further example is provided by Woods and Jeffrey (1998) in the UK, who noted that even within an inspection system, both educators and inspectors had to *negotiate* personal ways through structural constraints that could otherwise, at their worst, lead to feelings of de-professionalism. As such, childhood educators are able to, and need to, realise that power is fluid and moveable; there is no universal truth. As Carlone et al. (2010) argue, whilst discourses are powerful and often enduring, they are not static. Childhood educators mediate policy and need to position themselves to do so in order to maintain a professional identity that they relate to rather than one that is externally imposed. In turn, this will enable them to make contextual and informed decisions about the education of the children they are engaged with. Lea (2013) states that this is operating as a *policy entrepreneur*, an educator who questions the social, political and economic contexts that policy intends to address in order to make the best decision for particular children.

Importantly, in order for childhood educators to position *within* policy, there is a need to explicitly consider their personal values, and what influences are placed upon their professional identity. In order to undertake such reflective practice, it may be useful to consider the five *dimensions* that combine in the formation of professional identity, as stated by Wenger (1998, cited in Sachs, 2001, p. 154):

> These are: (1) identity as *negotiated experiences* where we define who we are by the ways we experience our selves through participation as well as the way we verify our selves; (2) identity as *community membership* where we define who we are by the familiar and the unfamiliar; (3) identity as *learning trajectory* where we define who we are by where we have been and where we are going; (4) identity as *nexus of multi membership* where we define who we are by the way we reconcile our various forms of identity into one identity; and (5) identity as *a relation between the local and the global* where we define who we are by negotiating local ways of belonging to broader constellations and manifesting broader styles and discourses.

It is argued that these five dimensions interact as educators wrestle with the social, cultural and political influences on the formation of their identity.

 — POINTS FOR DISCUSSION —

Consider Wenger's (1998) five dimensions of identity formation as a framework. What are the most significant influences on your own sense of professional identity?

FOCUS ON THEORY

Political interest in childhood education has increased across the globe and this interest would seem to be grounded in neo-liberal ideology. The accompanying political discourse is one of control and regulation; it is one that desires a specific formation of professionalism that is managerial and outcome-focused, rather than one which is cooperative and child-centred. Resulting parameters of control, or algorithms of accountability, will inevitably influence both practice within childhood education and the formation of a childhood educator's professional identity. Quite simply: 'ideologies and praxis encounters can challenge one's sense of professionalism' (Harwood and Tukonic, 2015, p. 36).

Childhood educators must consider how they can *position* themselves and mediate policy to ensure it is context-focused for the best needs of a particular child (Lea, 2013). Of course, the problem remains that 'as society becomes more complex so does the business of translating and interpreting policy into practice' (Lea, 2013, p. 21). It may be the case that if educators are to genuinely attempt to facilitate children's holistic development, in a meaningful way, they need to reflect on the 'ambiguities, tensions and debates' wrapped up in political discourse (Adams et al., 2015, p. 15). Only then will a childhood educator be able to *negotiate* a professional identity that they can relate to (Sachs, 2001), one whereby the childhood educator is a 'critically reflective emotional professional' (Osgood, 2010, p. 119) rather than one that is externally imposed.

There are real concerns felt internationally that a broader, enriching approach to childhood education is being threatened by this discourse bound in performativity and accountability (Adams et al., 2015, p. 1). It would appear that this discourse is inadvertently developing new definitions of professionalism which could potentially threaten childhood educators' perceptions of their own professional identity. It is imperative that those engaged in childhood education question the power and values that are underpinning policy decisions and producing a specific discourse, in particular the discourse that surrounds what *quality* childhood education should be. The challenge is made explicit by Lea (2013, p. 17): practitioners must explore their own values and *position* themselves within policy, understanding that political discourse 'opens a space for certain identities and closes down others' (Apple, 2013, p. 7).

SUMMARY

It is clear that much of the current and dominant political discourse and policies that emanate from such discourses, will impact significantly on children and those adults tasked with their education. Political interest in childhood education has greatly increased across the globe, with much of this apparent interest being grounded within neo-liberal ideologies, at the heart of which is an emphasis on enabling children to be *ready* for the next stage of their development and ultimately *ready* for work – practice that childhood educators will then be accountable for.

—— **EXTENDED AND RECOMMENDED READING** ——

Campbell-Barr, V. and Leeson, C. (2016) *Quality and Leadership in the Early Years: Research, Theory and Practice*. London: Sage.

> An excellent examination of how policy, discourse and practice are influenced by debates around quality and leadership.

Dahlberg, G., Moss, P. and Pence, A. (2013) *Beyond Quality in Early Childhood Education and Care: Languages of Evaluation* (Routledge Education Classic Edition). London: Routledge.

> An interesting text that examines defining and measuring quality in early childhood and the tendency to reduce philosophical issues of value to technical and managerial levels.

Reed, M. and Walker, R. (eds) (2014) *A Critical Companion to Early Childhood*. London: Sage.

> A critical and provocative text examining a range of interrelated topics, including professionalism, curriculum and policy.

 Don't forget to visit **https://study.sagepub.com/contemporarychildhood** for a selection of free SAGE journal articles, web links, additional case studies, activities, and PowerPoints to help you revise.

REFERENCES

Adams, K., Monahan, J. and Wills, R. (2015) 'Losing the whole child? A national survey of primary education training provision for spiritual, moral, social and cultural development', *European Journal of Teacher Education*, 38(2): 119–216.

Apple, M.W. (2013) *Can Education Change Society?* Abingdon: Routledge.

Beck, J. (2008) 'Governmental professionalism: re-professionalising or de-professionalising teachers in England', *British Journal of Educational Studies*, 56(2): 119–43.

Bolivar, A. and Domingo, J. (2006) 'The professional identity of secondary school teachers in Spain', *Theory and Research in Education*, 4(3): 339–55.

Campbell-Barr, V. and Leeson, C. (2016) *Quality and Leadership in the Early Years: Research, Theory and Practice*. London: Sage.

Carlone, H.B., Haun-Frank, J. and Kimmel, S.C. (2010) 'Tempered radicals: elementary teachers' narratives of teaching science within and against prevailing meanings of schooling', *Cultural Studies of Science Education*, 5: 941–65.

Casey, C. (1995) *Work, Self and Society: After Industrialism*. London: Routledge.

Clarke, J. (1995) 'Doing the right thing: manageralism and social welfare', Paper presented to ESRC Seminar: Professionals in Late Modernity, Imperial College, London, 26 June.

Commons Education Select Committee (2016) *1st Report: The Role of Regional Schools Commissioners*. Available at: www.publications.parliament.uk/pa/cm201516/cmselect/cmeduc/401/40102.htm (accessed 26 September 2016).

Department for Education (DfE) (2013) More Great Childcare: Raising Quality and Giving Parents More Choice. Available at: www.gov.uk/government/uploads/system/uploads/attachment_data/file/219660/More_20Great_20Childcare_20v2.pdf (accessed 2 March 2016).

Goodson I.F. (2003) *Professional Knowledge, Professional Lives: Studies in Education and Change*. Maidenhead: Open University Press.

Harwood, D. and Tukonic, S. (2015) 'The glass ceiling effect: mediating influences on early years educators' sense of professionalism', *Journal of the Canadian Association for Young Children*, 40(1): 36–54.

Heimer, L.G. and Klefstad, E. (2015) '"It's not really a menu because we can't pick what we do": context integration in kindergarten contexts', *Global Studies in Childhood*, 5(3): 239–54.

James, A.L. (2010) 'Competition or integration? The next steps in childhood studies', *Childhood*, 17(4): 485–99.

Lea, S. (2013) 'Early years work, professionalism and the translation of policy into practice', in Z. Kingdon and J. Gourd (eds), *Early Years Policy: The Impact on Practice*. London: Routledge.

Meyerson, D.E. (2004) 'The tempered radicals: how employees push their companies – little by little – to be more socially responsible', *Stanford Social Innovation Review*, Fall: 13–22.

Miller, L. (2008) 'Developing professionalism within a regulatory framework in England: challenges and possibilities', *European Early Childhood Education Research Journal*, 16(2): 255–68.

Moss, P. (2014) *Transformative Change and Real Utopias in Early Childhood Education: A Story of Democracy, Experimentation and Potentiality*. Abingdon: Routledge.

Moss, P. (2015) 'There are alternatives! Contestation and hope in early childhood education', *Global Studies of Childhood*, 5(3): 226–38.

Moss, P. and Dahlberg, G. (2008) 'Beyond quality in early childhood education and care: languages of evaluation', *New Zealand Journal of Teachers' Work*, 5(1): 3–12.

Murray, J. (2013) 'Becoming an early years professional: developing a new professional identity', *European Early Childhood Education Research Journal*, 21(4): 527–40.

Obama, B. (2016) State of the Union Address (https://medium.com/@WhiteHouse/president-obama-s-2016-state-of-the-union-address-7c06300f9726#.e0gq7pi8j).

Osgood, J. (2006) 'Deconstructing professionalism in early childhood education: resisting the regulatory gaze', *Contemporary Issues in Early Childhood*, 7(1): 5–14.

Osgood, J. (2010) 'Reconstructing professionalism in ECEC: the case for the critically reflective emotional professional', *Early Years: An International Research Journal*, 30(2): 119–33.

Parker, G. (2015) 'Distributed leadership in English schools in 2014', *Management in Education*, 29(3): 132–8.

Penninckx, M., Vanhoof, J., De Maeyer, S. and Van Petegem, P. (2015) 'Effects and side effects of Flemish school inspection', *Educational Management Administration & Leadership*, 1–17.

Range, B.G., Duncan, H.E., Day Scherz, S. and Haines, C.A. (2012) 'School leaders' perceptions about incompetent teachers: implications for supervision and evaluation', *NASSP Bulletin*, 96(4): 302–22.

Ryan, M. and Bourke, T. (2013) 'The teacher as reflexive professional: making visible the excluded discourse in teacher standards', *Discourse: Studies in the Cultural Politics of Education*, 34(3): 411–23.

Sachs, J. (2001) 'Teacher professional identity: competing discourses, competing outcomes', *Journal of Educational Policy*, 16(2): 149–61.

Spencer-Woodley, L. (2013) 'Accountability: tensions and challenges', in Z. Kingdon and J. Gourd (eds), *Early Years Policy: The Impact on Practice*. London: Routledge.

Tuval, S. (2014) 'Teachers living with contradictions: social representations of inclusion, exclusion and stratification in Israeli Schools', *Papers on Social Representations*, 23: 10.1–10.25.

Wenger, R. (1998) *Communities of Practice: Learning, Meaning and Identity*. Cambridge: Cambridge University Press.

Wiggins, K. (2016) 'Three-quarters of teachers are thinking of quitting … and this moving letter helps to explain why'. Available at: www.tes.com/news/school-news/breaking-news/exclusive-three-quarters-teachers-are-thinking-quitting-and-moving (accessed 20 December 2016).

Woods, P. and Jeffrey, B. (1998) 'Choosing positions: living the contradictions of Ofsted', *British Journal of Sociology of Education*, 19(4): 547–70.

9

THE DIGITAL CHILD

Why you should read this chapter

You probably own, or have access to, at least one digital device and it is most probably integral to your everyday life. Society is infused with digital technology and children are increasingly using this technology. They are growing up in a society where technology is changing rapidly and impacting on their daily lives. However, changes in the field of education happen much slower and it is important to consider how education is changing to utilise this new technology. Palaiologou (2016) asks the following questions: to what extent are early years settings and classrooms ready to accept the digital child of the twenty-first century? How can they use children's digital experiences to create learning environments that are consistent with their home experiences? How can they use digital media to actively engage parents in their children's learning? These are 'big' questions with no easy answers but this chapter aims to help you to begin to consider them.

By the end of this chapter, you should be able to:

- develop knowledge and understanding of how the lives of children have been changed by digital media
- consider the potential of digital media to transform children's lives
- reflect on the challenges of keeping children safe in an increasingly networked and online world.

WHAT IS A DIGITAL CHILD?

Children today are looking towards a future which is unknown and many may work in jobs which don't yet exist. However, what is clear is that along with the skills of creativity, critical thinking, flexibility and teamwork, having an ability to engage with digital technologies to locate information and resources, communicate and collaborate will be crucial (Dudeney et al., 2013). Today's children and young people accept digital technology as part of their lives in the same way that the older generation accepts the use of electricity as an everyday occurrence. Therefore, a 'digital child' may be described as a child who is living in a time and a culture where digital technology is readily available and widely used for everyday life, including entertainment, education and communication.

There has been a revolution in terms of the functionality and uptake of portable, networked technologies, and educators, in particular, are keen to capitalise on the potential application of such technologies for school education (Lynch and Redpath, 2014). Indeed, since they first appeared in 2010, iPads and other similar tablet devices have been heralded for their potential to transform education (Kucirkova, 2014). However, children's digital footprints often begin at birth and, as many children grow up in media-rich homes, they are in daily contact with a wide range of digital tools (Chaudron, 2015). Young children have been born into this new digital age and children are immersing themselves at younger and younger ages into new technologies (Teichert and Anderson, 2014). Therefore, young children have increasing exposure and access to digital technology. In a recent European study across six countries which explored children's and their families' experiences with digital technology, it was shown that it is an important part of children's lives but it is balanced with other activities such as outdoor play and non-digital toys (Chaudron, 2015). However, there are concerns about the amount of screen time that children have. In a recent survey of more than 1000 parents, it is reported that time spent watching TV by children under 5 has increased from 2.4 to 2.6 hours per day over the past year, and that 73 per cent of under-5s are using a tablet or computer compared to 23 per cent in 2012. Children are using tablets or computers by the age of 2 and when they reach 6 more than 40 per cent are using them every day (ChildWise, 2015). Older children, aged 8–11, are also spending more hours per week online (10.5 hours in 2014 vs 9.2 hours in 2013) (Ofcom, 2014). Similarly, in a recent UK report exploring play and creativity in pre-school children's use of apps, it is reported that 65 per cent of 3–7-year-olds have access to a tablet computer, and parents reported that children under 5 use tablets for an average of 1 hour and 19 minutes on a typical weekday (Marsh et al., 2015). Therefore, it is clear that digital devices play a huge role in the lives of many children today and will continue to do so in the future.

However, there are concerns that increasing screen time with a range of technologies can lead to a range of negative outcomes such as childhood obesity, sleep disturbance, harmful commercialisation and violence (see Ernest et al., 2014).

 —— POINTS FOR DISCUSSION ————————————

- Consider your own use of 'screens'. How many hours of 'screen time' might you have in a day? Do you think this has increased over the last few years and, if so, why?
- Think about some young children you might know. Which 'screens' do they use most, and when and how are they using them?
- Do you think that children spend too much time in front of 'screens'?
- What do you think are the benefits and drawbacks of 'screen time' for children?

DIGITAL MEDIA

There is a growing range of digital media available for children to use but the type of medium, how children engage with it and the amount of time spent with any technology is largely dependent on the family context (Livingstone et al., 2015). Therefore, parents' choices of digital devices, where they are located and their habits and rules in using them all influence their children's use. Let us briefly look at some of the different media that many children use regularly.

TELEVISION

TV has always been a hugely popular medium since its introduction in the 1930s. The introduction of colour TV in the UK in the late 1960s changed the viewing of television with an enhanced sense of actually being there (National Media Museum, 2011). Smart TVs go further with built-in internet capabilities, allowing viewers to use the TV like a computer. Ofcom (2014) reports that TV is the media activity that children aged 5–15 would prefer to use when given the choice and it is the media device they would miss most. It also reports that it is the only media device used every day by the majority of children aged 5–15. However, there has been a decrease in the number of children having a TV in the bedroom. Perhaps this is due to the fact that children can now watch TV programmes on mobile devices anywhere in the home and therefore there is less need to have a static device in particular rooms. This recent data show that TV, despite the growing range of other digital media devices, is still a very important medium for young children and they are spending a lot of time watching it.

TABLET COMPUTERS

A tablet computer (commonly shortened to tablet) is a small portable computer with touch-screen technology and a pop-up keyboard. Many have built-in cameras and microphones and they are popularised by their user-friendly interface. In 2010, Apple launched the iPad which was the first mass-market tablet and was to be a new category of device in between the mobile phone and the computer. Other Android tablets quickly followed as popular devices.

In a recent European study, the tablet computer was revealed as the favourite media device due to the size of its screen, its portability and its ease of use (Chaudron, 2015). Similarly, Ofcom (2014) reported a significant increase in access to, ownership of and use of tablet computers by children of all ages, with 70 per cent of children aged 5–15 now having access to a tablet computer at home. Children are also almost twice as likely to go online using a tablet computer. Whilst many parents value the educational use of tablets (Livingstone et al., 2015), it has been shown that the most common use of tablets is to play games, hence children use them primarily for entertainment rather than for educational purposes (Livingstone et al., 2014). In their exploratory study on young children and digital technology in the UK, Livingstone et al. (2014) found that popular games were running games such as 'Temple Run', aim-and-shoot games such as 'Angry Birds', and games related to popular films such as 'Frozen'.'Minecraft' was also widely played. Children are also increasingly watching YouTube on tablets; ChildWise (2015) talks about the irresistible rise of YouTube and how it is now the number one site for both boys and girls. It is reported that past concerns about the availability of unacceptable material have largely disappeared with parents now happy to let even young children use it. So we can see that tablet devices have a growing popularity and importance in children's digital lives, particularly for leisure.

SMARTPHONES

Playing games is not limited to tablets as many games can also be played on smartphones. A smartphone is a mobile phone with highly advanced features such as touch-screen display, Wi-Fi connectivity and web-browsing capabilities. Chaudron (2015) claims that smartphones are a melting-pot device as they are very versatile in their use, allowing children to watch videos, play games, send messages, take pictures and make video and phone calls. While many children may not own a smartphone, they will use their parents' smartphones regularly.

ChildWise (2015) reported that 35 per cent of pre-school children used a parent's mobile phone and Ofcom (2014) found that 40 per cent of children aged 5–15 owned their own phone; this rose to 80 per cent for children aged 12–15. More children are going online using a mobile phone than in previous years and the mobile phone is the most popular device for 12–15s for social and creative activities, such as arranging to meet friends, messaging, and posting and sharing photos.

SOCIAL MEDIA

Social media are computer-mediated tools that allow people to exchange information, ideas, pictures and videos in virtual communities and networks. Children's social media presence often begins before birth as parents share ultrasound images to announce the imminent arrival of a baby, and the joys of early childhood are often shared on Facebook, Instagram, Flickr and elsewhere (Leaver, 2015). Many social media sites have age limits for use that are not policed and therefore many children are using a variety of these. Facebook is the most popular social media site among 12–15s and their use of Instagram has doubled to 36 per cent since 2013. A significant number of 12–15s also use other social media sites such as SnapChat (Ofcom, 2014). ChildWise (2015) reports that Facebook is slowly losing ground to Instagram and Snapchat and that vloggers (video bloggers) are the new media stars for the younger generation.

— 🔍 —— CASE STUDY 9.1 —————————————————

Jenny is 10 years old. She has an older brother and sister who both have Facebook accounts. Her teenage sister also has Instagram and Snapchat accounts. She has asked her parents if she can join Facebook and Instagram since she says all her friends in primary school are on these social media sites (the minimum age for these sites is 13). Her parents aren't so sure but give in and allow her to join, as long as her sister is allowed to see her account and monitor what she is posting and who she is friends with. Jenny posts daily pictures of her kitten on Instagram. She also views her friends' pet pictures and sends them messages. She is following some of her favourite pop stars and some reality TV stars as she likes to talk about these with her friends in school. She is 'friends' with lots of her classmates on Facebook and likes to talk about her weekend and what she has been watching on TV. Her parents listen to her talking about these things and occasionally ask to see her Facebook and Instagram pages. They don't use social media and don't quite understand why their children need to use social media when they see their friends every day anyway.

FOCUS ON THEORY

Gardner and Davis (2013) refer to the current generation of young people growing up in a world of digital media as the 'App Generation' (you can see professor Howard Gardner talking about his book and how apps can shape young people and affect their lives at www.youtube.com/watch?v=F8E4u5uVJiI). Marc Prensky (2001) promoted the popular concept of Digital Natives and Digital Immigrants. Digital Natives are the 'native speakers' of the digital language of computers, video games and the internet, whilst those who have not been born into the digital world but have become fascinated by it and adopted many aspects of new technology are the Digital Immigrants. The important distinction, according to Prensky, is that Digital Immigrants always retain their 'accent', that is, their foot in the past. In the above example of Jenny and her family, Jenny is the Digital Native who is communicating and sharing her interests with her friends online through Facebook and Instagram. She knows what timelines and chats are and she knows how to tag, like, poke and unfriend someone. She wants to follow and have followers. However, much of this terminology is alien to her parents and they are the Digital Immigrants. They are interested in technology but don't use social media and they show their 'accent' by preferring more traditional ways of keeping in touch with people such as the phone and face-to-face contact, without understanding young people's desire to be connected with their peers in a continuous manner. However, Prensky cautions that one of the biggest problems facing education today (he wrote this 14 years ago but many would argue it is still relevant today) is that teachers who may be Digital Immigrants are speaking an outdated language. By that, he is not referring to the language of social media but rather to an awareness of the skills that Digital Natives have acquired through years of interaction and practice. He means that Digital Immigrants have little or no understanding that Digital Natives like to receive information fast, they like to multi-task, they prefer their graphics to their text and they thrive on instant gratification and frequent rewards. This can be seen as a generational divide, and as technology continues to race ahead this generational divide may persist and will continue to be a challenge in education. However, it is important not to assume that all young children are Digital Natives and to understand that some can feel overwhelmed when faced with new digital devices or websites (Plowman and McPake, 2012).

POINTS FOR DISCUSSION

- Consider your parents' (or other family members of their generation) and your own use of digital media. Can you appreciate Prensky's concept of Digital Natives and Digital Immigrants?
- Do your parents or older family members use social media and, if so, which sites do they use? What are their purposes for using social media? Are they similar or different to yours?

THE AFFORDANCES OF DIGITAL MEDIA

Affordance refers to the properties of an object that make clear how it should be used and which draw attention to its potential for particular uses. In the case of digital media, we are interested to know how digital media can be used in different ways to other, more traditional resources. We have seen earlier in this chapter that there is a variety of digital media that children use on a regular basis. We cannot address the affordances of all of them here, so, since tablet devices are the favourite media device of children (Chaudron, 2015), we will look at some examples of the affordances of tablets.

We have read earlier in this chapter about the increasing popularity of tablet devices and it is suggested that this is due to the particular affordances of these devices, which include their portability, affordability and efficiency (Flewitt et al., 2015). Many research studies refer to the novel features of tablet devices: they are portable and lightweight; they eliminate the need for separate input devices such as a mouse or keyboard; and they are designed to accommodate apps which have child-friendly, intuitive designs (Kucirkova, 2014). Indeed, it is reported that, in contrast to traditional computers, touch-screen tablets provide an easier to use and more intuitive interface for a child (McManis and Gunnewig, 2012). Children can take their tablet to any room in the house and also out and about to restaurants, shops and on holiday. They don't need to be at a desk but can lie on the floor or be in any position where they feel comfortable. A search of young children using tablets on YouTube shows very young children using tablets like it is second nature to them; they are seen tapping, swiping and pinching with ease. Neumann and Neumann (2014) discuss how touch-screen tablets have the physical features to facilitate early literacy learning as they are book-like in shape and are in the form of a notepad that detects and responds to finger touch. Story-making apps enable children to incorporate sounds, images, text and design into their stories which can enhance children's creativity (Kucirkova and Sakr, 2015). In a study on pre-school children's mark-making development, it was found that tablets supported mark-making interaction and enabled more mark making in a shorter time period (Price et al., 2015). Another recent study using e-workbooks on tablets with children aged 6–7 years, reported on the immediate feedback on the correctness of answers as a positive aspect of tablets, along with increased pupil persistence in solving tasks (Fekonja-Peklaj and Marjanovič-Umek, 2015).

These few examples from research illustrate how tablets can enhance learning. What recent research highlights is how tablet devices can not only enhance educational experiences but transform them, and the challenge that this brings (Merchant, 2012). Lynch and Redpath (2014) believe that this transformative work is possible but warn of a risk that tablets will emerge as tools that can be used in established classroom practices with some added interactive multimedia appeal. Similarly, Flewitt et al. (2015) caution that if innovative uses of new technologies are absent from the classroom, then we risk failing to turn on a powerful switch that can light up this generation's learning.

On a similar note, it is argued that it is not the device that makes the difference to children's learning but rather it is the pedagogy contextualising the use of the tablet that will make the difference to children's learning (Kucirkova, 2014). It is both interesting, and perhaps surprising, to note that in a recent report from the Organisation for Economic Co-operation and Development (OECD, 2015), it is stated that, in general, countries that have invested heavily in ICT for education have seen no appreciable improvement in student achievement in reading, mathematics or science over the past ten years. However, the report also suggests that a readiness to integrate technology into teaching, the accessibility of devices, the digital skills curriculum and a teacher's own skills and training in how to use devices to enhance student learning, are all key factors in whether computers will impact on children's achievement. Therefore, having tablet devices in classrooms is not going to make a difference to achievement unless teachers are properly trained to use them effectively in learning and teaching.

The OECD report also makes it clear that all students need to be equipped with basic literacy and numeracy skills first so that they can participate fully in the hyper-connected, digitised societies of the twenty-first century. This theme of balance with other, traditional forms of learning is echoed by other writers. For example, in the study on pre-school children's mark making mentioned previously, the authors recognised the benefits and affordances of the iPad as opposed to using physical paper and paint. However, they also acknowledged the limitations of the iPad in this activity. They recognised that children did not have the opportunity to blend colours on screen the way they would with real paint on paper, and they also highlighted that, by using the screen, they missed out on the sensory experience of physical paint. They argued, therefore, for the use of technology as a supplement rather than a replacement for certain kinds of activities (Price et al., 2015). Kucirkova (2014) suggests that there is a dominant misunderstanding regarding the troubled relationship between digital and non-digital resources; she believes that this has led to practice which tries to position technology and traditional approaches in opposition to each other, rather than viewing them as complementary teaching approaches.

STARTING WHERE CHILDREN ARE: THE IMPORTANCE OF CHILDREN'S LEARNING EXPERIENCES AT HOME

As we have discussed earlier, this second decade of the new millennium has brought rapidly changing technologies. McTavish (2014, p. 320) highlights how adults have to grapple with how they integrate this technology into their lives, but 'for young children born into this technological epoch, there is no choice; it is simply a way of being'. These children are arriving in early childhood settings and schools with a wide variety of experiences, including those with a range of media. As professionals who are working with children, we have to meet them in the world in which they live and therefore we need to know about children's experiences of new technologies in the home. So let us look more closely at some of the issues here.

CHILDREN AND THEIR USE OF DIGITAL TECHNOLOGY AT HOME

We have already looked at some statistics around children's use of technology earlier in this chapter. Many of these recent reports are telling us that young children lead active, varied lives in which technology plays an important part (Livingstone et al., 2014). For these young children, the experiences offered by digital devices are fairly straightforward: fun and relaxation, either to pass the time when alone or to share with siblings and friends. In recent reports by the National Literacy Trust, it is interesting to note the role of technology in the reading and writing of children and young people aged 8–16 years old. Over 29,000 children and young people from across the UK took part in this survey. It was reported that levels of reading enjoyment improved in 2013 for the first time since 2005. More children and young people in 2013 reported that they read daily outside class – many said they read technology-based materials, such as websites, text messages, emails and instant messages as well as fiction, comics, lyrics and poems. The proportion of children and young people reading e-books is also increasing (Clark, 2014). Whilst it is concerning to note that nearly 25 per cent of children and young people say they rarely or never write outside of class, technology-based formats such as text messages, social networking messages and emails are the most common formats of writing for those who do (Clark, 2014). So whilst schools maintain what Yelland et al. (2008) refer to as a 'heritage curriculum' where value is attached to print texts, children themselves are appropriating and using digital technology for their own purposes in their daily lives. Let us look at this by drawing on a body of work known as the New Literacy Studies.

FOCUS ON THEORY

The New Literacy Studies (Gee, 1996; Street, 1997) take a sociocultural view of literacy and are based on the view that reading and writing only make sense when they are studied in the context of social and cultural practices. Reading and writing are seen as social practices rather than technical skills to be learned in formal education. Street uses the concept of 'social literacies' and argues that, if literacy is a social practice, then it varies with the different contexts in which it is used. This move from an 'autonomous model' of literacy to an 'ideological' model of literacy makes it hard to justify teaching only one particular form of literacy, and so New Literacy Studies have given rise to the notion of 'multiple literacies' which vary with time and

(Continued)

(Continued)

place and are embedded in specific cultural practices. Indeed, Street (1997) proposed nearly 20 years ago that any curriculum for literacy needs to capture the richness and complexity of actual literacy practices and give value to the different literacies that are employed in home contexts. So if we consider the literacy practices of the children and young people which were reported in the recent National Literacy Trust survey above, we can see that they are using technology-based formats of reading and writing as tools for building and maintaining social relationships, for getting things 'done' and for deeply personal and internal purposes. In these social contexts, literacy has real meaning, relevance and purpose for children and failure to acknowledge this could result in school being seen as irrelevant and archaic (McTavish, 2014).

PARENTS' PERSPECTIVES ON CHILDREN AND DIGITAL TECHNOLOGY

Recent reports suggest that parents see digital technologies as positive but challenging (Chaudron, 2015; Livingstone et al., 2014). Parents can see the benefits of digital technology and emphasise the potential for knowledge acquisition, hand–eye coordination and enhanced communication skills. Parent beliefs are important because they set the context for digital experiences at home and parents are the gatekeepers for creating and shaping children's learning environments at home. However, parents also play a key role in managing their children's digital media use from a young age as many see risks for their children, ranging from inappropriate content being accessed to the health and social impacts of using digital technology. Many parents even build the use of digital media into their reward–punishment system, using the right to access digital devices as an incentive for doing homework, cleaning and tidying up, or withdrawing access as a form of punishment. Chaudron (2015) claims that both of these strategies serve to reinforce the desirability of the digital object.

A recent study by Livingstone et al. (2015) into families with children aged 0–8 years, divides families into three groups with regards to their mediation of children's use of digital devices. The report found that lower income, less educated families had a relatively high device ownership at home but had more restrictive parental mediation strategies (such as limiting time and location of use) as parents were worried about the use of digital media. In lower income, more educated families, parents were more confident in their digital skills and had more active mediation in their children's use of digital media (such as talking about activities and sitting nearby while their child was online). Higher income, more educated families had different strategies to manage restrictions on digital device use, with efforts to promote offline activities. Therefore, this report claimed that socio-economic status influences parental practices and beliefs when it comes to managing their children's digital lives. What is clear is that parents play a key role in supporting their children's use of and interaction with digital media, and Neumann and Neumann (2014) argue that early childhood educators should work with families to adopt a pedagogical approach that builds on children's home digital experiences to support emergent literacy learning in the classroom.

CHILDREN'S DIGITAL LIVES IN THE NEW MILLENNIUM

The Institute of Education at the University of London has carried out a range of surveys on children who were born around the beginning of the new millennium, known as the Millennium Cohort Study (IOE, 2014). A recent survey on these children, who were then aged around 11, found some of the important features of contemporary 11-year-olds' lives. The study reports that age 11 represents a pivotal moment in children's lives as they are anticipating the transition from primary to secondary schooling and are on the cusp of adolescence and all that this brings, physically, emotionally and educationally. It was found that the ever-increasing reliance on technology for entertainment and communication is a key part of the lives of the children in this study across all social groups. Nearly three-quarters of 11-year-olds in the study had their own mobile phone, 96 per cent had access to a computer and 95 per cent were linked to the internet at home. Over half of all 11-year-olds used the internet most days when they were not at school and 17 per cent of those in the study said they spent three or more hours per day watching TV. Social media was a key part of many children's lives, providing them with new ways to communicate with each other and new definitions of what friends are. So what does this mean for our children in this new millennium?

MORAL PANICS

There has been a succession of moral panics about the impact of new technology on language, education and society at large, including children. This is certainly not a recent phenomenon. Dudeney et al. (2013) suggest that this pattern of mistrust is repeated with the arrival of each new communications technology: the telegraph; postcards; the telephone; comic books; television; CDs and DVDs; mobile phones; and now the new digital tools of today. Marsh (2010) describes how many people look back at the more traditional realms of children's culture with a sense of regret and a feeling of a loss of childhood innocence. There is even some alarm that children's play is disappearing in this new media age.

CHILDREN'S CULTURE

However, Jenkins (2015) believes these polarised debates between 'technology as harmful' (it is nothing more than a distractor or an electronic babysitter) and 'technology as saviour' (apps will somehow fix anything) should be avoided with a more empowering view through a third way which sees technology as a powerful complement. Children's cultural interests have certainly changed but children use these media interests to shape their play and literacy practices in new ways. Marsh (2014) explains Levi-Strauss's concept of bricolage where the creator, the bricoleur, draws on whatever is to hand in order to create something new. Therefore, children may be seen as bricoleurs when they engage with new media texts, and they may draw on a range of experiences from TV, the internet, apps and other artefacts of personal interest when they play, either on their own or with friends. Marsh (2014) also refers to the concept of 'mediascapes', where a popular aspect within children's culture, such as the film *Frozen*, can have a huge scope of associated artefacts, such as DVDs, computer games, toys, dressing-up clothes, music, bed linen, lunchboxes, stationery, Facebook pages and much more. Jenkins et al. (2006) refer to this flow of media into every aspect of children's daily lives as 'transmedia'. These transmedia texts can provide 'big worlds' with rich literacy resources and memorable characters which can allow for children to have 'thick play' (Mackay, 2009), which is play that is repeated and intensive, a playing and replaying that develop deeper literary understanding. It is this thick play that will enable children to critique and challenge the stereotypes, settings and messages within popular media. Hence, Wohlwend (2015) challenges what she calls the commonplace conception that popular culture is harmful and inappropriate for young children. Rather, educational professionals should engage with the children they teach in order to discern the nature of their cultural worlds and how those worlds might find a place in the classroom, since they have the potential to motivate and engage as well as enable pupils to extend their critical engagement with their own cultural practices (Marsh, 2010).

E-SAFETY FOR CHILDREN IN A DIGITAL WORLD

As we know from reading this chapter so far, all the evidence points to the fact that digital exposure for most children is increasingly inevitable. Whilst we have discussed many of the positive outcomes of digital technology for children, we cannot fail to have read or heard about the negative sides of using digital technology. Some of these have been shown to be life-altering or even life-ending (Binford, 2015), and therefore it is essential that we look at e-safety issues for children.

THE CHALLENGES AND POTENTIAL OF THE DIGITAL AGE

Evans (2014) discusses how young people surf the internet for pleasure and play, to gather information and engage in and sustain many of their day-to-day relationships. She also reports that social media play a crucial role in their everyday lives as they are the 'new, cool cultural hangouts, having replaced the street corner or public park of old' (2014, p. 154). She maintains that young people used to explore and experiment with their identity by physically going out into their world; however, this exploration can now be achieved in the comfort and privacy of their bedrooms – 'when grappling with questions such as "Who am I?" cyberspace can provide the answers' (Evans, 2014, p. 155). More and more young children are engaging with media as parents themselves are providing the opportunities for them to do so. Parents have increasingly invested in computers, internet access and mobile technologies as they have been positioned as offering opportunities for children, and Livingstone (2009, cited in Willett, 2015, p. 1062) describes the 'great expectations' which surround families' investment in computers and the internet, particularly of 'new opportunities for self-expression, sociability, community engagement, creativity and new literacies'. Therefore, providing digital technology has become a sign of good parenting, with the social and entertainment aspects of these devices being downplayed in favour of the educational selling point (Willett, 2015). Whilst there are many educational opportunities for children in using digital media, as this chapter has presented, there has also been a range of research which presents the risks in their use. For example, in a recent large-scale study, Brindova et al. (2015) reported that watching television for more than three hours per day is correlated with adverse symptoms such as headaches, irritability and depression. In another recent study, Boniel-Nissim et al. (2015) showed that there was a relationship between the amount of online communication and life satisfaction. More peer communication is experienced as positive up to a point but too much communication is associated with lower measures of life satisfaction. This concurs with an ONS (2015) report on children's mental health and well-being in the UK, which highlights that children who spend more than three hours per day on social media sites are more than twice as likely to suffer with poor mental health.

 —— POINTS FOR DISCUSSION ————————————————

Some writers have coined the term 'Facebook envy', where increased use of social media sites such as Facebook can result in feelings of envy, negative comparisons with one's own life and depression. Consider your own use of social media and discuss this notion of envy:

(Continued)

(Continued)

- How do celebrities present their lifestyles through social media?
- How do some of your friends convey their lifestyles and do you think these are realistic?
- Have you experienced feelings of envy when using social media and, if so, why?
- How do you think we can help children avoid the negative comparison trap when using social media?

There is also a range of other risks which are mentioned in the media on an almost daily basis: sexting, child pornography, cybersurveillance, cyberbullying, revenge porn, grooming and trolling. These are only a few examples of digital interactions that have a unique and potentially devastating impact on children (Binford, 2015). All of these issues are very complex but let us briefly look at two of them.

Sexting has become common for many adolescents who are at a critical and vulnerable stage of development. However, if the person featured in the sexting image is below the age of 16 in the UK, then the possession or circulation of the image by other adolescents could be a criminal offence. Therefore, what can be seen as a private sharing of information can result in life-altering, permanent public impact (Binford, 2015). If compromising images go into the public domain, it can also trigger harassment and mocking of the person in the image, and many children and young people are totally unaware of the permanence of images on the internet and the impact of that digital footprint on their future lives.

Cyberbullying is an evolving social phenomenon and Purdy and McGuckin (2015) discuss how it can take place at any time of the day or night, can happen outside of school, be anonymous and have a potential worldwide audience. They further highlight how existing guidance and legislation on bullying is often outdated when applied to cyberbullying, and they report the growing frustration of school leaders around the lack of clarity on the boundaries between home and school and the responsibility for dealing with cyberbullying issues.

THE DIGITAL CHILD AND THE UNITED NATIONS CONVENTION ON THE RIGHTS OF THE CHILD

In 2013, the United Nations Committee on the Rights of the Child issued General Comment No. 17 on the right of the child to rest, leisure, play, recreational activities, cultural life and the arts. The growing role of electronic media in children's lives was acknowledged and the potential benefits were highlighted along with the perceived risks and harm for children. The Committee encouraged the introduction of measures to empower and inform children to enable them to act safely online and to become confident and responsible citizens of digital environments (UN, 2013). However, Binford (2015) believes that the Committee did not go nearly far enough in providing strategies for how to protect the Digital Child. He argues that the child's right to privacy and the child's right to be forgotten are core issues and that children have a right to grow up in a state of relative privacy where they can engage in age-appropriate conduct that will prepare them for adult life. He also argues that children cannot be held hostage to juvenile indiscretions that prevent the development of a dignified public identity. The three Ps of the UNCRC are children's *participation* rights, *provision* rights and *protection* rights, and Livingstone (2014) highlights that there can be difficulties when children's rights to provision and participation (for example, their right to access and use the internet) conflict with their right to protection (for example, protection from inappropriate content, data exploitation, bullying). It is agreed that the international community has more to consider if it wants to adequately protect and guide the next generation, as its members try to navigate the new digital frontier (Binford, 2015).

ROLE OF PARENTS IN THEIR CHILDREN'S DIGITAL SAFETY

In a recent study (Chaudron, 2015), parents are reported as perceiving the opportunities for their children in using digital technologies but they are also concerned about the potential risks. Economic consequences, incidental inappropriate content, health and social impacts were all suggested as key concerns. In a similar study, parents were concerned about the following issues: a sense that this technology was out of their control; the damaging effects of instant gratification; children being so absorbed in the technology that they ignore those around them; violent, scary or gory content and strong language (Livingstone et al., 2014). Another recent report claimed that around a quarter of parents are concerned about who their child is in contact with online (Ofcom, 2014).

Parents use a range of mediating strategies in relation to their children's use of digital technology, such as setting time limits, having social rules such as no digital activity during dinner, having set places in the house for using devices, using content filters, supervision of their children and talking to their children about online safety. However, what is very clear from recent studies is that some parents underestimate the risks of the use of technology by their children, and there is a pressing need for greater parental awareness of potential risks and for the development and promotion of communication strategies outlining how parents can talk to young children about managing online risks (Gray et al., 2016; Livingstone et al., 2014).

 **POINTS FOR DISCUSSION**

Look at the website 'Internet matters' which is an independent, not-for-profit organisation which helps parents to keep their children safe online: www.internetmatters.org/

There is a vast array of accessible guides, advice and videos for parents of children of all ages. Select one resource, read/watch it and consider:

- Have you learned anything from it?
- How useful is this for parents?
- How might early years practitioners and teachers use this site to aid parents' understanding of how to help their children stay safe online?

SUMMARY

In describing the growth of digital media, Naughton (2012, p. 182) stated that 'anybody hoping that the turbulence wrought by the internet will eventually subside, and that things will eventually level out, is doomed to disappointment'. Evans (2014) agrees and states that online technology has expanded at a dizzying rate and will only continue to do so. In this chapter, we have investigated the complexities and potential benefits and challenges in the use of digital media with children. We have seen that digital exposure for most children is inevitable and, whilst there are some polarised debates and controversies on children's use of digital media, there is also growing awareness of technology as a powerful complement to children's education. Therefore, the challenge for early years professionals and teachers is to find that balanced approach and negotiate these choppy waters as we rethink learning in the digital age.

 EXTENDED AND RECOMMENDED READING

Flewitt, R., Messer, D. and Kucirkova, N. (2015) 'New directions for early literacy in a digital age: the iPad', *Journal of Early Childhood Literacy*, 15(3): 289–310.

Provides an interesting account of the opportunities and challenges in using iPads in early literacy learning.

Livingstone, S., Marsh, J., Plowman, L., Ottovordemgentschenfelde, S. and Fletcher-Watson, B. (2014) *Young Children (0-8) and Digital Technology: A Qualitative Exploratory Study - National Report - UK*. London: London School of Economics and Political Science.

Provides an overview of young children and digital technology in the UK.

Don't forget to visit **https://study.sagepub.com/contemporarychildhood** for a selection of free SAGE journal articles, web links, additional case studies, activities, and PowerPoints to help you revise.

REFERENCES

Binford, W. (2015) The Digital Child, Social Science Research Network (http://ssrn.com/abstract=2563874).

Boniel-Nissim, M., Tabak, I., Mazur, J., Borraccino, A., Brooks, F., Gommans, R., et al. (2015) 'Supportive communication with parents moderates the negative effects of electronic media use on life satisfaction during adolescence', *International Journal of Public Health*, 60(2): 189–98.

Brindova, D., Dankulincova Veselska, Z., Klein, D., Hamrik, Z., Sigmundova, D., van Dijk, J.P., et al. (2015) 'Is the association between screen-based behaviour and health complaints among adolescents moderated by physical activity?', *International Journal of Public Health*, 60(2): 139–45.

Chaudron, S. (2015) *Young Children (0–8) and Digital Technology: A Qualitative Exploratory Study across Seven Countries*. Luxembourg: Publications Office of the European Union.

ChildWise (2015) *The Monitor Pre-School Report: Key Behaviour Patterns Among 0–4 Year Olds*. London: ChildWise.

Clark, C. (2014) *Children's and Young People's Reading in 2013: Findings from the 2013 National Literacy Trust's Annual Survey*. London: National Literacy Trust.

Dudeney, G., Hockly, N. and Pegrum, M. (2013) *Digital Literacies*. London: Routledge.

Ernest, J.M., Causey, C., Newton, A.B., Sharkins, K., Summerlin, J. and Albaiz, N. (2014) 'Extending the global dialogue about media, technology, screen time and young children', *Childhood Education*, 90(3): 182–91.

Evans, S. (2014) 'The challenge and potential of the digital age: young people and the internet', *Transactional Analysis Journal*, 44(2): 153–66.

Fekonja-Peklaj, U. and Marjanovič-Umek, L. (2015) 'Positive and negative aspects of the IWB and tablet computers in the first grade of primary school: a multiple-perspective approach', *Early Child Development and Care*, 185(6): 996–1015.

Flewitt, R., Messer, D. and Kucirkova, N. (2015) 'New directions for early literacy in a digital age: the iPad', *Journal of Early Childhood Literacy*, 15(3): 289–310.

Gardner, H. and Davis, K. (2013) *The App Generation*. London: Yale University Press.

Gee, J.P. (1996) *Social Linguistics and Literacies: Ideology in Discourses*. London: Taylor & Francis.

Gray, C., Dunn, J., Moffett, P. and Mitchell, D. (2016) *Digital Technology in the Early Years Classroom*. Belfast: Stranmillis University College.

IOE (2014) Millennium Cohort Study: Initial findings from the age 11 survey (www.cls.ioe.ac.uk/page.aspx?&sitesectionid=1330&sitesectiontitle=MCS+age+11+initial+findings).

Jenkins, H. (2015) Tap, Click, Read: An interview with Lisa Guernsey and Michael Levine (http://henryjenkins.org/2015/10/tap-click-read-an-interview-with-lisa-guernsey-and-michael-levine-part-two.html).

Jenkins, H., Purushotma, R., Clinton, K., Robison, A.J. and Weigel, M. (2006) *Confronting the Challenges of Participatory Culture: Media Education for the 21st Century*. Chicago: The John D. and Catherine T. MacArthur Foundations.

Kucirkova, N. (2014) 'iPads in early education: separating assumptions and evidence', *Frontiers in Psychology*, 5(715): 1–3.

Kucirkova, N. and Sakr, M. (2015) 'Child–father creative text-making at home with crayons, iPad collage and PC', *Thinking Skills and Creativity*, 17: 59–73.

Leaver, T. (2015) 'Researching the ends of identity: birth and death on social media', *Social Media and Society*, 1–2.

Livingstone, S. (2014) 'Children's digital rights: a priority', *Intermedia*, 42(4/5): 20–4.

Livingstone, S., Marsh, J., Plowman, L., Ottovordemgentschenfelde, S. and Fletcher-Watson, B. (2014) *Young Children (0–8) and Digital Technology: A Qualitative Exploratory Study – National Report – UK*. London: London School of Economics and Political Science.

Livingstone, S., Mascherone, G., Dreier, M., Chaudron, S. and Lagae, K. (2015) *How Parents of Young Children Manage Digital Devices at Home: The Role of Income, Education and Parental Style*. London: EU Kids Online, LSE.

Lynch, J. and Redpath, T. (2014) 'Smart technologies in early years literacy education: a meta-narrative of paradigmatic tensions in iPad use in an Australian preparatory classroom', *Journal of Early Childhood Literacy*, 14(2): 147–74.

Mackay, M. (2009) 'Exciting yet safe: the appeal of thick play and big worlds', in R. Willett, M. Robinson and J. Marsh (eds), *Play, Creativity and Digital Cultures*. London: Routledge. pp. 92–107.

McManis, L.D. and Gunnewig, S.B. (2012) 'Finding the education in educational technology with young learners', *Young Children*, 67: 14–24.

McTavish, M. (2014) '"I'll do it my way!": A young child's appropriation and recontextualization of school literacy practices in out-of-school spaces', *Journal of Early Childhood Literacy*, 14(3): 319–44.

Marsh, J. (2010) *Childhood, Culture and Creativity: A Literature Review*. Newcastle: Creativity, Culture and Education.

Marsh, J. (2014) 'From the wild frontier of Davy Crockett to the wintery fjords of Frozen: changes in media consumption, play and literacy from the 1950s to the 2010s', *International Journal of Play*, 3(3): 267–79.

Marsh, J., Plowman, L., Yamada-Rice, D., Bishop, J.C., Lahmar, J., Scott, F., et al. (2015) Exploring Play and Creativity in Pre-schoolers' Use of Apps: Report for early years practitioners (http://techandplay.org/tap-media-pack.pdf).

Merchant, G. (2012) 'Mobile practices in everyday life: popular digital technologies and schooling revisited', *British Journal of Educational Technology*, 43(5): 770–82.

National Media Museum (2011) Television: Colour television in Britain (www.nationalmediamuseum.org.uk/~/media/Files/NMeM/PDF/Collections/Television/ColourTelevisionInBritain.pdf).

Naughton, J. (2012) *From Gutenberg to Zuckerberg: What You Really Need to Know about the Internet*. London: Quercus.

Neumann, M. and Neumann, D. (2014) 'Touch screen tablets and emergent literacy', *Early Childhood Education Journal*, 42: 231–9.

OECD (2015) *Students, Computers and Learning: Making the Connection* (PISA). Paris: OECD Publishing.

Ofcom (2014) Children and Parents: Media use and attitudes report (http://stakeholders. ofcom.org.uk/market-data-research/other/research-publications/childrens/children-parents-oct-14/).

ONS (2015) Insights into Children's Mental Health and Well-being (https:// barrycarpentereducation.com/2015/11/24/insights-into-childrens-mental-health/).

Palaiologou, I. (2016) 'Children under five and digital technologies: implications for early years pedagogy', *European Early Childhood Education Research Journal*, 24(1): 5–24.

Plowman, L. and McPake, J. (2012) 'Seven myths about young children', *Childhood Education*, 89(1): 27–33.

Prensky, M. (2001) 'Digital natives, digital immigrants: Part 1', *On the Horizon*, 9(5): 1–6.

Price, S., Jewitt, C. and Lanna, L.C. (2015) 'The role of iPads in pre-school children's mark making development', *Computers and Education*, 81: 131–41.

Purdy, N. and McGuckin, C. (2015) 'Cyberbullying, schools and the law: a comparative study in Northern Ireland and the Republic of Ireland', *Educational Research*, 57(4): 420–36.

Street, B. (1997) 'The implications of the "new literacy studies" for literacy education', *English in Education*, 31(3): 45–59.

Teichert, L. and Anderson, A. (2014) 'I don't even know what blogging is: the role of digital media in a five-year-old girl's life', *Early Child Development and Care*, 184(11): 1677–91.

UN (2013) General Comment No. 17 on the Right of the Child to Rest, Leisure, Play, Recreational Activities, Cultural Life and the Arts (Art. 31), 17 April, CRC/C/GC/17 (www.refworld.org/docid/51ef9bcc4.html).

Willett, R.J. (2015) 'The discursive construction of "good parenting" and digital media: the case of children's virtual world games', *Media, Culture and Society*, 37(7): 1060–75.

Wohlwend, K. (2015) 'Making, remaking and reimaging the everyday: play, creativity and popular media', in J. Rowsell and K. Pahl (eds), *Routledge Handbook of Literacy Studies*. London: Routledge. pp. 548–60.

Yelland, N., Lee, L., O'Rourke, M. and Harrison, C. (2008) *Rethinking Learning in Early Childhood Education*. New York: Open University Press.

10

INTERNATIONAL PERSPECTIVES

Why you should read this chapter

All of us who work with children are influenced by the historical, economic and political cultures in which we practice. In more recent decades, practice has come to be increasingly influenced by factors across the globe. Massive migration in recent years has meant that practitioners will now almost certainly find themselves working with children from a number of different countries.

By the end of this chapter you should:

* have knowledge and understanding of how children across the globe are having their lives shaped by different political, cultural and economic contexts
* understand the potential of technology to transform children's lives
* understand the impact of conflict on children's lives
* have explored the challenges faced by societies in properly resourcing children's learning and development across the globe.

INTERNATIONAL VARIATIONS IN PRACTICE

A little over a decade ago, Hicks (2004, p. 19) commented on how:

> We can only understand life today in our own communities if it is set in the wider global context. What happens elsewhere in the world constantly impacts on our daily lives even if we may not have been aware of it ... Climate change, energy use, economic growth, wealth and poverty, and violent conflict affect our local communities and day-to-day living ... The forces of globalization, engineered by the rich world, are binding the world more closely together, but are also being more fiercely resisted than ever before.

Childhood is understood differently across the globe and one only has to view news programmes and read popular newspapers to see, at first hand, how different cultures, societies and communities have developed in the way in which they view and, more fundamentally, treat their children. Sorin (2005, p. 14) has noted that:

> The construct of childhood innocence comes at a price – it positions children as incompetent, vulnerable and dependent; a blank slate ready to be moulded by adults. While a need to protect children from harm is a very real concern in these violent and terror-ridden times, it is a concern that protection is becoming surveillance and control and children are not being given rights or opportunities to act on their own behalf.

The twentieth and twenty-first centuries have witnessed a shift away from churches and philanthropists overseeing the welfare and education of children to greater involvement by government, with increasing involvement from professionals such as child psychologists and social workers and a significant rise in bureaucracy (Cregan and Cuthbert, 2014). Two decades ago, Richardson (1990, cited in Hicks, 2004, p. 20) identified two traditions within the field of education as follows:

> The one tradition is concerned with learner-centred education, and the development and fulfilment of individuals. This tradition is humanistic and optimistic, and has a basic trust in the capacity and will of human beings to create healthy and empowering systems and structures ... The second tradition is concerned with building equality, and with resisting the trend for education merely to reflect and replicate inequalities ... it is broadly pessimistic in its assumption that inequalities are the norm wherever they are not consciously and strenuously resisted.

It is not possible for schools to function outside of political and economic influence. Each of these dimensions has its own unique but interrelated factors. Wood (2004), for example, drew attention to how debates surrounding education and its link to economic factors have been successively heightened through comparisons being drawn by governments with other countries. Wood drew particular attention, for example, to how publications in the UK during the 1990s, such as those by Ofsted (1996), had suggested that children in the UK were achieving less than their peers in the Pacific Rim countries, especially China, Japan and South Korea. Wood emphasised that the debates had intensified when Asian tiger economies appeared to be thriving, leading to a 'flurry of reports' from Her Majesty's Inspectorate (HMI) calling on the UK government to learn how schools were organised and children were being taught in these other countries. Elsewhere, she suggested, governments were paying increased attention to international comparisons.

In the decade following 1985, South Korea evolved into one of the leading steel producers in the world, Singapore developed its educational infrastructure to become a notable competitor on the world stage, and the USA, under the presidency of Bill Clinton, moved to proposing how every state across the USA should work to incorporate rigorous standards into its schools. More recently, the Strong Start for America's Children Act 2013 highlighted the impact that quality interventions in the early years and notably from birth, such as home visiting and increased investment, would have on the future learning of young children. The Act proposed free early years education for children in low-income families with a key focus on those aged 4 years. As a result of the Act, there has been increased spending on pre-school programmes, with President Obama stressing in his 2015 State of the Nation speech that childcare was a 'must have' for all working parents. Drawing a comparison with the UK, Fitzgerald and Kay (2016, p. 120) have, however, offered the following rather cautionary note in regard to the Act and current practice across the USA:

> In comparison to the UK, there are distinct similarities ... However, the issues of quality are different, with national quality regulations and inspection in the UK providing better conformity of standards than in the USA. Similarly, more regulatory attention to staff qualifications and suitability seems to be evident in the UK as opposed to the USA.

Across the globe, provision for the education of children in the early years is highly variable and all-too-frequently determined largely by economic and political legacies. In Ireland, for example, there is no state provision for children before the age of 3, other than a variety of voluntary and community initiatives mostly financed by parents or local communities. The *Growing up in Ireland Survey* (McGinnity et al., 2013), cited in Palaiologou et al., 2016, p. 61, made reference to the fact that in Ireland around 40 per cent of children aged 9 months were in receipt of regular childcare. The survey also reported on how 42 per cent of children not being cared for by their parents were being cared for by relatives, most typically grandparents, that 31 per cent were being cared for by adults who were not relatives, usually childminders, and that 27 per cent of children were cared for in a local centre. Dunphy goes on to indicate how, in recent years, the cost of childcare has, for many parents, become a major concern, to such an extent that in 2014 the European Commission openly called on Ireland to address the issue, with the result that in January 2015 the Irish government agreed to set up a committee aimed at bringing forward plans for childcare that would be more affordable.

O'Toole (2013) had emphasised in an article in the popular Irish newspaper *The Irish Times*, how widespread childcare provision and practice was a relatively recent trend in Ireland, with statistics from a longitudinal study, *Growing Up in Ireland*, revealing that 38 per cent of 9-month-olds and 50 per cent of 3-year-olds were in some form of fixed childcare outside of the home. O'Toole reported on how UNICEF, in 2008, placed Ireland joint bottom of the league of 25 countries in relation to the quality and accessibility of early childhood care and education services.

In regard to pre-school provision, O'Toole (2013) recently commented on how the quality of childcare can typically be assessed by examining 'the structural features of the setting' such as the adult–child ratio and group size, and the education level of carers and the daily interactions experienced by the child. She went on to emphasise how parents can gain insights into the nature and quality of interactions by asking the following questions:

> are caregivers generally in good spirits when interacting with my child? Do they smile often at my child and make frequent eye contact? Do they make positive physical contact by holding hands, giving pats on the back, giving cuddles? Do they respond to my child's vocalisations? Do they take a positive approach even if my child is having trouble managing his/her emotions or behaviour?

O'Toole stressed, however, that many parents will have limited contact with the adults who care for their children when they leave their child at the provision and when they then pick them up, or because of the turnover in staff at their child's setting. She drew particular attention to the:

> detrimental effects of stress on the ability to provide sensitive caregiving [which] are well-documented. Quality childcare is dependent on qualified staff who have a good understanding of child development, are paid decent wages and enjoy good working conditions, including supports and resources.

O'Toole (2013) emphasised that many cost-benefit analyses have demonstrated how, with early investment in children, countries can maximise the potential of their citizens and, thereby, reap a range of benefits for the whole population. She went on to highlight how findings from research into childcare in the early years has been unequivocal, warning that if we fail to invest now in our children then we will find ourselves having to pay substantially more in the future because of failure to promote healthy development in the early years. O'Toole also drew attention to the fact that Scandinavian countries typically spend 1 per cent of their GDP on early childhood care and education in the early years and that, in contrast, Ireland's investment is a fraction of this.

In Wales, the situation regarding provision in the early years remains fluid. Palaiologou et al. (2016, p. 58), for example, have drawn attention to the Donaldson Review (2015), *Successful Futures*, which proposed a radical overhaul of the Welsh curriculum for 3–16-year-olds. The situation in Scotland also remains fluid, as indicated by the Children and Young People (Scotland) Act 2014, which highlighted the importance of increased funding for pre-school children and free school meals for primary-aged children (Palaiologou et al., 2016, p. 51). Northern Ireland offers a similar picture with its publication *Learning to Learn Framework* (DENI, 2013), which emphasised the need to raise standards, increase access and equality and close the performance gap (Palaiologou et al., 2016, p. 46). Elsewhere, in Europe, the situation is quite different. Generally considered to be leaders in childcare provision, Scandinavian countries such as Sweden, Norway and Finland have, for example, set very high benchmarks for early years provision; these countries have developed a strong commitment to care in early childhood that has been historically, politically and economically supported. Unlike many other countries in Europe, as well as across the globe, and unlike many children in Ireland, young children in Finland who are born into lower socio-economic families are provided with high-quality care during their pre-school years rather than, as Fitzgerald and Kay (2016, p. 121) suggest, 'suffering a postcode lottery as to quality'.

Only a decade ago, Coulby (2004, p. 54) commented: 'One of the benevolent effects of looking at education from an international or even a comparative perspective may be that it provides a shock with regards to anomalous practice in one's own system.' Coulby has drawn particular attention to the whole issue of inclusion and how this differs across European countries as follows:

> The whole industry of detailed categorization (labelling) and separate, special provision (segregation) is absent in countries such as Italy and Norway. All children are educated together in the least restrictive environment with the maximum of social and curricular integration. The glacial progress towards inclusion in the UK reflects a society which too readily rejects and segregates children on the basis of perceived difference. (p. 54)

He went on to demonstrate the differences amongst countries in Europe regarding their perceptions of education and, in particular, the content of their curricula, proposing that this was largely due to the historical roles played by different states in 'nation-building through education':

> In all states in Europe, though much more in Greece, Latvia, Romania and the UK and much less in Norway and Finland, the teaching of history, national language and social and cultural subjects is infused with nationalism ... Schools in Norway teach children to be citizens of Norway and the world, schools in England teach children to be citizens of England, confident that that means citizens of the world; schools in Latvia teach children to be citizens of Latvia in contradistinction to the world. (Coulby, p. 54)

In drawing attention to the political influence, or what some classify as 'interference', Merz and Swim (2011, p. 305) suggest that 'Most public school principals and teachers wrestle with developing and implementing a vision amongst the imposition of mandates'. Indeed, Cox (2011, p. 3) has argued that in England the culture of primary schooling:

> has been sustained, at least in part, by a performance orientation towards education and a target-driven political agenda ... Added to this, there has been the overriding expectation, over the past two decades or so, that teachers must comply with policy initiatives.

The result, Cox suggested, has been a process of overloading and over-prescribing of teachers. Others have argued that quality teachers will leave the profession if this process continues. In 2012, Daniel Boffrey, the policy editor of the popular UK newspaper *The Observer*, reported as follows:

> Morale among state school teachers is at 'rock bottom', according to a former chief inspector of schools, who speaks out today as unions warn that a 'perfect storm' of government meddling threatens an exodus of talent from the profession ... The pressure on teachers includes tougher targets [and] a new Ofsted grading system that threatens the current rating of most schools ... Many teachers have also complained of dilapidated conditions in the schools they work in. (p. 1)

Since then, significant numbers of teachers have left the profession.

Powell and Goouch (2014) have drawn attention to the variations in and increased demand for childcare, which has coincided with the increase in women entering the workplace. They indicate how in 2008 some 30 per cent of children under 3 years of age were enrolled in dedicated facilities for childcare in those states that make up the Organisation for Economic Cooperation and Development (OECD) and that there were significant variations amongst these countries (OECD, 2006, 2011). They cited, for example, Chile, Mexico, Hungary, Poland and the Czech Republic having less than 10 per cent of children enrolled in childcare, whilst Denmark, Iceland and Norway had over 50 per cent of children enrolled. Powell and Goouch (2014) have also stressed how findings from global research have led many countries to make a much greater investment in the early years, combining care with education, which of course varies in degree depending on political, economic and, crucially, historical and cultural factors.

An important issue in regard to combining education with care has been the need to ensure quality. Powell and Goouch have cited the findings of Ackerman and Barnet (2009) who, in examining outcomes for children of 3 years and older in the USA on the provision of childcare for those under 3 years of age, found that 'increases in provision of the former appeared to have led to increases in the latter but lacked policy attention to quality, which they found to be generally poor' (p. 45).

— ✈ —— POINTS FOR DISCUSSION ──────────────

What key elements can be identified that separate 'care' and 'education' in practice with pre-school children? Can 'care' and 'education' be described as learning? If so, how and if not, why not?

In regard to Scotland, Burton (2012, p. 4, cited in Powell and Goouch, 2014, p. 45) has suggested that 'care and education are not separate in terms of the benefits they bring for children and families, but ... in our systems of funding, provision and staffing'. Here, one is drawn to explore distinctions between the different cultures and histories that have come to be formed across the globe and the extent to which traditions and beliefs have come to inform and define provision for children from their first years. The case of Northern Ireland offers an interesting example, where, for generations, many children from their earliest years have often been placed in early years settings on the grounds of religion.

CHILDREN AND CONFLICT

Outside of the UK, political involvement has, all too often, led to conflict, as can be seen by recent events across the globe. On 26 January 2016, for example, UNICEF posted an appeal on its website in which it hoped to raise £806 million for the crisis in Syria. It reported on how over six million children, who have remained inside Syria, are in urgent need of humanitarian assistance with two million children living in hard-to-reach and besieged areas that are difficult to reach. Millions of children in Syria, as well as those who have left, have lost their families and loved ones as well as their homes. Children have been facing unimaginable violence, have little if any food and clean water and are increasingly facing disease and malnutrition as well as exploitation by adults. UNICEF (2016) commented on how conflict and extreme weather are driving large numbers of children from their homes and submitting millions more to serious shortages of food and starvation, violence and abuse and disease; all of this in addition to significant risks to their education. In the same release on its website, UNICEF reported that some 246 million children, i.e. one in every nine of the world's children, now live in conflict zones. In 2015, children living in those countries and areas touched by conflict were 'twice as likely to die of mostly preventable causes' prior to reaching 5 years of age, than children living in other countries. Staggeringly, UNICEF also reported how, in 2015, over 16 million children were born into conflict, i.e. one in every eight births.

Conflict involving children and their families has often arisen from racism. Racism can be observed in most places in the world and presents itself in many guises, ranging from the most 'subtle' types to those that are openly extreme and distasteful to many. Recently, Fitzgerald and Kay (2016, p. 110), for example, offered the following, in regard to the Czech Republic, which, they reported:

> is one of the Eastern European states that was accused by the European Monitoring Centre on Racism and Xenophobia of over-readiness to identify Roma children as having learning disabilities and sending them to special schools on the basis of faulty diagnoses ... However, many educationalists in the Republic support the idea of special provision for Roma children because of the difficulties they are seen to encounter and present in mainstream schools.

Conflict has also led to starvation. Across the globe, we continue to witness accounts of hunger and starvation. Sadly, this is not just confined to developing countries. It is not only starvation, however, that poses major concerns for society as a whole, for there are increasing numbers of children who are overeating or eating too many foods which are potentially harmful to them. Many children are, in effect, growing up with poor nutrition associated all-too-often with a lack of oversight or poor understanding, on the part of parents, of what constitutes good nutrition. Much of this is due to changes in lifestyle.

 POINTS FOR DISCUSSION

View the YouTube video clip entitled 'Poverty Britain's Hungry Children', at www.youtube.com/watch?v=ekHA8_SDwjA, shown on Channel 4 News and published on YouTube on 4 September 2013, which explores the effects of austerity and poverty on children in the UK. Then consider how primary schools and early years settings can work with parents to support them in developing better nutrition for those families who need it.

GROWTH OF TECHNOLOGY

Technology is reaching into almost every corner of the globe and though it is generally recognised as being beneficial, especially by parents (Vittrup et al., 2016), there are those who express caution. Just over a decade ago, Hicks (2004, p. 19), for example, commented on how science was once viewed as holding all of the answers, whilst now 'science and technology are seen as contributing to contemporary problems, from the storage of nuclear waste to carbon emissions as a factor in global warming'.

Byron (2008) alerted us to how research has indicated that individuals behave differently when using the internet and, rather worryingly, that individuals' 'moral codes' can alter due to the lack of gatekeepers on the internet. There is also an absence of visual cues from important 'others' that children can use in moderating their interactions with those they communicate with via technology. Byron argues that this process can be very difficult for children who are already attempting to learn and internalise the basic social rules, boundaries and parameters of the 'offline world'. They may, he proposes, typically lack those skills and abilities that allow them to critically evaluate, interpret and make sense of information they come into contact with and thereby form accurate judgements about, in terms of how to behave online (2008, p. 5). Byron went on to emphasise how all practitioners and parents have a key role in ensuring that children remain safe whilst still exploring and enjoying new technology. This new technological culture, characterised by a high level of responsibility, spans both parents and children and needs to be supported by government as well as industry and the public sector (p. 13).

GENDER

Knowles (2013, cited in Knowles and Holmström, 2013, p. 37) has outlined some of the complexities central to the issue of gender, as follows:

> At birth, usually depending on primary sex characteristics, children are normally determined as being boys or girls, male or female. However, although male and female can be termed biological distinctions, many argue that we have control over how we manifest our *gender*, particularly in terms of our behaviours, attitudes, values and beliefs. When identifying our gender we may say we are male, female or transgender, and there is considerable argument over whether the way we manifest that gender is genetic or learnt behaviour.

In recent years, the issue of 'gender' has received increasing attention in the media and this has, perhaps, been most noticeable in attempts at 'opening up' debates into the nature of transgenderism in young people. It has been estimated that in the UK there are between 300,000 and 500,000 individuals who are transgender, with this estimation continuing to grow as increased awareness, transparency and legislation take place. This is not the case in all countries. Making reference to the earlier work of Fausto-Sterling (2000), Knowles and Holmström indicate how:

> not only are there instances where there is ambiguity about the primary sex characteristics that are present at birth, where 'scientists, medical professionals, and the wider public have made sense of (or ought to make sense of) bodies that

present themselves as neither entirely male nor female' (Fausto-Sterling, 2000, p. 3), but also there is more to being male or female than the physical characteristics of the body. That is to say: 'labeling someone a man or a woman is a social decision'. (2013, p. 37)

The issue of transgenderism, like that of homosexuality, affects children all over the world, with the extent of the impact being, more often than not, driven by religious, historical and cultural factors. Societies across the globe deal with these issues in different ways. In 2011, for example, the UK Government released a report, *Advancing Transgender Equality: A plan for action* (GOV.UK, 2011, p. 6), in which it set out a clear commitment to tackling issues relating to transgender in young children's lives, indicating that prejudice and discrimination not only blight the lives of individuals but also 'undermine the principles upon which this country prides itself'. The then government reported that it was 'committed to making transgender equality a reality' (p. 5). The report stressed the importance of tackling bullying, and in doing so acknowledged that whilst progress had been made there was still much to achieve: 'Whilst the experiences of transgender pupils are least likely to be reflected in data and research … we know that over 70 per cent of boys and girls who express gender variant behaviours are subject to bullying in schools' (p. 5).

The report emphasised that tackling transphobic bullying is crucial to addressing behaviour that is not acceptable and to ensuring that society increases in its tolerance:

> This Government is committed to tackling transphobic bullying and we want to support schools to act as leaders and advocates for change. We have already issued anti-bullying guidance to support head teachers … including transphobic bullying … We are also issuing separate statutory guidance to extend head teachers' powers to respond to pupils who bully other pupils outside the school premises, and are reforming Ofsted schools' inspections to give all forms of prejudice-based bullying more prominence. But there is still a long way to go. (GOV.UK, 2011, p. 5)

PROVISION FOR CHILDREN THROUGHOUT THE WORLD

The provision that has been made for children throughout the world has been of such a varied nature. Whilst many children have been well provided for, growing up in homes where they are nurtured and cared for, many have not. Countless numbers of children have, for example, over past generations, been removed from their birth parents for a multitude of questionable reasons; all-too-frequently this has involved acute and monumental emotional pain and distress on both the part of parents and their children. Children have, for example, been removed from their mothers and placed in orphanages because they were born outside of marriage, as was so often the case in countries such as Ireland. Others were sent abroad to developing countries, most notably the colonies of Australia and Canada. Many children who were transported, experienced extremely harsh lives including penury, hard labour and abuse (including sexual abuse), but received little or no formal education' (Cregan and Cuthbert, 2014, p. 125). Between 1854 and 1930, an estimated 200,000 children from the eastern cities of the USA were put on 'orphan trains' and sent into the west where they were then placed with families who needed help with managing everyday chores (Cregan and Cuthbert, 2014). Startlingly, it has been reported (in 2014) that the last time children were transported from England to Australia was as recently as 1967 when they sailed from the port of Liverpool, meaning a child of 10 years of age at the time is now in their 50s.

ECONOMIC COSTS OF CHILDHOOD

There is no escaping the notion that childhood and the economy are inextricably linked. Politicians worldwide are paying more and more attention to childhood education, seeing it as pivotal to the economy and a country's ability to compete in the global economic 'race'. To emphasise the point, the Department for Education (2013, p. 6) explicitly states that effective childcare is vital in ensuring that the UK can compete in the global race; this is actioned through providing help for parents going back to work and, importantly, readying children for school and, eventually, employment. In essence, many childhood policies stem from a political perspective that views society as 'subject to the logics of commodification, marketisation, competition and cost-benefit analysis' (Apple, 2013, p. 6).

A useful starting point when considering the cost of childhood is the amount faced by families in raising a child. Bingham (2015) reported that recent research carried out by the Centre for Economic and Business Research (CEBR) has shown that the basic outlay for bringing up a child in the UK has risen 50 per cent faster than inflation over more than a decade. There are variations between regions but the overall figure has increased by 63 per cent since 2003 to £229,251 at present. Bingham (2015), citing the CEBR research, highlights a stark reality of these costs, noting 29 per cent of parents' gross annual income is spent on raising a child. Interestingly, there are broader implications as there were indications that parents had postponed having their next child or limited the size of their family for financial reasons.

Whilst these costs raise interesting debate, we should not hide from the notion that the political focus is not on the increasing expense faced by individual families, but more on the outcomes of childhood for the broader economy, in particular those implications often associated with child poverty. Walker and Griggs

(2008, p. 1) identified the serious consequences of child poverty for both individuals and society, noting that they include 'losses to the economy through reduced productivity, lower educational attainment and poor health'. UNICEF (2014, p. 2) emphasised this further, stating that 'poverty can also set children on the lifelong trajectory of low education levels and reduced productivity, and undermine their physical and mental health'.

Hirsch (2013, p. 1) summarises that the economic cost of child poverty is 'influenced by four variables: the level of child poverty itself; levels of benefits and earnings; general levels of public spending; and specific policies which direct public spending towards children in low income families.' He continues to calculate that the total cost in the UK of child poverty increased from £25 billion in 2008 to £29 billion in 2013. Disconcertingly, he suggests that if levels of child poverty in 2020 are realised, the cost would increase to £35 billion, approximately 3 per cent of GDP (UNICEF, 2014, p. 2), implying that this spiralling of cost results from creating and sustaining *intergenerational cycles of poverty*, as 'children living in poverty are more likely to become impoverished adults and have poor children'.

The stark short-, medium- and long- term implications for the economy emanating from child poverty were discussed by Walker and Griggs (2008), who undertook a literature review around the costs of child poverty for individuals and society, on behalf of the James Rowntree Foundation. The consequences for the economy stemming from the impact of poverty on children's health, employment opportunities, behaviour and family relationships, were highlighted:

- From a health perspective, Walker and Griggs (2008) highlight how a host of studies have connected children from low-income families with an increased risk of poor physical (e.g. diabetes, asthma) and mental health (e.g. depression). As children from low-income families are more likely to experience health problems but also accumulate health risks as they grow older, there are implications for healthcare spending but also, as Walker and Griggs (2008, p. 4) state, 'costs for the economy through sickness absence and lower productivity'.
- From an educational perspective, Walker and Griggs (2008, p. 5) argue that there is a growing base of evidence that links childhood poverty to poor educational outcomes, and they succinctly state that 'a workforce with lower skill levels, lower educational attainment and limited aspirations reduces productivity, economic growth and a country's capacity to compete in the global economy'. Whilst we must not ignore the personal and social implications of poor education and child poverty on employment opportunities, if we consider this purely from an economic standpoint, having a significant proportion of the adult population out of work is detrimental to the economy not only in terms of productivity, but also in terms of benefit payments and loss of taxes (p. 5).

- From a behavioural perspective, Walker and Griggs (2008) imply that whilst there is no consensus on the direct association between childhood poverty and crime, there are suggestions that growing up in low-income households can lead to an increased likelihood of being excluded from school, risk-taking behaviour, aggression and potential involvement in crime. Again, there is no escaping the social and emotional effects of crime, but taking a strict economic viewpoint, the 'economic costs of youth anti-social and criminal behaviour include the youth justice system, pupil referral units and other school-related services' (p. 5).
- From a family relationship perspective, Walker and Griggs (2008, p. 6) hold back from giving figures for the burden placed on services to families due to childhood poverty, but remind us that 'what should be considered in any calculation is the three billion pounds spent by local authorities each year on social services directed at children'.

With such huge social and economic costs associated with child poverty, it is understandable and right that politicians want to eliminate it. As Hirsch (2013, p. 4) noted, there is a powerful incentive to devote resources to 'fulfilling the commitment, enshrined in the Child Poverty Act 2010, of its eradication'. UNICEF (2014, p. 2) summarise the situation: 'While the largest costs of child poverty are borne directly by children themselves, society also pays a high price through reduced productivity, untapped potential and the costs of responding to chronic poverty. Child poverty damages children's life chances and harms us all.'

Investment in early childhood education and care is gaining growing global interest because of this; Barnett and Nores (2012, p. 1) argue that the interest stems from 'evidence of the importance of environmental influences on early cognitive and social development, the human and economic costs of poor developmental trajectories for children in poverty, and the potential for early interventions to alter those developmental trajectories'. Whilst there have been numerous international research studies identifying the positive benefits associated with early childhood education, relatively few have calculated the economic value of these benefits (p. 1). However, Barnett and Nores (2012) note that the few studies that have considered economic benefits across the globe have painted a positive picture and indicated good reasoning for investment.

THE READYING CULTURE

Political drivers of the economy and global competition ('the global race') have resulted in a discourse of 'readiness', where the purpose of education is to 'ready' children for the next stage of their *development*, moving from early years *preparation* for schools ('school ready') through to school *preparation* for work ('work ready' or in President Obama's (2016) terminology, 'job-ready'). 'Readiness' associated with economic and employment debates is evident in a range of government narratives; as an example, the Department for Education (2013, p. 6) explicitly states that 'great childcare is vital to ensuring we can compete in the global race, by helping parents back to work and readying children for school and, eventually, employment'. The result of such comments is that educators are faced with decisions on what is deemed necessary for this staged *readiness*, decisions that will eventually dictate the mechanisms of control and regulation that will be put in place. Structures, curriculum, preferred pedagogy and standards for training all emanate from the focus of ensuring children are *ready*.

There are clear implications for both children and childhood educators. Kohn (2006) implies that when there is a 'readying' culture, where children lead 'controlled' lives in trying to reach the expectations of externally imposed standards, this may lead to self-alienation and undermine children's holistic well-being. In short, the very essence of creativity and excitement for learning can be threatened by pressures to perform and become *ready* for the next stage of their development. Supporting this fear, in March 2016, Lucy Ward from the popular UK newspaper *The Guardian* reported on how recent research funded by the Lego Foundation had indicated that both parents and schools were ignoring the benefits of play in early childhood education; a focus on knowledge of the '3 Rs' is seemingly replacing the opportunity to develop creativity, problem solving and empathy through play-based activities. Countering this view slightly, it is possible to at least initially view the concept of 'readiness' as positive; it seems to make sense to 'future proof'. Such 'future proofing' would, in principle, enable children to transition between phases of their lives more easily and potentially have greater opportunities for social mobility. However, this message has been interpreted slightly differently by Moss (2015, p. 235) who suggests that 'future proofing' children from a political perspective is about 'creating flexible souls able to respond effortlessly to changing market demands and training them up to participate in the "global race"'. Importantly, moving on from this point, Moss argues that childhood educators can challenge and mediate this message. Competition can be questioned. Collectivism can be supported. Indeed, rather than *future proof*, Moss (2015) directs us to consider Facer's (2011, p. 15) vision where educational environments have a role of *future building*, allowing 'young people and communities to contest the visions of the future that they are being presented with … to fight for viable futures for all'.

The issue that must be explored by those engaged in childhood education relates to how the *message*, how the discourse and narrative, can be mediated. Without this, practitioners could be unintentionally indoctrinating children – far from the *future-building* vision espoused by Facer. Within all policy, there are hidden assumptions that operate and these can have an impact on both cultural and sub-cultural values but also on individuals and their values (Lea, 2013).

SUMMARY

All adults working with children will increasingly have to pay attention to the historical, cultural, economic and political structures within which they practise; education is now a global process and countries can no longer exist in isolation. Huge migration in recent decades has meant that many practitioners now find themselves working with children from a range of different countries and cultures.

 —— **EXTENDED AND RECOMMENDED READING** ——

Cregan, K. and Cuthbert, D. (2014) *Global Childhoods*. London: Sage.

A very useful text, which brings together a great deal of information and offers many reasons as to why practitioners need to think more globally about their practice.

Don't forget to visit **https://study.sagepub.com/contemporarychildhood** for a selection of free SAGE journal articles, web links, additional case studies, activities, and PowerPoints to help you revise.

REFERENCES

Ackerman, D.J. and Barnet, W.S. (2009) *What Do We Know About the Impact of Publicly Funded Preschool Education on the Supply and Quality of Infant/Toddler Care?* New Brunswick, NJ: National Institute for Early Education Research (NIEER).

Apple, M.W. (2013) *Can Education Change Society?* Abingdon: Routledge.

Ariès, P. (1962/1986) *Centuries of Childhood: A Social History of Family Life*. London: Penguin Books.

Barnett, W.S. and Nores, M. (2012) *Investing in Early Childhood Education: A Global Perspective*. Keynote Address at the 'Early Childhood: Secure Childhood. Promising Future' conference, Riyadh, Saudi Arabia, November.

Bingham (2015) 'Average cost of raising a child in UK £230,000', *The Telegraph*. Available at: www.telegraph.co.uk/news/uknews/11360819/Average-cost-of-raising-a-child-in-UK-230000.html (accessed 12 April 2016).

Boffrey, D. (2012) 'Schools "face talent drain" as teachers' morale dives', *The Observer*, 13 March, p. 1.

Burton, S. (2012) Address to Scottish Trades Union Congress by Sarah Burton, Policy Development Manager, Children in Scotland at the Annual Conference of the STUC, Inverness, 23 April.

Byron, T. (2008) *Safer Children in a Digital World: The Report of the Byron Review*. Nottingham: DCSF Publications.

Coulby, D. (2004) 'Education in Europe', in S. Ward (ed.), *Education Studies: A Student's Guide*. London: RoutledgeFalmer.

Cox, S. (2011) *New Perspectives in Primary Education*. Maidenhead: Open University Press.

Cregan, K. and Cuthbert, D. (2014) *Global Childhoods*. London: Sage.

Department for Education (DfE) (2013) More Great Childcare: Raising quality and giving parents more choice. Available at: www.gov.uk/government/uploads/system/uploads/attachment_data/file/219660/More_20Great_20Childcare_20v2.pdf (accessed 2 March 2016).

Department for Education in Northern Ireland (DENI) (2013) *Learning to Learn: A Framework for Early Years Education in Northern Ireland*. Bangor: DENI.

Donaldson, G. (2015) *Successful Futures: An Independent Review of Curriculum and Assessment Arrangements in Wales*. Cardiff: Welsh Government.

Facer, K. (2011) *Learning Futures: Education, Technology and Social Change*. London: Routledge.

Fausto-Sterling, A. (2000) *Sexing the Body: Gender Politics and the Construction of Sexuality*. New York: Basic Books.

Fitzgerald, D. and Kay, J. (2016) *Understanding Early Years Policy* (4th edn). London: Sage.

GOV.UK (2011) Advancing Transgender Equality: A plan for action, December (www.gov.uk/government/uploads/system/uploads/attachment_data/file/85498/transgender-action-plan.pdf).

Hicks, D. (2004) 'The global dimension in the curriculum', in S. Ward (ed.), *Education Studies: A Student's Guide*. London: RoutledgeFalmer.

Hirsch, D. (2013) *An Estimate of the Cost of Child Poverty in 2013*. Loughborough: Centre for Research in Social Policy, Loughborough University.

Knowles, G. (2013) 'Families, identity and cultural heritage', in G. Knowles and R. Holmström, *Understanding Family Diversity and Home–School Relations*. London: Routledge.

Knowles, G. and Holmström, R. (2013) *Understanding Family Diversity and Home–School Relations*. London: Routledge.

Kohn, A. (2006) *The Homework Myth: Why Our Kids Get Too Much of a Bad Thing*. Boston, MA: Da Capo Press.

Lea, S. (2013) 'Early years work, professionalism and the translation of policy into practice', in Z. Kingdon and J. Gourd (eds), *Early Years Policy: The Impact on Practice*. London: Routledge.

McGinnity, F., Murray, A. and McNally, S. (2013) *Growing up in Ireland: National Longitudinal Study of Children – Mother's return to work and childcare choices for infants in Ireland*. Dublin: The Stationery Office.

Merz, A.H. and Swim, T.J. (2011) '"You can't mandate what matters": bumping visions against practices', *Teacher Development*, 15(3): 305–18.

Moss, P. (2015) 'There are alternatives! Contestation and hope in early childhood education', *Global Studies of Childhood*, 5(3): 226–38.

Obama, B. (2016) State of the Union Address (https://medium.com/@WhiteHouse/president-obama-s-2016-state-of-the-union-address-7c06300f9726#.e0gq7pi8j).

Ofsted (1996) *Worlds Apart: A Review of International Surveys of Educational Achievement Involving England*. London: The Stationery Office.

Organisation for Economic Cooperation and Development (OECD) (2006) *Starting Strong II: Early Childhood Education and Care*. Paris: OECD.

Organisation for Economic Cooperation and Development (OECD) (2011) *PF3.2 Enrolment in Childcare and Pre-Schools*. Paris: OECD.

O'Toole, C. (2013) 'Lack of investment in early years care will cost society dear', *The Irish Times*. Available at: www.irishtimes.com/news/social-affairs/lack-of-investment-in-early-years-care-will-cost-society-dear-1.1409029 (accessed 20 February 2016).

Palaiologou, I., Walsh, G., MacQuarrie, S., Waters, J., Macdonald, N. and Dunphy, E. (2016) 'The national picture', in I. Palaiologou (ed.), *The Early Years Foundation Stage: Theory and Practice*. London: Sage.

Powell, S. and Goouch, K. (2014) 'International snapshots of provision for babies and young children', in G. Pugh and B. Duffy (eds), *Contemporary Issues in the Early Years* (6th edn). London: Sage.

Richardson, R. (1990) *Daring to be a Teacher*. Stoke-on-Trent: Trentham Books.

Sorin, R. (2005) 'Changing images of childhood: reconceptualising early childhood practice', *International Journal of Transitions in Childhood*, 1: 12–21.

UNICEF (2014) Child Poverty in the Post-2015 Agenda, UNICEF Briefs. Available at: www.unicef.org/socialpolicy/files/Issue_Brief_Child_Poverty_in_the_post-2015_Agenda_June_2014_Final.pdf (accessed 12 April 2016).

UNICEF (2016) Unicef Appeals for £806 million for Syria Crisis Response: Alarming figures highlight extent of humanitarian crisis. Available at: www.unicef.org.uk/Media-centre/Press-releases/Unicef-appeals-for-806-million-for-Syria-crisis-response-alarming-figures-highlight-extent-of-humanitarian-crisis/ (accessed 2 February 2016).

Vittrup, B., Snider, S., Rose, K.K. and Rippy, J. (2016) 'Parental perceptions of the role of media and technology in their young children's lives', *Journal of Early Childhood Research*, 14(1): 43–54.

Walker, R. and Griggs, J. (2008) *The Costs of Child Poverty for Individuals and Society: A Literature Review*. York: Joseph Rowntree Foundation. Available at: www.jrf.org.uk/sites/default/files/jrf/migrated/files/2301-child-poverty-costs.pdf (accessed 12 April 2016).

Ward, L. (2016) 'Children should learn mainly through play until age of eight, says Lego', *The Guardian*, 15 March (www.theguardian.com/education/2016/mar/15/children-learn-play-age-eight-lego).

Wood, K. (2004) 'International perspectives: the USA and the Pacific Rim', in S. Ward (ed.), *Education Studies: A Student's Guide*. London: RoutledgeFalmer.

Zelizer, V. (1985/1994). *Pricing the Priceless Child: The Changing Social Value of Children*. Princeton, NJ: Princeton University Press.

11

CONTEMPORARY ISSUES IN A GLOBAL SOCIETY

Why you should read this chapter

All societies and cultures are now influenced by global events. Practitioners working with children will increasingly find themselves managing the learning and development of children who are affected by events that may be occurring in other parts of the world.

By the end of this chapter you should:

- have increased your awareness of how global issues impact on children
- have examined the impact of poverty on the lives of children
- have explored the impact of obesity on children, the growth in sexualisation and commercialism and the relevance of the media and issues relating to mental health
- have examined the emergence of neuroscience and its contribution to education
- have reflected on professionalism and the importance of child-centredness in a changing world.

POVERTY AND LIFE CHANCES

Across the globe, countless numbers of children are living in a state of poverty, which can present in many different guises and on many different levels. Only a decade ago, the United Nations General Assembly (UNGA, 2006, para. 460) took what many considered to be a major advance in formulating agreement on what has become an internationally accepted means of viewing child poverty. In doing so, they emphasised that whilst severe deprivation of goods and basic services adversely affects everyone, 'it is most threatening and harmful to children, leaving them unable to enjoy their rights, to reach their full potential and to participate as full members of society'. A year later, the United Nations Children's Fund (UNICEF) (2007) emphasised that it was important to separate 'child poverty' from popular notions of poverty. In particular, they cautioned how attempts at measuring child poverty should not be 'lumped together' with measurements of general poverty, which typically focus on income levels; instead, they should also take into account access to basic social services, in particular diet and nutrition, clean and drinkable water, effective sanitation and shelter and, importantly, education.

Recent decades have seen increased acknowledgement and acceptance amongst governments across the globe that poverty significantly affects the life chances of countless numbers of children and, therefore, the success of societies and nations (Boyden et al., 2003; Corak, 2005; Delamonica and Minujin, 2007; Doek et al., 2009; Feeny and Boyden, 2003; Jones and Sumner, 2011). The UK government report *New Approach to Child Poverty: Tackling the Causes of Disadvantage and Transforming Families* (GOV.UK, 2011) indicated that some 800,000 children in families with a disabled member were living in relative poverty. The report also indicated that children from black and ethnic families were twice as likely to live in poverty as those from white families, and that 1.1 million children in lone-parent families were living in relative poverty. The numbers of children living in poverty have increased since then, with even greater recognition now being given to the fact that recent austerity and the downturn in the global economy have led to greater numbers of families experiencing quite severe poverty.

— ✈ — POINTS FOR DISCUSSION —————————

View the YouTube video entitled 'BBC World Debate Why Poverty?', at www.youtube.com/watch?v=KNIEb3injpc, which examines the 'causes' of and 'cures' for the continuing problems underlying severe poverty throughout the world. Then, consider what activities teachers might use to develop their pupils' understanding of themselves as individuals growing up in a global context.

OBESITY

Whilst poverty affects children throughout the world, other factors such as diet and nutrition impact on the lives of children. Obesity, in particular, has emerged as a significant issue across the globe and, not surprisingly, it is often associated with a growing importance that children, and even very young children, are giving to self-image. In China, for example, there have been significant changes in the lifestyle of much of the population over the past few decades, brought about by major economic growth. This has led to a marked increase in obesity, with the number of children considered as obese more than tripling between 1986 and 2010 (Ji et al., 2013; Yu et al., 2012, cited in Cregan and Cuthbert, 2014). The number of overweight children under the age of 5 increased from 32 million globally in 1990 to 42 million in 2013, with an increase from 4 to 9 million overweight or obese children being recorded in the World Health Organisation (WHO) African region during this same period (WHO, 2015a). A concerning fact is that the majority of children who are overweight or obese are growing up in developing countries with an estimated rate of increase being 30 per cent higher than that of under-developed countries. The WHO estimates that if current trends continue, the number of overweight or obese infants and young children across the globe will rise over the next decade to around 70 million in 2025.

Recently, the Health and Social Care Information Centre (HSCIC) (2015) reported that in England the number of children aged 4–5 years in their reception year in 2013/14 who were obese amounted to 9.5 per cent, which was higher than the previous year when it was 9.3 per cent, but, interestingly, fewer than the year 2006/07 when it was found to be 9.9 per cent. The HSCIC also reported the proportion of obese children across England aged 10–11 in Year 6 in 2013/14 to be 19.1 per cent, which was higher than in the previous year when it was 18.9 per cent, and higher than in 2006/07 when it was 17.5 per cent. Such statistics are indeed concerning and point to what some consider to be a worrying vision of childhood in forthcoming generations. Overweight and obesity typically lead to related health problems and in many cases psychological issues in childhood, associated, for example, with bullying and teasing and even social isolation. Equally concerning is the impact that obesity will have on the economies of respective countries where associated illnesses in children will place much greater pressure on health and social services at a time when many adults are living longer, and, therefore, placing enormous pressure on health and social services. In addition, concerns can be expressed in regard to the reduced contributions that obese children growing into obese adults might offer to the communities and societies in which they live. More recently, in January 2016, the Commission on Ending Childhood Obesity (WHO, 2016) presented its final report to the WHO following a two-year process to address very worrying levels of obesity and overweight children across the globe. The report made a number of recommendations to governments, aimed at reversing the growing and extremely worrying trend of children under 5 years of age becoming obese.

SEXUALISATION OF CHILDREN

When one takes time to look, one can see examples of the precocious sexualisation of children through commercialisation everywhere (Cregan and Cuthbert, 2014) – young children, for example, dressed like adults and presenting with adult-like behaviours, often connected by mobile phones to social websites. A particular concern expressed by many parents and professionals around the world is the increase in sexual activity amongst increasingly younger children. In a relatively recent report, *World Health Report: Reducing Risks, Promoting Health Life* (2002), the WHO offered the following very useful starting point for examining the sexualisation of children as it draws particular attention to the importance of 'sexual health' in children and how the concept of 'health' goes beyond just physical factors to address crucial aspects of emotional and social development:

> Sexual health is a state of physical, emotional, mental and social well-being related to sexuality; it is not the absence of disease, dysfunction or infirmity ... For sexual health to be attained and maintained, the sexual rights of all persons must be respected, protected and fulfilled.

Different generations have viewed sexual health in very different ways, with much of what is considered acceptable today being greatly frowned on in previous generations and even decades. In many western industrial societies, aspects of sexual activity were considered to be a taboo; not to be spoken about in public, kept almost totally private and, in some quarters, viewed as sinful. The situation today is, however, very different.

Less than a decade ago, Currie et al. (2008, cited in Cowie, 2012, p. 145) indicated that young people were becoming more sexually active at an earlier age. They reported that over 30 per cent of children in their study reported having sex by the age of 16 years and that this trend has been rising since the 1960s. They proposed that young people were experimenting more with sex and were less inhibited than the youth of earlier generations. Cowie noted how body piercing and having tattoos could demonstrate to others that young people had gone through the transition to adulthood. Cowie commented further in regard to this important transition as follows:

> The proof can be circulating intimate pictures of, for example, genital or belly button piercing, on the internet or by mobile phone ... They will often rely more on blogs and informal chat with one another in order to seek clarification about sexual behaviour. (p. 145)

Cowie also cited a survey undertaken by Barter (2009) who surveyed 1,353 young people between the ages of 13 and 17 and found that 88 per cent of those surveyed had engaged in some kind of intimate sexual relationship. A further study, cited by Cowie, was that undertaken by Moore and Rosenthal (2006) who indicated that 'young people are engaging in a wide range of sexual behaviours, including solo sex, anal and oral sex' (p. 145). A recent report commissioned by the Department for Education, *Letting Children be Children: Report of an Independent Review of the Commercialization and Sexualization of Childhood* (Bailey, 2011, p. 6), pointed to the pressure on children today to grow up too quickly, which:

> [takes two] different but related forms: the pressure to take part in a sexualized life before they are ready to do so; and the commercial pressure to consume the vast range of goods and services that are available to children and young people of all ages.

A more recent report by the NSPCC (Jütte et al., 2015), *How Safe are our Children? The most comprehensive overview of child protection in the UK*, noted that, in the UK, police recorded nearly 36,500 sexual offences against children in 2013 to 2014. The report emphasised that each of these parts of the UK had seen a 'sharp increase' in the numbers of sexual offences recorded against children 'in the past year', with a 26 per cent rise in those against children below the age of 16 years, and that this was probably due to the 'Yewtree effect', which is a greater willingness on the part of individuals to report abuse due to the number of recent high-profile sexual abuse cases reported in the media. A further reason given by the authors of the report was the possibility of 'improved compliance' in regard to standards of recording amongst some police forces, due to investigations into the nature of recording practices in November 2014, which, rather worryingly, demonstrated high levels of under-recording of sexual offences (2015, p. 26).

More recently, Elizabeth Rigby, the media editor for the popular UK newspaper *The Times* (Rigby, 2016, p. 13), made reference to how the 'sexting epidemic' in Britain is a 'time-bomb'. In the same newspaper, reporters Rachel Sylvester and Alice Thompson (Sylvester and Thompson, 2016, p. 12) quoted the chief constable of Norfolk who offered the following and rather worrying statistics, implying an aspect of development in young people that appears, at first hand, to be largely beyond the control of adults:

> In the late 1990s there were only 7,000 indecent images of children in circulation in Britain. Now, conservatively, I would say that there are 100 million ... There has been an 80 per cent increase in cases in the last three years, with police carrying out 70,000 child sexual abuse investigations last year.

SOCIAL FEARS

All children experience forms of anxiety from time to time. This can vary in degree, in extent and in occurrence and can be viewed against cultural norms and expectations. What makes one child experience anxiety and social fear might excite another child and embrace their interest and even enthusiasm. Children are different. Recently, raisingchildren.net.au (2016) reported on its website how children experience social anxiety when they are fearful of those situations where they might need to interact with others, or where they become the focus of attention. Typically, such children worry that others will think badly of them, and in some cases that they will perform some action that will be seen by others as embarrassing. Children affected can be very young and this type of anxiety has, according to the website, been diagnosed at as early a stage as 4 years old, with presenting behaviours and signs including nausea, blushing and even trembling.

Children with social anxiety may also present as being overly shy and may be observed to have problems with meeting other children either individually or within groups. They may also present as having few friends and can avoid situations where they may feel they will become the centre of attention. This may be particularly noticeable in the playground where time is unstructured by adults and children are faced with initiating interactions with others and joining in. All-too-often, the behaviours of such children can go unnoticed and may give little cause for concern because those affected are not overtly presenting with outward-facing problematic behaviours such as fighting and arguing, hitting and pushing. In itself, shyness is not a significant difficulty for most children and may even be considered normal. It only becomes a problem when this aspect of children's emotional and social state actually interferes adversely with their well-being and state of emotional balance.

MENTAL HEALTH

The World Health Organisation (WHO, 2015b) estimated in 2015 that across the globe 10–20 per cent of children and adolescents experience mental disorders, with 50 per cent of all mental illness starting by 14 years of age and neuropsychiatric conditions being the main cause of disability in young people. When untreated, problems impact significantly on children's development, their educational achievements and their ability to have fulfilling and productive lives. Children, the WHO emphasised, who have mental disorders 'face major challenges with stigma, isolation and discrimination, as well as lack of access to health care and education facilities, in violation of their fundamental human rights'. Children with mental health problems are typically at much greater risk of having physical health problems and are also more likely to be smokers. Those who present with eating disorders and the early onset of psychosis are especially at risk.

The extent of mental health problems in children and adolescents in the UK was recently reviewed in a report by the Department of Health (2015), *The Future in Mind: Promoting, protecting and improving our children and young people's mental health and well-being*. The report's picture for the UK was similar to the global estimation of the WHO (2015b), in that 50 per cent of mental health problems begin before the age of 14, with the DoH noting further that 75 per cent have developed by the age of 18. The report made reference to the work of Green et al.

(2005), in estimating that just under 10 per cent of school-aged children between 5 and 16 years had a mental disorder – this percentage amounted to over 800,000 children. A closer look at the survey indicated that over 300,000 of these children were aged between 5 and 10 years and over 500,000 were aged between 11 and 16 years. This would suggest that in an average class of 30 children around three will have a mental health disorder, with the most common categories being anxiety and depression, hyperkinetic disorders (severe ADHD) and conduct disorders. The survey noted that just over 500,000 children and young people had a conduct disorder, 290,000 an anxiety disorder, around 80,000 were seriously depressed and over 132,000 had ADHD which was severe.

A UK report, *What About the Children?*, produced by Ofsted and the Care Quality Commission (CQC) (Ofsted, 2013), took evidence from nine local authorities and partner agencies in addition to canvassing the views of parents, carers and children as well as practitioners and managers. The report drew attention to the rather worrying fact that one in six of the adult population, an estimated 9 million individuals, experience mental health problems, with estimates suggesting that 30 per cent of these adults have dependent children (between birth and 18 years of age). The report also offered evidence from a number of small studies of individuals with health difficulties, suggesting that at least 25 per cent of adults and probably many more, especially among young women in acute psychiatric hospital settings, might be parents. The report also made reference to recent findings from the NSPCC (Cuthbert et al., 2011), in which it was estimated that 144,000 babies below the age of 1 year live with a parent 'who has a common mental health problem'. The report also made reference to the National Treatment Agency for Substance Abuse, which collects data on individuals who use drug and alcohol services. This latter report estimated that around 200,000 adults are currently receiving some type of treatment for substance misuse problems and that, very worryingly, nearly a third or 30 per cent of these individuals were parents who lived with their children. The review undertaken by the NSPCC (Cuthbert et al., 2011) estimated that during the previous year (2010) some 19,500 infants under the age of 1 year were living in a home where their parent was a user of Class A drugs, with some 93,500 infants below the age of 1 year living in a household with a parent classified as a problem drinker.

A further report by ChildLine (NSPCC, 2014), *What's Affecting Children in 2013*, revealed how in 2012/13 it had received 2.4 million approaches, a rise of 28 per cent from the previous year. It also revealed that in 2013 it had offered counselling to 278,886 children and young people, with 10,961 of these having expressed to them concerns about another child. Worryingly, it reported a 50 per cent increase in contacts from 12-year-olds regarding self-harm, a 33 per cent rise overall in suicidal counselling and a 43 per cent increase in the age group 12–15. Sixty per cent of referrals were on behalf of young people who were actively suicidal, which represented a 14 per cent increase from 2011 to 2012. In regard to children under the age of 11, ChildLine reported the following:

There were 22,733 counselling sessions with this age group. 86 per cent of young people within this age group were aged 9-11. The youngest recorded age was five, for which there were 319 counselling sessions. Nearly one in four (24 per cent) children aged 11 and under who contacted ChildLine during 2012/13 were concerned about bullying. Counselling about physical abuse was proportionately higher (9 per cent) for this age group, compared with 12-15 year olds (6 per cent) and 16-18 year olds (3 per cent). There was also a 19 per cent growth in counselling about school and education problems among this age group. A third (33 per cent) of neglect counselling was with children aged 11 and under. When a child describes their life to ChildLine they rarely recognize that what they are experiencing is neglect. ChildLine counsellors who are trained to identify this type of abuse often determine when a child is being neglected.

Concerns about bullying also rose by 87 per cent compared with the previous year, with a rise of 69 per cent relating to anti-racist bullying. Nearly 40,000 children and young people approached ChildLine struggling with depression and unhappiness, which became a new 'concern category', introduced by ChildLine in 2012, and which includes feelings of sadness and low mood, loneliness, low self-esteem and low confidence and issues around body image, which, as yet, have not become so severe that they have been classified as severe depression or a mental health issue.

MEDIA AND MATERIALISM

It has been acknowledged for some time that children are being born into societies largely shaped and even defined by materialism, and that, increasingly, they are growing up too quickly (Elkind, 1981). Some (Cregan and Cuthbert, 2014, p. 52) have even gone as far as suggesting an 'impending crisis for children and childhood' in what they see as the Global North. Cregan and Cuthbert have also suggested that this crisis has been spreading to rapidly developing countries across the globe, for example Malaysia; in making reference to the work of Niner et al. (2013), they liken the impact of modernisation on young people in Malaysia to a '"social tsunami", which apocalyptically threatens to sweep away everything in its path' (p. 50). Cregan and Cuthbert have been more explicit in their concerns regarding the impact of materialism on those more affluent and developed countries in the Global North:

another set of apprehensions arises from the conditions of material affluence ... These include anxiety about the impact of technology on the lives of children; the precocious sexualization of children through age-inappropriate clothing, popular clothing and merchandise; the progressive sequestering and inactivity of children inside their home due to fears of dangers outside the home; and children's preoccupation with technologized entertainment. (p. 50)

Some years before Cregan and Cuthbert wrote the above, the UK newspaper the *Daily Telegraph* published a letter in 2006, signed by over 100 teachers, psychologists and other experts who were calling on the UK Government to 'prevent the death of childhood':

> Since children's brains are still developing, they cannot adjust – as full-grown adults can – to the effects of ever more rapid technological and cultural change. They still need what developing human beings have always needed, including real food (as opposed to processed 'junk'), real play (as opposed to sedentary, screen-based entertainment), first-hand experience of the world they live in and regular interaction with the real-life significant adults in their lives. (Fenton, 2006, p. 1)

Worryingly, Marsh and Bishop (2014, cited in MacBlain et al., 2015) recently reported on how children re-enacted aspects of a current television show, *The Jeremy Kyle Show*, where individuals talk openly about very personal, complex and adult issues in their lives. Marsh and Bishop discuss how such programmes may be considered as 'trash TV', 'in which a particular representation of people from lower socioeconomic groups is embedded which generally features immorality and depravity' (MacBlain et al., 2015, p. 168). The effects of media on children's brains have been debated for many years. These debates have coincided with a huge growth in research into the workings of the brain and how the functioning of the brain affects children's learning and development.

THE EMERGENCE OF NEUROSCIENCE

Recently, Hohnen and Murphy (2016, p. 75) referred to a 'movement across the world to integrate neuroscience into formal education' but in doing so also commented on how 'there continues to be a debate in the field about how fruitful a relationship this might be' (Ansari et al., 2011). Despite the fact that debate continues to exist in regard to this relationship, it is, nonetheless, important to acknowledge that the emerging field of neuroscience does have a great deal to offer in regard to our understanding of children's emotional, social and cognitive development (Whitebread and Sinclair-Harding, 2014).

Gray and MacBlain (2015, p. 11) have drawn attention to how, from the 30th week of gestation, the 'neural architecture' of the brain, which is often referred to as *wiring* or *hard wiring*, has been created, and it is this architecture that then supports learning in the child. They have also drawn attention to the fact that whilst it was previously believed children's brains were complete at birth, it is understood that, importantly, in addition to the 100 billion neurons that are present at birth, formed through a process of neurogenesis, parts of the brain continue to generate neurons throughout life and into adulthood. Such a view highlights the importance of seeking to further understand how aspects of brain functioning affect the course of development and learning throughout childhood and into adulthood. One important benefit of recognising that parts of the brain continue to generate throughout life has been the more recent emergence of neuroscience and, more particularly, neuropsychology. MacBlain (2014) further shows that, with advances in our understanding of the structure and functioning of the brain and particularly in the field of neuroscience, we are now coming to better appreciate how the development of the brain interfaces with children's environment and how this complex and necessary interaction impacts on learning and thinking. The importance of the genetic make-up inherited by children and the experiences they have in the environments in which they grow up is, therefore, now much better understood than even a decade ago.

Howard-Jones (2014) undertook what is an excellent and highly informed review of neuroscience and education, in collaboration with the Wellcome Trust, which considered 'the extent to which insights from the sciences of mind and brain influence, or are close to influencing, classroom practice' (p. 2). The review included a survey of teachers, parents and students in addition to a study of the neuroscience literature. The review offers a summary of education evidence in regard to approaches and interventions that have been based on, or have been claimed to be based on, neuroscientific evidence. The review has been structured around 18 topics, each of which was judged against the strength of evidence relating to its educational effectiveness and the 'distance that needs to be travelled for the neuroscience knowledge to be applied within the classroom'; it offers evidence of how aspects of neuroscience have successfully informed education, in addition to areas of neuroscience that can usefully inform education in the future. Within the body of the review, Howard-Jones stressed that:

> Anything that has an impact on learning will ultimately have a brain basis; the idea that our understanding about how the brain works could impact upon educational practice is therefore an attractive one. This idea has gained traction in the last 10-15 years (particularly in the last five years), with considerable discussion and a step change in the number of articles connecting the brain with education. (2014, p. 3)

In his review, Howard-Jones concluded that neuroscience and education is an area that offers great potential. Key findings from the review offer, for example, the following, in relation to our understanding of children's thinking when tasked with completing activities in the area of mathematics:

> Neuroscience has helped reveal the importance of both non-symbolic and symbolic representation of quantity in the earliest (and later) stages of mathematics education ... Students must learn to link these representations ... Mental rotation skills predict maths and science achievement and these skills are amenable to training, including by the playing of action video games ... Fingers may have a

special relationship with concepts of number ... Maths anxiety interferes with neu-rocognitive processes crucial to learning, with effects mediated by an individual's recruitment of cognitive control networks ... Cognitive neuroscience has made a substantial contribution to understanding how numerical abilities develop in young children and the foundational role of non-symbolic and symbolic representation in acquiring formal mathematical skills. We now understand that quantitative ability involves a number of components, and these include:

- a non-symbolic number system (or numerosity) which is the ability to quickly understand and approximate numerical quantities ... and is considered to be evi-dent in animals and present very early in human development
- a symbolic number system which is the ability to understand representations such as '3' or 'three', whose development is strongly linked to that of early language, beginning around 2-3 years old
- an ability to map between non-symbolic and symbolic systems, which appears linked to the use of fingers and develops through early childhood. (p. 13)

It is clear from the review undertaken by Howard-Jones that neuroscience has a great deal to offer practitioners working with young children. It is now generally accepted (Kokkinaki and Vasdekis, 2015; MacBlain, 2014; Whitebread, 2012) that the field of neuroscience has much to offer education and our understand-ing of children's thinking, emotional and social development, and, therefore, their learning.

REFLECTIONS ON PROFESSIONALISM

A New Zealand study of pupils', and more particularly their teachers', views on enhancing self-worth in the classroom (Cushman and Cowan, 2010, cited by Brown Hajdukova et al., 2014) found that both groups were unanimous in perceiving how positive relationships between pupils and their teachers led to students having better feelings about themselves, which then impacted posi-tively on the pupils' learning. More importantly perhaps, Brown Hajdukova et al., in drawing on the earlier work of Birch and Ladd (1998), also make the point that negative pupil–teacher relationships in primary school can be associated with pupils' low academic achievement, poor self-direction and dis-engagement from school. There is, however, a limit to what teachers and early years practitioners can achieve in their direct work with children. Much also needs to happen outside of schools and early years settings, as was previously proposed by the theoretical work of Bronfenbrenner who viewed other factors such as culture, economy, politics, and so on, as having both a direct and indi-rect impact on children's development and their learning (Gray and MacBlain, 2015). Mathers et al. (2014, p. 62) have highlighted the importance of early years practitioners having appropriate qualifications as well as continuing professional development. They also emphasised the importance of staff–child ratios in ensuring the quality of provision:

> research shows that both quality and children's outcomes (e.g. language skills, social skills and secure attachments) are better where ratios are higher, and there is particularly convincing evidence that ratios are important for under 3s … In the GLF [Graduate Leader Fund; Mathers et al., 2011] evaluation, rooms with fewer children per staff member offered higher overall quality, as well as higher quality personal care routines and a more appropriate and individualized schedule for infants and toddlers. (2014, p. 63)

CHILD-CENTREDNESS IN A CHANGING WORLD

All children have a right to grow up safe from harm. Children from all cultures can, however, find themselves subjected to neglect and even abuse. Different races, cultures and ethnicities have different approaches to bringing up children. Whilst remaining sensitive to the differences, professionals must also maintain a clear line about what is acceptable and what is not. In the UK, the Children Act 1989 promoted the view that all children and their parents should be considered as individuals, and that family structures, culture, religion, ethnic origins and other characteristics should be respected. The thinking that underpinned this Act has subsequently been built on offering more enlightened views about how professionals work with children and their families. Elsewhere, other cultures have demonstrated models of thinking that encompass empathy, sensitivity and very helpful ways of conceptualising learning in childhood. The Scandinavian notion of 'maskrosbarn', for example, is one where children are viewed as hardy 'dandelions' who thrive and grow no matter what the circumstances are; even when there is poor support from parents, these 'dandelion' children become resilient and are able to cope adequately when in stressful situations. In contrast, 'orkidebarn' children are viewed as being like the orchid flower – delicate and weak and 'prone to withering' (Ellis and Boyce, 2008: 184). In regard to 'orkidebarn' children, it is possible to reflect on how early years environments could potentially be damaging if learning is essentially adult-led (Snelling, 2016). The following case study, cited by MacBlain and Bowman (2016, pp. 79–80), now offers a most revealing insight into how a senior manager at an early years setting placed children at the very centre of their practice. The case also highlights the tensions that currently exist for many practitioners working in early years settings, in particular in terms of ownership of their own practice and how they might, for example, accommodate 'orkidebarn' children.

— 🔍 —— CASE STUDY 11.1 ————————————————————

I can remember it vividly, the moment where the light bulb went off in my head. I was in a room of 200 people ... It was clear when networking that all of the changes we had seen as early years teachers were resulting in us losing our way and what we all knew as sound pedagogical principles and practices, such as sustained shared thinking, outstanding learning environments, relationships and attachment theory, as well as many other key ideas, things that had previously excited us, were being forgotten and lost. On return I embarked on a research project and held consultations with the staff ... We recognized the importance of curriculum areas such as mathematics and literacy but felt that the environment and resources would ensure that children still developed their knowledge and that our priority was to give children the character to cope with higher-order thinking and knowledge. My research focused on two curricula in the main: Te Whãriki in New Zealand and Reggio Emilia in Italy ... What was crucial about both of these curricula was the significant impact they were having on outcomes for children, and still today the UK fails to build an early years curriculum using these outstanding examples of good practice ... The emphasis on the child being unique as a learner, with a strong set of skills and knowledge was not new, but having this central to our EYFS curriculum was, as demonstrated in the flawed Development Matters document, uninspiring, with a compartmentalized learning that fails to enable teachers and practitioners to look at the child holistically. What does it mean to be 22–36 months in maths? ... Early years education is ... a springboard to later stages of formal education, as opposed to a distinct developmental phase. Sadly this continues throughout children's lives with preparation for tests, Key Stage 1, Key Stage 2, SATs and secondary schooling. Teaching in this way is going to lead to a breakdown in childhood, where children are frightened to have a go and make mistakes, as well as lead to significant mental health issues for our children.

This case offers real insights not only into how practice at the nursery evolved but also how an understanding of the wider learning experiences of children and their families and the physical learning environment can inform and lead to good practice. The case also demonstrates the tensions that can exist between practitioners in the early years and those responsible at government level for making decisions typically based on political ideologies. This is certainly the case throughout the world, where practitioners can find themselves constrained by politicians. Take, for example, the recent proposal by the UK Government to turn every school in England into an academy, even though the teaching unions and a large number of teachers are against this happening.

SUMMARY

This chapter has addressed important aspects that lie at the very heart of our understanding of childhood universally. All of us are now influenced by events that happen across the world, and increasingly practitioners will find themselves tasked with responding to issues in childhood that are globally determined. Poverty and the over-commercialisation and over-sexualisation of children continue to define much of childhood. This is in addition to the growing crisis of obesity. All those working with children in the world today need to turn much greater attention to these factors and work to ensure that children have greater opportunities to grow up in societies and communities that celebrate different and more 'natural' values.

 EXTENDED AND RECOMMENDED READING

Formby, S. (2014) *Practitioner Perspectives: Children's use of Technology in the Early Years*. London: National Literacy Trust.

An interesting and informative text that explores many of the implications of technology and its impact on young children.

Howard-Jones, P. (2014) *Neuroscience and Education: A Review of Educational Interventions and Approaches Informed by Neuroscience*. University of Bristol: Education Endowment Foundation (https://educationendowmentfoundation.org.uk/public/files/Publications/EEF_Lit_Review_NeuroscienceAndEducation.pdf).

An excellent review of the potential that neuroscience has for our understanding of children's learning and thinking, and, more particularly, of how practice can be informed so that access to the curriculum for many children with varying learning needs can be improved.

Palaiologou, I. (2012) *Ethical Practice in Early Childhood*. London: Sage.

An interesting and challenging text that examines in detail aspects of undertaking research with young children.

 Don't forget to visit **https://study.sagepub.com/contemporarychildhood** for a selection of free SAGE journal articles, web links, additional case studies, activities, and PowerPoints to help you revise.

REFERENCES

Ansari, D., Coch, D. and De Smedt, B. (2011) 'Connecting education and cognitive neuroscience: where will the journey take us?', *Educational Philosophy and Theory*, 43(1): 37–42.

Bailey, R. (2011) *Letting Children be Children: Report of an Independent Review of the Commercialization and Sexualization of Childhood*. London: DfE.

Barter, C. (2009) 'In the name of love: exploitation and violence in teenage dating relationships', *British Journal of Social Work*, 39: 211–33.

Birch, S.H. and Ladd, G.W. (1998) 'Children's interpersonal behaviors and the teacher–child relationship', *Developmental Psychology*, 34: 934–46.

Boyden, J., Eyber, C., Feeny, T. and Scott, C. (2003) *Children and Poverty: Experiences and Perceptions from Belarus, Bolivia, India, Kenya and Sierra Leone*. Richmond, VA: Christian Children's Fund.

Brown Hajdukova, E., Hornby, G. and Cushman, P. (2014) 'Pupil–teacher relationships: perceptions of boys with social, emotional and behavioural difficulties', *Pastoral Care in Education: An International Journal of Personal, Social and Emotional Development*, 32(2): 145–56.

Corak, M. (2005) *Principles and Practicalities in Measuring Child Poverty for the Rich Countries*. Florence: UNICEF Innocenti Research Centre.

Cowie, H. (2012) *From Birth to Sixteen: Children's Health, Social, Emotional and Linguistic Development*. London: Routledge.

Cregan, K. and Cuthbert, D. (2014) *Global Childhoods*. London: Sage.

Currie, C., Roberts, C. and Morgan, A. (2008) *Health Behaviour in School-aged Children: International Report from 2005/2006 Study*. Geneva: WHO.

Cushman, P. and Cowan, J. (2010) 'Enhancing student self-worth in the primary school learning environment: teachers' views and students' views', *Pastoral Care in Education*, 28: 81–95.

Cuthbert, C., Rayns, G. and Stanley, K. (2011) *All Babies Count: Prevention and Protection for Vulnerable Babies – A review of the evidence*. London: NSPCC.

Delamonica, E.E. and Minujin, A. (2007) 'Incidence, depth and severity of children in poverty', *Social Indicators Research*, 82: 361–74.

Department of Health (DoH) (2015) *The Future in Mind: Promoting, Protecting and Improving our Children and Young People's Mental Health and Well-being*, DoH/NHS England Publication Gateway Ref. No 02939 (www.gov.uk/government/publications/improving-mental-health-services-for-young-people).

Doek, J.E., Shiva Kumar, A.K., Mugawe, D. and Tsegaye, S. (2009) *Child Poverty: African and International Perspectives*. Antwerp: Intersentia.

Elkind, D. (1981) *The Hurried Child: Growing Up Too Fast Too Soon*. Reading, MA: Perseus Publishing.

Ellis, B. and Boyce, W. (2008) 'Biological sensitivity to context', *Current Directions in Psychological Science*, 17(3): 183–7.

Feeny, T. and Boyden, J. (2003) *Children and Poverty: A Review of Contemporary Literature and Thought on Children and Poverty – Rethinking the causes, experiences and effects*. Richmond, VA: Christian Children's Fund.

Fenton, B. (2006) 'Junk culture "is poisoning our children"', *Daily Telegraph*, 12 September, p. 1.

GOV.UK (2011) *A New Approach to Child Poverty: Tackling the Causes of Disadvantage and Transforming Families*. Norwich: The Stationery Office.

Gray, C. and MacBlain, S.F. (2015) *Learning Theories in Childhood* (2nd edn). London: Sage.

Green, H., McGinnity, A., Meltzer, H., Ford, T. and Goodman, R. (2005) *Mental Health of Children and Young People in Great Britain, 2004: A Survey Carried out by the Office for National Statistics on Behalf of the Department of Health and the Scottish Executive*. Basingstoke: Palgrave Macmillan.

Health and Social Care Information Centre (HSCIC) (2015) Statistics on Obesity, Physical Activity and Diet: England 2015 (http://digital.nhs.uk/catalogue/PUB16988/obes-phys-acti-diet-eng-2015.pdf).

Hohnen, B. and Murphy, T. (2016) 'The optimum context for learning: drawing on neuroscience to inform best practice in the classroom', *Educational & Child Psychology*, 33(1): 75–90.

Howard-Jones, P. (2014) *Neuroscience and Education: A Review of Educational Interventions and Approaches Informed by Neuroscience*. University of Bristol: Education Endowment Foundation (https://educationendowmentfoundation.org.uk/public/files/Publications/EEF_Lit_Review_NeuroscienceAndEducation.pdf).

Ji, C., Chen, T. and the Working Group on Obesity in China (WGOC) (2013) 'Empirical changes in the prevalence of overweight and obesity among Chinese students from 1985 to 2010 and corresponding preventive strategies', *Biomedical Environmental Science*, 26(1): 1–12.

Jones, N. and Sumner, A. (2011) *Child Poverty, Evidence and Policy: Mainstreaming Children in International Development*. Bristol: The Policy Press.

Jütte, S., Bentley, H., Tallis, D., Mayes, J., Jetha, N., O'Hagan, O., et al. (2015) *How Safe are our Children? The Most Comprehensive Overview of Child Protection in the UK*. London: NSPCC.

Kokkinaki, T. and Vasdekis, V.G.S. (2015) 'Comparing emotional coordination in early spontaneous mother–infant and father–infant interactions', *European Journal of Developmental Psychology*, 12(1): 69–84.

MacBlain, S.F. (2014) *How Children Learn*. London: Sage.

MacBlain, S.F. and Bowman, H. (2016) 'Teaching and learning', in D. Wyse and S. Rodgers (eds), *A Guide to Early Years and Primary Teaching*. London: Sage.

MacBlain, S.F., Long, J. and Dunn, J. (2015) *Dyslexia, Literacy and Inclusion: Child-centred Perspectives*. London: Sage.

Marsh, J. and Bishop, J. (2014) '"We're playing Jeremy Kyle!" Television talk shows in the playground', *Discourse: Studies in the Cultural Politics of Education*, 35(1): 16–30.

Mathers, S., Ranns, H., Karemaker, A.M., Moody, A., Sylva, K., Graham, J. and Siraj-Blatchford, I. (2011) *Evaluation of the Graduate Leader Fund: Final Report*. DFE-RB144. London: DfE.

Mathers, S., Roberts, F. and Sylva, K. (2014) 'Quality in early childhood education', in G. Pugh and B. Duffy (eds), *Contemporary Issues in the Early Years* (6th edn). London: Sage.

Moore, S. and Rosenthal, D. (2006) *Sexuality in Adolescence: Current Trends*. London: Routledge.

National Society for the Prevention of Cruelty to Children (NSPCC) (2014) *What's Affecting Children in 2013? Can I Tell You Something – ChildLine Review 2012/13*. London: NSPCC.

Niner, S., Ahmed, Y. and Cuthbert, D. (2013) 'The "social tsunami": media coverage of child abuse in Malaysia's English-language newspapers in 2010', *Media, Culture & Society*, 35(4): 435–53.

Office for Standards in Education (Ofsted) (2013) *What About the Children? Joint Working between Adult and Children's Services when Parents or Carers have Mental Ill Health and/or Drug and Alcohol Problems*. Manchester: Ofsted.

Raisingchildren.net.au (2016) Social Anxiety in Children (http://raisingchildren.net.au/articles/social_anxiety.html).

Rigby, E. (2016) 'Teenagers' sexting out of control, says Labour', *The Times*, 22 March.

Snelling, C. (2016) 'Is the 2014 Early Years Foundation Stage framework meeting the social and emotional needs of preschool children who have additional learning needs?' Unpublished Master's dissertation, University of St Mark & St John, Plymouth.

Sylvester, R. and Thompson, A. (2016) 'Children grow up watching porn and think it's normal', *The Times*, 22 March.

UNICEF (2007) *UN General Assembly Adopts Powerful Definition of Child Poverty*. New York: UNICEF.

United Nations General Assembly (UNGA) (2006) *Promotion and Protection of the Rights of Children: Report of the Third Committee*. New York: United Nations.

Whitebread, D. (2012) *Developmental Psychology and Early Childhood Education*. London: Sage.

Whitebread, D. and Sinclair-Harding, L. (2014) 'Neuroscience and the infant brain', *Nursery World*, 20 Oct.–2 Nov.: 21–4.

World Health Organisation (WHO) (2002) *World Health Report: Reducing Risks, Promoting Healthy Life*. Geneva: WHO.

World Health Organisation (WHO) (2015a) Facts and Figures on Childhood Obesity. Available at www.who.int/end-childhood-obesity/facts/en/ (accessed 30 October 2015).

World Health Organisation (WHO) (2015b) Child and Adolescent Mental Health. Available at www.who.int/mental_health/maternal-child/child adolescent/en/ (accessed 20 January 2016).

World Health Organisation (2016) Report of the Commission on Ending Childhood Obesity (ECHO). Available at www.who.int/end-childhood-obesity/final-report/en/ (accessed 30 March 2016).

Yu, Z., Han, S., Chu, J., Xu, Z., Zhu, C. and Guo, X. (2012) 'Trends in overweight and obesity among children and adolescents in China from 1981 to 2010: a meta-analysis', *PLoS One*, 7(12): e51949.

INDEX

2012 Framework 22–3
  child protection and safeguarding 24
  core areas of learning and development 22, 24
  core belief 22
  limited paperwork 24
  ongoing assessment 23
  over-arching principles 23
  training/qualifications/skills of providers 24

absence of care 13
accountability 150, 152, 153, 154, 155, 157, 163
Adams et al. 149
additional needs *see* special educational needs
  (SEN)
ADHD (Attention Deficit Hyperactivity
  Disorder) 115, 116, 211
adoption 100
Adoption and Children Act (2002) 100
Adoption and Children (Scotland) Act (2007) 100
Advancing Transgender Equality: A plan for action
  (GOV.UK, 2011) 196
affective psychological process, Bandura 50
affordances of digital media 173–4
agency 31
Ainsworth, M. 52
Alaca et al. 38
Alderson, P. and Morrow, V. 34
algorithms of accountability 150, 152, 154, 155,
  157, 163
Allen, V. and Fernandez, C. 132–3
*Annual Report of Her Majesty's Chief Inspector of
  Education, Children's Services and Skills 2015:
  Early Years, The* (Ofsted, 2015b) 68, 69–70
App Generation 172
Apple, M.W. 149, 197
apps 173
assessment
  2012 Framework 23
  best practice 76
  children with EAL 76
  early years 67–70
  effective and purposeful 71–2
  ethical issues 75
  formal 67
  informal 67
  primary years 70–4

Association of Teachers and Lecturers (ATL) 60
asylum seekers
  definition 96
  supporting families and children 97
attachment 52–3
Aubrey, C. 133
austerity 16–18
  and education, financial cost 17
Aynsley Green, A. 12

Baby P 3, 132–3
Baby Tax Credit 58
Bandura, A. 49–51
Barnardo's 18
Barnett, W.S. and Nores, M. 199
Barter, C. 208
Beck, J. 159
behaviour
  child poverty 199
  internalised models of 13
  online 195
'being' versus 'becoming' dualism 32
belief systems 73
benefit cuts 58
bereavement 53–5
Binford, W. 181
Bingham (2015) 197
Boffrey, D. 192
Bolivar, A. and Domingo, J. 158–9
Boniel-Nissim et al. 179
Bousted, M. 60
Bowlby, J. 52
brain
  development of 213–14
  interface with children's environment 214
  neural architecture of 213
breakfast clubs 60
bricolage, concept of 178
Brindova et al. 179
British Association for Early Childhood
  Education (2012) 24
Bronfenbrenner, U. 95, 113–14, 215
Brooks et al. 76–7, 77
Brown et al. 215
Brown, G. 21
buddy systems 61

bullying 212
  cyber 180
  transphobic 196
Byron, T. 195

CAF (Common Assessment Framework) 130–1
Campbell-Barr, V. and Leeson, C. 150, 151–2
care
  absence of 13
  children in 58–9
  combining with education 192–3
  see also childcare
Care Quality Commission (CQC) 211
caregivers 190
carers, children as 18–19
Carlone et al. 161, 162
Centre for Economic and Business Research
    (CEBR) 197
Centre for Social Justice (CSJ) 87
challenges, children facing 50
Chaudron, S. 170, 176
child-centred pedagogy 157
child-centredness 216
child labour 5
child poverty 197–9
  behavioural perspective 199
  educational perspective 198
  family relationship perspective 199
  health perspective 198
  increase in 206
  measuring 206
child protection 24, 188
childcare
  grandparents and 93–4
  increased demand for 192
  in Ireland 189–90
  in Northern Ireland 191
  quality of 190
  reliance on relatives for 122
  in Scandinavia 191
  in Scotland 191
  in Wales 191
  working parents and 189
childhood
  death of, preventing 213
  economic costs of 197–9
  perceptions of 3, 4–5, 5–6
  as a unitary phenomenon 5
Childhood Bereavement Network (CBN) 53
childhood education
  challenging political discourse 163
  discourse of control 150, 151
  government attention to 149, 150
  hidden reasoning 150

childhood education cont.
  influence of economics on 149
  investment and economic benefits 199
  neo-liberal ideology 149, 158, 163
  policies 148, 149
  quality in 148, 150
  recognition of 149–50
childhood educators see teachers
childhood innocence 188
Childhood Studies 31–2
ChildLine 211–12
childminders 122–3
children
  as active social agents 153
  adoption by same-sex couples 100
  as adults-in-waiting 4
  behaviour online 195
  conflict and 193–4
  as expert, concept of 32
  future proofing 200
  gifted 15, 41
  investment in 190
  provision for, worldwide 196–7
  sexual offences against 209
  sexualisation of 208–9
  see also UNCRC (United Nations Convention
    on the Rights of the Child)
Children Act (1989) 216
Children Act (2004), Section 14 129
Children and Families Act (2014) 14, 15, 139
Children and Young People (Scotland) Act
    (2014) 191
Children and Young People's Mental Health
    Coalition (CYPMHC) 53
  2012 guide 115
children in care 58–9
Children's Centres 58
children's perspectives
  challenges and tensions in listening to 34–5
  childhood studies 31–2
  current views on 30–1
  innovative methods for eliciting views 37–8
  research, methods for seeking 36–7
  research process, involvement in 39–42
Children's Research Advisory Group (CRAG)
    39–40
children's security 12–13
Children's Society 30
Children's Trusts 134
ChildWise 170, 171
China, obesity in 207
Christensen, P. and James, A. 38
Christensen, P. and Prout, A. 36
chronosystem 114

Civil Partnership Act (2005) 99
Clark, A. 4
Clarke, J. 158
Claxton, G. 67–8
Climbié, V. 3, 132
Code of Practice (SEN, 2015) 14, 15
cognitive neuroscience 215
cognitive psychological process, Bandura 50
cognitive system, Marzano 73
Commission on Ending Childhood Obesity 207
Committee on the Rights of the Child (UNCRC)
    180–1
  children expressing themselves 33, 36
  General Comment No. 7 (2005) 33
  General Comment No. 12 (2009) 33
  General Comment No. 14 (2013) 33
  General Comment No. 17 (2013) 181
commodification of education 149
common inspection framework 78, 79
Commons Education Select Committee report
    (2016) 154
community membership 162
complex families 86, 101
computers, poorer children's access to 16
conduct disorder 115
confidentiality 137
conflict, children and 193–4
consent 137
contemporary political ideology 149–51
control, in education 151–6
Cook, D. 19
Coulby, D. 191
counselling 211–12
Cowie, H. 208
  on stresses of childhood 4, 12
Cox, S. 192
Cregan, K. and Cuthbert, D. 31, 212
Crowley, K. 55
Cullis, A. and Hansen, K. 16
culture
  children's 178
  LGBT-headed families 101
  refugee families 98
Curran, A. 55–6
Currle et al. 208
cyberbullying 180

Daily Telegraph, The 20, 213
data dashboards 152–3
decision making, children at the centre of 14, 15
democratic professionalism 157–8
Department for Education (DfE) 60, 150
  Letting Children be Children report (2011) 209
  readiness 200

Department of Education Northern Ireland
    (DENI) 13–14
Department of Health (DoH) 210
depression 212
deprivation 16
Deprivation and Risk: The Case for Early
    Intervention (Action for Children, 2010) 16
designer employees 158, 160
Development Matters in the Early Years Foundation
    Stage (EYFS, 2012) 24
Diagnostic and Statistical Manual of Mental
    Disorders (DSM-5) 115
digital child
  children's learning experiences at home 174–5
    digital technology, use of 175
    parents' perspectives 176–7
  concept of 168–9
  digital media 169–74
  e-safety 178
    cyberbullying 180
    digital age, challenges and potential of
      179–80
    role of parents 181
    sexting 180
    and the UNCRC 180–1
  new millennium, in the 177–8
    children's culture 178
    moral panics 177
Digital Immigrants 172
digital media
  affordances of 173–4
  children's use at home 175
  investment by parents 179
  parents' perspectives 176–7
  smartphones 170–1
  social media 171
  tablet computers 168, 170
  technology, growth of 194–5
  television 169–70, 179, 213
Digital Natives 172
discourse see political discourse
discrimination 101–2
displacement, global 95
diversity 14
divorce 86, 87
Dockett et al. 35, 36
domestic violence 13
Donaldson Review (2015), Successful
    Futures 191
drugs, parental use of 12, 211
drunkenness 4
Dudeney et al. 177
Dunn et al. 39
dyslexia 15

e-safety 178–81
Early Childhood Action 20
Early Childhood Education and Care (ECEC) 122
early years
  children's participation 30
  education
    free 69, 139
    high political profile 69
    high-quality 69
    importance of play 24
    in Ireland 189–90
    provision of 68
    stronger provision of 68
    transition from nurseries 69
  emerging curricula and proposed initiatives
      22–4
  experiences and significant events 3
  identification and assessment 67–70
  professional love 57–8
  quality of experiences 68
  rights of children 33
  self-efficacy and 51
  settings 12, 13, 15, 57–8
    inclusion of LGBT families 101–2
  teachers, challenges facing 15
Early Years Foundation Stage (EYFS) 22–3
Early Years Register 22
ecological model of human development 114
Ecological Systems Theory 95
economics, education and 149
education
  for children in hospitals 61–2
  combining with care 192–3
  commodification of 149
  comparative achievements of rich/poor
      children 17
  economics and 149
  equality, tradition of building 188
  free 69, 139
  impact of poverty and austerity 16–18
  learner-centred, tradition of 188
  nationalism and 191
  neuroscience and 214–15
  political influence in 192
  tablet computers and 173
  technology and 168
  UK comparisons with other countries 188–9
  see also childhood education; early years,
      education
Education Act (1981) 14
Education, Health and Care (EHC) plans 113, 139
Education Scotland (ES) 60
educational attainment, link with deprivation 16
educators see teachers

effective teaching 71–2, 152, 215
Einarsdottir, J. 34
emotional apprenticeship of children 68
emotional disorder 115
emotional intelligence (EI) 48–9, 138
emotional memories 53–4
emotions
  managing 49
  perceiving 49
  reasoning with 49
  understanding 49
  in young children 48
  see also social and emotional functioning
employment
  ages of children 5
  longer working hours 120–1
  maternal rates of 122
English as an Additional Language (EAL) 13, 14
  categories of pupils learning 76–7
Equality Act (2010) 101
Equality Act (Sexual Orientation) Regulations
      (NI, 2006) 101
ethical issues 75
ethical symmetry 36
Evans, S. 179, 182
Every Child Matters initiative (DfES) 128, 131
  Green Paper 130
exercise play 21
exosystem, Bronfenbrenner model 114
exploration, play and 20–1
expressing views, children's right to 33, 36
external surveillance systems 151–2

Facebook 171
Facer, K. 200
families
  breakdown of 87
  complex 86, 101
  divorce and 86, 87
  fathers 88–91
  grandparents 91–5
  LGBT 99–102
  mothers 88–9
  refugee and asylum-seeking 95–9
  separation in 86
  step-families 86–7
  see also parenting; parents
fantasy play 21
Father Institute 91
  Fathers Reading Every Day (FRED) 91
  Fathers' Story Week 91
fathers
  deficit approach to fathering 89
  effective involvement of 90–1

fathers *cont.*
  gay 101
  importance in families 88
  as the invisible parents 88
  listening to 110
  and mothers' interactions with their children
      88–9
  nature of involvement 89
  unique roles 88
  young 89–90
fear 55
Feuerstein, R. 73–4
Field, F. 16
Findler, L. 94
Finland, childcare in 191
first language 76–7
Fitzgerald, D. and Kay, J. 122, 132, 189
  on racism 194
Flewitt et al. 173
Forest Schools 21
free education 69, 139
free school meals (FSM) 17
Freeman, M.A. 34
Froebel, F. 2
Fromm, E. 56, 58
future-building vision 200
Future in Mind, The report (DoH, 2015) 30, 210–11

Gallagher, L. and Gallagher, M. 32
Gardner, H. and Davis, K. 172
Garmezy, N. 54
gender 195–6
gender dysphoria 100, 101
Gibb, N. 150–1
Global North 212
global society, contemporary issues in
  child-centredness 216
  media and materialism 212–13
  mental health 210–12
  neuroscience, emergence of 213–15
  obesity and self-image 207
  poverty and life chances 206
  professionalism 215–16
  sexualisation of children 208–9
  social fears 209–10
Goleman, D. 49, 53–4
  on emotional memories 54
Good Childhood Report, The (Children's Society,
    2015) 30
Good Schools Guide 41
Goodson, I.F. 157
government discourse *see* political discourse
grandparents
  childcare and 93–4

grandparents *cont.*
  cultural knowledge, passing on 92
  families and 91–2
  health and well-being 94–5
  historian, as role of 92
  role in families 92–3
  valued role in China 92
Gray, C. and MacBlain, S.F. 5, 70, 213
Green et al. 210–11
Grotberg, E. 54–5
growing up, experiences of 5–6
Growing up in Ireland Survey (2013) 189

handwriting 41
happiness 48, 51
Hartas, D. 15
Harwood, D. and Tukonic, S. 156–7
Hattie, J. 71–2
Health and Social Care Information Centre
    (HSCIC) 207
Health in Pregnancy Grant 58
Health Visitor Implementation Plan (2011-15) 139
Healthy Child Programme Review 139, 140
Heimer, L.G. and Klefstad, E. 148, 153, 154
heritage curriculum 175
heteronormativity 101
Hicks, D. 188, 194
high-quality education 151, 153
high-stakes inspection 160
HighScope 58
Hirsch, D. 198, 199
Hohnen, B. and Murphy, T. 213
homosexuality 99, 101
hospitals, children in 61–2
housing, cost of 121
Howard-Jones, P. 214–15
'the hundred languages of children' 36

'I am' illustration 54, 55
'I can' illustration 55
'I have' illustration 54–5
Ideal Family 3
identification 67
  best practice 76
  early years 67–70
  effective and purposeful 71–2
  ethical issues 75
  primary years 70–4
ideology
  contemporary political, and philosophy
      149–51
  government 148
  neo-liberal 149, 158, 163
  underpinning childhood education policy 148

Ihmeideh, F.M. 88
illness 61–2
immigrants 96
inclusion 14–15, 191
industrialisation 4
information sharing 128, 131
information sub-set, Marzano 73
initiatives, early years education 22–4
Insecurely attached: ambivalent infants 52
Insecurely attached: avoidant infants 52
inspections 77, 78, 79
  role of leadership 78, 79
  Schools and Parents report (Ofsted, 2011) 119–20
  undesirable side-effects of 160
Instagram 171
Institute for Public Policy Research 93
Institute of Education (IOE) 177
Integrated Review (NCB, 2015) 138–40
integrated services 133
An Intelligent Look at Emotional Intelligence (ATL) 68
intentionality 74
inter-agency working 133
International Labour Organisation (ILO) 5
international perspectives
  children and conflict 193–4
  economic costs of childhood 197–9
  gender 195–6
  international variations in practice 188–93
  provision for children, worldwide 196–7
  readying culture 199–200
  technology, growth of 194–5
interventions
  children at 2½ years 140
    additional support 140
  involving parents 137, 140
  by professionals 115
investment of meaning 74
involvement, Laevers' 5-point scale 51–2
inward migration 13–14
iPads 170, 174
Ireland, childcare in 189–90
isomorphism 158

James, A. and Prout, A. 2, 30, 31
James, O. 120–1
  on love bombing 57
Jarvis, M. 110–11
Jenkins et al. 178
Jenkins, H. 178
joined-up working 133

Kanyal, M. and Gibbs, J. 34
Kenner, C. 77
kindergarten, notion of 2

knowledge domain, Marzano 73
Knowles, G. 86
Knowles, G. and Holmström, R. 195–6
Kohn, A. 200
Kornhaber, A. 92
Kring et al. 115–16, 137–8
Kucirkova, N. 174
Kuczera et al. 67

Laevers, F. 51–2
Laming report 132
language play 21
Lea, S. 152, 161, 162
Leach, E. 102
league tables 152–3
learning
  best practice 76
  children with EAL 76–7
  defining 70
  effective 71–2
  emotions and 48
  impact of loss in childhood 53–5
  Leuven Well-being and Involvement Scales
    51–2
  self-efficacy and 51
  Social Interactionist Theory of 74
  see also optimum learning environments
*Learning Behaviour Principles and Practice: What
  Works in Schools* report (DfES, 2006) 61
Learning to Learn Framework (DENI, 2013) 24, 191
learning trajectory 162
LeDoux, J. 53–4
legislation, protection of children 4
Letting Children be Children report (DfE, 2011) 209
Leuven Well-being and Involvement Scales 51–2
Levy, R. and Thompson, P. 32, 39
LGBT (lesbian, gay, bisexual and transgender)
  families
  cultural acceptance 101
  inclusion in early years settings and
    schools 101–2
  issues, legal changes regarding 99–100
  research about 100–1
life chances 206
limited capacity, working memory 119
listening to children 34–5, 36
  Mosaic approach 37–8
literacy skills 66, 67, 174
  New Literacy Studies 175–6
Livingstone et al. 170, 176
Livingstone, S. 34
local authorities (LAs) 61–2
Local Safeguarding Children's Board's
  Regulations (2006) 129

Locke, J. 4
locomotor play 21
long-term memory 119
looked-after children 58–9
loss, in childhood 53–5
love 55–8
love bombing 57
low achievement 75–6
low-income families 16
LSCBs (Local Safeguarding Children Boards) 128–30
    objectives 129
    Ofsted reviews 129–30
Lundy, L. 34
Lundy, L. and McEvoy, L. 40
Lupton, R. 16
Lynch, J. and Redpath, T. 173

MacBlain, S.F. 214
macrosystem, Bronfenbrenner model 114
Malaguzzi, L. 2
Malaysia 212
maltreatment
    emotional 13
    physical 13
managerial professionalism 157–8
Manning et al. 86, 87
mantras 32, 37
mark-making 173
Marriage (Same Sex Couples) Act (2013) 99
Marsh, J. 177, 178
Marsh, J. and Bishop, J. 213
Marzano, R. 72–3, 74
maskrosbarn 216
mastery, model of 151
materialism 212–13
maternal employment rates 122
mathematics 151
Mathers et al. 215–16
McDowall Clark, R. 5
    on the regulation of childhood 19
McKinney, S. 5
McTavish, M. 174
mediascapes 178
mediated learning experience (MLE) 74
memory 119
mental health 210–12
    disorders 210–11
mental sub-set, Marzano 73
Merz, A.H. and Swim, T.J. 192
mesosystem, Bronfenbrenner model 95, 114
metacognitive system, Marzano 73
Meyerson, D.E. 161
microsystem, Bronfenbrenner model 95, 114

migrants 13
Millennium Cohort Study (IOE) 177
Miller, L. 158
Miller, L. and Pound, L. 68–9
monitoring and evaluation 77–9
Moore, S. and Rosenthal, D. 208–9
moral panics 177
Morgan et al. 90
Morton, K. 57–8
Mosaic approach 37–8
Moss, P. 149, 150, 151, 153, 200
Moss, P. and Dahlberg, G. 152, 153
mothers
    and fathers' interactions with their children 88–9
    unique roles 88
motivational psychological process, Bandura 50
multi-agency panel 133
multi-agency teams 133
multi-agency working 133–4
    challenges of 134–5
    inter-professional practice 134
multi-professional perspectives
    evolving perspectives 128
    initiatives 138–40
    integrated review at 2½ years 138–40
    multi-agency working, challenges of 134–5
    professionals and parents working together 135–8
    safeguarding 128–34
multi-sensory representations, working memory 119
multiculturalism 13–14
multilingualism 14
multiple literacies 175–6
Murray, J. 156, 159
    on internal and external views of professional identity 159
Mykkänen et al. 38

National Association for Language Development in the Curriculum (NALDIC, 2012) 13
    on multilingual children 14
National Children's Bureau (NCB) 138–40
National Literacy Trust 175, 176
National Society for the Prevention of Cruelty to Children (NSPCC) 4, 12, 209
    children in care 58–9
National Treatment Agency for Substance Abuse 211
Naughton, J. 182
negotiated experiences 162
neo-liberal ideology 149, 158, 163

Neumann, M. and Neumann, D. 173, 177
neuroscience 213–15
  see also brain
New Approach to Child Poverty: Tackling the Causes of Disadvantage and Transforming Families (GOV.UK, 2011) 206
New Literacy Studies 175–6
new sociology of childhood 31–2
  dualisms 32
newcomer children 14
nexus of multi membership 162
Nicholson, N. 110
Nikiforidou, Z. and Anderson, B. 128
non-symbolic number system 215
Northern Ireland
  childcare 191
  divorce rate 86
  Early Years (0–6) Strategy (DENI, 2010) 30
  inward migration 13–14
  Learning to Learn: A Framework for Early Years Education and Learning (DENI, 2013) 24
  mainstream schooling of children with SEN 15
  Way Forward for Special Educational Needs and Inclusion, The (DENI, 2009a) 17
NSPCC *see* National Society for the Prevention of Cruelty to Children (NSPCC)
nuclear family 102
numeracy skills 66, 67, 174
nursery schools
  refugee children 98
  transition from 69
nurture groups 59–60
  Nurture Group Network (NGN) 59
nutrition 194

Obama, B. 149, 189
obesity 207
OECD (Organisation for Economic Co-operation and Development) 174
Office for National Statistics (ONS) 121–2
Ofsted 22–3
  Annual Report of Her Majesty's Chief Inspector of Education, Children's Services and Skills 2015: Early Years, The (2015b) 68, 69–70
  best practice in children's learning 76
  early years educational provision 68
  Early Years Foundation Stage (EYFS) 22–3
  'The future of education inspection: understanding the changes' document 78
  inspections 77
  parents' conduit to 111
  recommendations for reform of 78

Ofsted *cont.*
  Report of Her Majesty's Chief Inspector of Education, Children's Services and Skills 2013–14 Social Care, The (2015) 134–5
  review of SEN 75
  reviews of LSCBs 129–30
  Schools and Parents report (2011) 119–20
  welfare requirements notices 23
  What About the Children? report (2013) 211
online games 170
oppositional defiance disorder (ODD) 138
optimum learning environments
  challenges today 66–7
  children with EAL 76–7
  identification and assessment 67
    early years 67–70
    ethical issues 75
    primary years 70–4
  low achievement and underachievement 75–6
  monitoring and evaluating practice 77–9
orkidebarn children 216
orphan trains 197
Osgood, J. 151, 157, 158
O'Toole, C. 190
outcome-focused pedagogy 157
outcome-oriented pedagogy 158
outdoor play 21

Palaiologou et al. 191
Palaiologou, I. 30, 37, 133
Palmer, S. 66
Parent Management Training (PMT) 137–8
Parent View initiative 111
parental leave 89
parenting
  positive and effective 22
  shared roles 88–9
  shared-time 87
parents
  children's digital safety 181
  children's use of media 121
  difficult childhood school experiences of 111–12
  drug taking 12, 211
  investment in digital technology 179
  listening to 110–19
    assurance of teachers' qualifications 110–11
    conduit to Ofsted 111
    intervention by professionals 115
    involvement of fathers 110
    Parent View initiative 111
    support mechanisms 111
    teachers' home visits 112

parents *cont.*
   perspectives on children and digital
      technology 176–7
   problem drinking 12
   working, childcare for 189
   working patterns 120–3
      changing nature of 121–2
      childcare, reliance on relatives 122
      childminders 122–3
      longer hours 120–1
      maternal employment rates 122
      rising costs of living 121
   working with 119–20
   working with professionals 135–8
   see also families
Parker, G. 154
participation, children's
   balance with child protection 34
   in research 30, 35
participation rights, UNCRC 181
Paton, G. 20
Patterson, G. 137
Pearce, C.
   on early years care 57
   on Insecurely attached: ambivalent infants
      52–3
pedagogy
   child-centred 157
   outcome-focused 157
   outcome-oriented 158
performative professionalism 157
performativity culture 153
perspectives
   children's *see* children's perspectives
   international *see* international perspectives
   multi-professional *see* multi-professional
      perspectives
philosophy 149–51
photo-elicitation 38
photographs 38
photovoice methodology 38
physical abuse 13
physical sub-set, Marzano 73
play
   as all-inclusive cure 19
   benefits to children 20, 200
   differences from previous eras 19
   exploration and 20–1
   importance in early years education 24
   language 21
   locomotor 21
   outdoor 21
   physical
     exercise play 21

play *cont.*
   rhythmical stereotypes 21
   rough-and-tumble play 21
   political tensions about 20
   pretend 21
   sociodramatic 21
   technology and 19
   thick 178
Pleck et al. 89
policy
   childhood education policies 148, 149
   and practice 148
policy entrepreneurs 148, 162
political discourse
   contemporary political ideology and
      philosophy 149–51
   defining high-quality education 151
   dominance of 151
   neo-liberal ideology 149, 158, 163
   policy and practice 148
   policy entrepreneurs 148, 162
   professionalism 156–63
      democratic versus managerial
         professionalism 156–8
      professional identity 158–61, 162
      regulation, control and accountability
         151–6, 163
      tempered radicals 148, 161–2
   see also childhood education
political ideology, contemporary 149–51
post-traumatic stress disorder (PTSD) 97
poverty 16–18, 206
   and education, financial cost 17
   educational underachievement 17
   see also child poverty
Powell, S. and Goouch, K. 192
practice
   monitoring and evaluating 77–9
   policy and 148
practitioners *see* teachers
pregnancy, teenage 4
Prensky, M. 172
pretend play 21
*Pricing the Priceless Child: The Changing Social
   Value of Children* (Zelizer) 4–5
primary years 70–4
Prime areas, 2012 Framework 23, 24
principled professionalism 157
professional identity 148, 151, 153, 154, 158–61
   continual negotiation of 159
   crisis of 160
   dimensions of 162
   internal and external views of 159
   self-perceptions of 158–9, 160

professional identity *cont.*
  social legitimacy 159
professional love 57–8
professional standards 154–5
professionalism 215–16
  defining 151
  democratic versus managerial 156–8
  fixed 159
  glass ceiling 157
  performative 157
  political discourse and 151
  principled 157
professionals, working with parents 135–8
protection, child 24, 188
  balance with child participation 34
protection rights, UNCRC 181
Prout, A. 5, 32
provision rights, UNCRC 181
psychodynamic tradition 56
Punch, S. 36
Pupil Premium 60
Purdy, N. and McGuckin, C. 180

quality
  childcare 190
  in childhood education 69, 148, 150
    defined by political discourse 151, 153
  of experiences, early years education 68
Quennerstedt, A. 38

racism 194
readiness, discourse of 199–200
reading 175
reciprocity 74
referrals 134
refugees
  definition 96
  global displacement 95
  importance of education/school for
    children 98
  physical and psychological problems 97
  post-migration factors 97
  pre-migration factors 97
  social exclusion 97
  supporting families and children 97
  trans-migration factors 97
regulation, in education 151–6
rehearsal, working memory 119
Removing Barriers to Literacy report
  (Ofsted, 2011) 66
*Report of Her Majesty's Chief Inspector of
  Education, Children's Services and Skills
  2013–14 Social Care, The* (Ofsted, 2015)
  134–5

research
  buddy partnership approach 39
  children's participation in 30, 35, 38, 39–42
    benefits of 39
  photo-elicitation 38
  photovoice methodology 38
  power differentials between adult researchers
    and children 35, 39
resilience 54
rhythmical stereotypes 21
Richardson, R. 188
Rigby, E. 209
rights 181
  of children 15, 33, 36
  see also UNCRC (United Nations Convention
    on the Rights of the Child)
risk 128
Roaf, C. 134
Rogoff, B. 32
Rotherham child abuse scandal 3, 128, 136
rough-and-tumble play 21
Rousseau, J.-J. 4
running away 4, 12
Ryan, M. and Bourke, T. 154, 157

Sachs, J.
  on the control of the market 155
  democratic professionalism 157
  on education as commodity 149
  fixed view of professionalism 159
  on managerial professionalism 157
  on the professional standards movement
    154–5
Sadowski, C. and McIntosh, J. 87
safeguarding 24, 128–34
  Baby P case 132–3
  CAF (Common Assessment Framework) 130–1
  LSCBs (Local Safeguarding Children Boards)
    128–30
  multi-agency working 133–4
    challenges of 134–5
  responsibility of all 128
  Victoria Climbié case 132
same-sex marriages 99–100
Sarkadi et al. 88
Savile, J. 3
Schools and Parents report (Ofsted, 2011) 119–20
Schostak, J. 3
Scotland
  childcare 191
  divorce rate 86
  separation of education and care 193
secure attachment 52, 53
security, children's 12–13

selection psychological process, Bandura 50
self-confidence 49, 56
self-efficacy 49–52
self-esteem 15, 49, 54, 55–6
self-image 207
self-system, Marzano 72–3
SEN (special educational needs) and/or
    disabilities 14
  2012 Framework *see* 2012 Framework
  education in mainstream schools 15
  Ofsted review 75
  rights of children 15
SENCos (Special Educational Need
    Co-ordinators) 112
Senior, J. 128
separation 86
serious case reviews (SCRs) 131
Sex Discrimination (Gender Reassignment)
    Regulations (NI, 1999) 101–2
sexting 180, 209
sexualisation of children 208–9
shared-time parenting 87
short-term memory 119
Singapore 189
smartphones 170–1
Smith et al. 20–1
Snapchat 171
Social and Emotional Aspects of Learning (SEAL)
    programme 138
social and emotional functioning
  attachment and the learning environment
    52–3
  emotional intelligence (EI) 48–9
  fear and love 55–8
  learning, happiness and well-being 48
  loss in childhood 53–5
  self-efficacy 49–52
  support outside of the home
    breakfast clubs 60
    buddy systems 61
    children in care 58–9
    children in hospitals 61–2
    initiatives supporting young children 58
    nurture groups 59–60
social fears 209–10
social inclusion, refugees 97, 98
social inequity 5
Social Interactionist Theory of learning 74
social literacies 175
social media 171
socioculturalism 32
sociodramatic play 21
Sorin, R. 2, 188
South Korea 189

Special Education Needs Disability Act (SENDA,
    2001) 14
special educational needs (SEN) *see* SEN (special
    educational needs) and/or disabilities
Specific areas, 2012 Framework 23, 24
standards
  behaviour-heavy 157
  professional 154–5
  raising 78
  standardisation for teachers and children 155
  standardised testing 153
starvation 194
Statements of Special Educational Needs 15
*Statutory Framework for the Early Years Foundation
    Stage, The* (DfE, 2012) *see* 2012 Framework
*Statutory Framework for the Early Years Foundation
    Stage, The* (DfE, 2014b) 22, 24
Steinberg, S.R. and Kincheloe, J.L. 2
step-families 86–7
storymaking apps 173
Street, B. 176
Strong Start for America's Children Act (2013) 189
structural cognitive modifiability 74
suicidal thoughts 4, 12, 211
  counselling for 211
Sure Start Maternity Grant 58
Sutton Trust 17
symbolic number system 215
Syria 193

tablet computers 168, 170
  affordances of 173–4
tasks 50
teachers
  accountability regimes 154
  autonomy of 159
  belief systems 73–4
  best practice 76
  challenging political discourse 163
  expectations of pupils 72
  glass ceiling to professionalism 157
  good 72
  leaving the teaching profession 192
  as mediators 73
  morale of 192
  policy and 148
  as policy entrepreneurs 148, 162
  positive relationships with pupils 215
  professional development 110–11
  quality in childhood education 148, 150
  readiness and 200
  regulation and control, impact of 154
  self-efficacy and collective efficacy 160
  standardised testing, concerns about 153

teachers *cont.*
　　as tempered radicals 148, 161–2
　　see also professional identity
teaching
　　children with EAL 13, 14, 76–7
　　effective 71–2, 152, 215
　　newcomer children 14
　　staff-child ratios 216
technology *see* digital media
teenage pregnancy 4, 90
Tekin, A.K. 85
television 169–70, 179
　　Jeremy Kyle Show, The 213
tempered radicals 148, 161–2
testing, standardised 153
theoretical perspectives 32
therapeutic relationships 138
thick play 178
tick-box professionals 160
Tisdall, E.K.M. and Punch, S. 34
touch-screen tablets 173
transgenderism 100, 195–6
transmedia 178
Tuval, S. 161

UNCRC (United Nations Convention on the
　　Rights of the Child) 29, 33–4
　　Article 12 33, 40
　　three Ps 181
　　UK ratification 33
　　see also Committee on the Rights of the Child
　　　(UNCRC)
underachievement 75–6
　　educational 17–18
underage sex 4
unhappiness 212
UNHCR (United Nations Refugee Agency) 96
UNICEF (United Nations Children's Fund) 193
　　on child poverty 199
　　measuring child poverty 206
United Nations Convention on the Rights of
　　the Child (UNCRC) *see* UNCRC (United
　　Nations Convention on the Rights of the
　　Child)
United Nations Convention Relating to the
　　Status of Refugees (1951) 96
United Nations General Assembly (UNGA) 206
United States of America (USA) 189

universalism 158
universities, focus on childhood 5
*Unsure Start: HMCI's Early Years Annual Report
　　2012/13 Speech 2014* (Wilshaw) 16–17

voice, parents 110–23
Vygotsky, L. 32

Waldegrave, H. and Simons, J. 78
Wales
　　childcare in 191
　　divorce rate 86
Walker, R. and Griggs, J. 197–9
Ward, L. 200
*Way Forward for Special Educational Needs and
　　Inclusion, The* (DENI, 2009a) 17
welfare requirements notices 23
well-being 48
　　Laevers' 5-point scale 51–2
Wenger, R. 162
What About the Children? (CQC) (Ofsted, 2013)
　　211
What's Affecting Children in 2013 (ChildLine)
　　211
Whitebread, D. 119
　　on emotions 48
Wiggins, K. 155–6
Wilshaw, M. 17
　　on financial costs 17
　　on leadership for raising standards 78
　　on leadership to drive improvements 79
　　on poverty and education 16–17
　　underachievement of children 17–18
Wohlwend, K. 178
Wood, E. 69
Wood, K. 188–9
Woods, P. and Jeffrey, B. 161–2
working memory 119
World Health Organisation (WHO) 207
　　mental disorders in children 210
　　*World Health Report: Reducing Risks, Promoting
　　　Health Life* (2002) 208
writing 175

Yewtree effect 209
Young Minds 30

Zelizer, V. 4–5